JOURNAL FOR THE STUDY OF THE NEW TESTAMENT
SUPPLEMENT SERIES
89

Executive Editor
Stanley E. Porter

JSOT Press
Sheffield

Word and Glory

On the Exegetical and Theological Background of John's Prologue

Craig A. Evans

Journal for the Study of the New Testament
Supplement Series 89

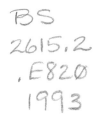
Copyright © 1993 Sheffield Academic Press

Published by JSOT Press
JSOT Press is an imprint of
Sheffield Academic Press Ltd
343 Fulwood Road
Sheffield S10 3BP
England

Typeset by Sheffield Academic Press
and
Printed on acid-free paper in Great Britain
by Biddles Ltd
Guildford

British Library Cataloguing in Publication Data

Evans, Craig A.
    Word and Glory: On the Exegetical and
    Theological Background of John's
    Prologue. - (JSNT Supplement Series, ISSN
    0143-5108; No. 89)
    I. Title II. Series
    226.5

ISBN 1-85075-448-9

CONTENTS

Word and Glory: On the Exegetical and Theological Background of John's Prologue presents the results of an investigation into the question of the origin and background of the Johannine Prologue (that is, Jn 1.1-18). The book is narrowly focused in that it speaks to recent claims that the most natural and illuminating background for understanding the Prologue is to be found in Gnosticism, particularly as represented by the Coptic tractate from Nag Hammadi, the *Trimorphic Protennoia*. At the same time the book is broadly focused in that it speaks to the more encompassing question of Johannine Christology and context. The opening chapter reflects the narrower concerns and provides the necessary historical background to the study. Although many of the details of Rudolf Bultmann's classic hypothesis have been discarded, the essence of his proposal, that Johannine Christology is fundamentally indebted to a Gnostic myth, still exerts influence in some quarters. Bultmann's use of late Mandaean sources provides the occasion to work out criteria for assessing the relative value of sources that offer 'parallels'. Lateness, of course, does not necessarily disqualify a given source, but it does increase the burden of proof and so necessitates the employment of rigorous criteria. The second chapter reviews the major Gnostic contenders today, such as the Coptic codices from Nag Hammadi. Parallels that have been adduced from these writings are reviewed against the criteria worked out in the first chapter.

The third chapter examines the biblical parallels and sources that have been adduced, including those that are quite obvious and generally are universally acknowledged (such as Gen. 1 and Exod. 34) and those that are perhaps not so well known (such as Prov. 8 and Sir. 24). The important issue that concerns this chapter is the question of how much these biblical parallels account for the themes and Christology of the Prologue and what, if anything, is left unexplained. The fourth chapter investigates related exegeses, paraphrases and interpretive traditions. Numerous parallels are adduced, most of which antedate the Fourth Gospel. Philo's *logos*, the targumic *memra*, and various Moses traditions are given special attention. The evidence of these two chapters suggests that the interpretive context of the synagogue is the most likely provenance of Johannine Christology in general and the Prologue in particular. The evidence further suggests that Gnostic mythology probably had nothing to do with the formulation of Johannine Christology.

This conclusion is tested further in the fifth chapter, which widens the scope of the study by examining various other indicators of provenance. The Fourth Evangelist's knowledge of Palestine, particularly Judea and Jerusalem, his acquaintance with targumic and midrashic diction and interpretive traditions, his repeated reference to the threat of being excluded from the synagogue, and his general indebtedness to the Old Testament for his Christology support the conclusions reached in Chapters 3 and 4. The sixth chapter offers several critical comments touching method, particularly with respect to the assessment of parallels. The chapter also speaks to historical matters (which Johannine critics often ignore) that add further support to the conclusions of the previous chapters.

The appearance of two books in 1989 and 1990 prompted me to undertake this investigation. The first was Martin Hengel's *The Johannine Question*.[1] For me this important book was a breath of badly needed fresh air. Instead of tiring the scholarly community with another subjective 'close reading' of the text, Hengel reexamines the historical evidence, both external and internal, relating to the question of authorship (which I treat briefly in the sixth chapter). The result is a clearer understanding of both the author and his Gospel, an understanding that is almost always documented by solid evidence. I was impressed when in the fall of 1987 I heard Professor Hengel read portions of this book to students and faculty of Princeton Theological Seminary. I was even more impressed when I read the book. The anticipated appearance of the longer and more detailed German version will no doubt offer still more grist for the mill.[2]

The second book that persuaded me that the present study is needed was the second volume of the Festschrift for James M. Robinson,

---

1.   London: SCM Press; Philadelphia: Trinity Press International, 1989.

2.   Since I wrote this preface the book has appeared, entitled *Die johanneische Frage: Ein Lösungsversuch* (WUNT, 67; Tübingen: Mohr [Paul Siebeck], 1993).

Gnosticism and the Early Christian World.[1] Of particular interest were essays by Gesine Robinson and Jack T. Sanders which either assumed or argued that Bultmann's hypothesis, though not always his arguments, is correct and that documents like the *Odes of Solomon* and the *Trimorphic Protennoia* provide us with the best available parallels to Johannine thought. I found these essays disturbing not so much because their conclusions are at points quite erroneous, but because they exhibit insufficient awareness of the problems attending the utilization of documents that significantly postdate the writings of the New Testament. I found these essays, as well as the earlier studies of Bultmann and James Robinson, puzzling in that ancient writings which offer better parallels and which unquestionably antedate the Fourth Gospel are either minimized or ignored altogether. It is rather like straining at the gnat and swallowing the camel.

I hope in this book to accomplish three things: (1) to clarify the interpretive background of the Johannine Prologue; (2) to clarify the provenance of the Fourth Gospel itself; and (3) to establish criteria for evaluating 'parallels', especially those found in documents that postdate the New Testament.

I salute my colleagues here at Trinity, as well as those who gather monthly at Vancouver School of Theology for a time of friendly discussion. It was in this setting that an early and much shorter form of this book was given an airing.

C.A. Evans
Trinity Western University
Langley, British Columbia
January, 1993

1.   J.E. Goehring *et al.* (eds.), *Gnosticism and the Early Christian World* (Sonoma, CA: Polebridge, 1990).

ABBREVIATIONS

AB	Anchor Bible
ABRL	Anchor Bible Reference Library
AGJU	Arbeiten zur Geschichte des antiken Judentums und des Urchristentums
AGSU	Arbeiten zur Geschichte des Spätjudentums und Urchristentums
AnBib	Analecta biblica
ANTJ	Arbeiten zum Neuen Testament und Judentum
ArBib	The Aramaic Bible
ATR	*Anglican Theological Review*
AusBR	*Australian Biblical Review*
AUSS	*Andrews University Seminary Studies*
BBR	*Bulletin for Biblical Research*
BDB	F. Brown, S.R. Driver and C.A. Briggs, *Hebrew and English Lexicon of the Old Testament*
BETL	Bibliotheca ephemeridum theologicarum lovaniensium
BEvT	Beiträge zur evangelischen Theologie
BFCT	Beiträge zur Förderung christlicher Theologie
BHT	Beiträge zur historischen Theologie
Bib	*Biblica*
BibOr	Biblica et orientalia
BJS	Brown Judaic Studies
BNTC	Black's New Testament Commentaries
BTB	*Biblical Theology Bulletin*
BTSt	Biblisch-theologische Studien
BU	Biblische Untersuchungen
BZ	*Biblische Zeitschrift*
BZAW	Beihefte zur *Zeitschrift für die alttestamentliche Wissenschaft*
BZNW	Beihefte zur ZNW
CBQ	*Catholic Biblical Quarterly*
CBQMS	*CBQ* Monograph Series
CH	Calwer Hefte
CJT	*Canadian Journal of Theology*
CRINT	Compendia rerum iudaicarum ad Novum Testamentum
CSR	*Christian Scholar's Review*
EPRO	Etudes préliminaires aux religions orientales dans l'empire romain

EstBíb	*Estudios bíblicos*
ExpTim	*Expository Times*
FRLANT	Forschungen zur Religion und Literatur des Alten und Neuen Testaments
GA	Gesammelte Aufsätze
GNS	Good News Studies
GTS	Gettysburg Theological Studies
HBT	*Horizons in Biblical Theology*
HNT	Handbuch zum Neuen Testament
HNTC	Harper's New Testament Commentaries
HTKNT	Herders theologischer Kommentar zum Neuen Testament
HTR	*Harvard Theological Review*
HTS	Harvard Theological Studies
ICC	International Critical Commentary
IKZ	*Internationale Katholische Zeitschrift* (*Communio*)
Int	*Interpretation*
JAC	*Jahrbuch für Antike und Christentum*
JBL	*Journal of Biblical Literature*
JBT	*Jahrbuch für biblische Theologie*
JETS	*Journal of the Evangelical Theological Society*
Jew Enc	*The Jewish Encyclopedia*
JJS	*Journal of Jewish Studies*
JNES	*Journal of Near Eastern Studies*
JQR	*Jewish Quarterly Review*
JSNTSup	*Journal for the Study of the New Testament*, Supplement Series
JSOTSup	*Journal for the Study of the Old Testament*, Supplement Series
JSP	*Journal for the Study of the Pseudepigrapha*
JTS	*Journal of Theological Studies*
KEK	Kritisch-exegetischer Kommentar über das Neue Testament
LCL	Loeb Classical Library
LD	Lectio divina
LTR	*Lutheran Theological Review*
MB	Le monde de la Bible
MHUC	Monographs of the Hebrew Union College
NCB	New Century Bible
NCE	M.R.P. McGuire *et al.* (eds.), *New Catholic Encyclopedia*
Neot	*Neotestamentica*
NHC	Nag Hammadi Codex
NHS	Nag Hammadi Studies
NovT	*Novum Testamentum*
NovTSup	*Novum Testamentum*, Supplements
NTS	*New Testament Studies*
NumSup	*Numen: International Review for the History of Religions*, Supplements

QD	Quaestiones disputatae
QR	Quellen der Religionsgeschichte
RevThom	*Revue thomiste*
RevQ	*Revue de Qumran*
RGG	*Religion in Geschichte und Gegenwart*
RSR	*Recherches de science religieuse*
SANT	Studien zum Alten und Neuen Testament
SBL	Society of Biblical Literature
SBLDS	SBL Dissertation Series
SBLMS	SBL Monograph Series
SBLTT	SBL Texts and Translations
SBS	Stuttgarter Bibelstudien
SBT	Studies in Biblical Theology
ScEccl	*Sciences ecclésiastiques*
ScEs	*Science et esprit*
Scr	*Scripture*
SEÅ	*Svensk exegetisk årsbok*
SJT	*Scottish Journal of Theology*
SJLA	Studies in Judaism in Late Antiquity
SNT	Studien zum Neuen Testament
SNTSMS	Society for New Testament Studies Monograph Series
SPB	Studia postbiblica
Str–B	[H. Strack and] P. Billerbeck, *Kommentar zum Neuen Testament aus Talmud und Midrasch*
SubBib	Subsidia biblica
TD	*Theology Digest*
TDNT	G. Kittel and G. Friedrich (eds.), *Theological Dictionary of the New Testament*
THKNT	Theologischer Handkommentar zum Neuen Testament
TLZ	*Theologische Literaturzeitung*
TRu	*Theologische Rundschau*
TU	Texte und Untersuchungen
TynBul	*Tyndale Bulletin*
TZ	*Theologische Zeitschrift*
VC	*Vigiliae christianae*
WBC	Word Biblical Commentary
WF	Wege der Forschung
WMANT	Wissenschaftliche Monographien zum Alten und Neuen Testament
WUNT	Wissenschaftliche Untersuchungen zum Neuen Testament
ZNW	*Zeitschrift für die neutestamentliche Wissenschaft*
ZTK	*Zeitschrift für Theologie und Kirche*

Chapter 1

INTRODUCTION: IN SEARCH OF THE JOHANNINE CONTEXT

Introduction

Years ago Rudolf Bultmann argued that the background of the Johannine Prologue, as well as the entire Gospel itself, was to be found in Gnosticism, especially as seen in the Odes of Solomon and some of the Mandaean writings.[1] The fact that the latter writings post-dated the Fourth Gospel by several centuries was not viewed as problematic, since it was assumed that the traditions they contained were consider-

---

1. R. Bultmann, 'Der religionsgeschichtliche Hintergrund des Prologs zum Johannesevangelium', in H. Schmidt (ed.), *EYXAPIΣTHPION: Studien zur Religion und Literatur des Alten und Neuen Testaments*, II (2 vols.; Göttingen: Vandenhoeck & Ruprecht, 1923), pp. 3-26; *idem*, 'Die Bedeutung der neuerschlossenen mandäischen und manichäischen Quellen für das Verständnis des Johannesevangeliums', *ZTK* 24 (1925), pp. 100-46. Both of these studies have been reprinted in *Exegetica: Aufsätze zur Erforschung des Neuen Testaments* (ed. E. Dinkler; Tübingen: Mohr [Paul Siebeck], 1967), pp. 10-35, 55-104. An English translation of the first has appeared in J. Ashton (ed.), *The Interpretation of John* (London: SPCK; Philadelphia: Fortress Press, 1986), pp. 18-35. See also Bultmann's comments in *The Gospel of John: A Commentary* (Oxford: Basil Blackwell; Philadelphia: Westminster Press, 1971), pp. 17-18; and *idem*, 'γινώσκω, γνῶσις, κτλ', *TDNT*, I, pp. 689-719, esp. pp. 708-13. For an older commentary that understands the Fourth Gospel from this perspective, see W. Bauer, *Das Johannesevangelium* (HNT, 6; Tübingen: Mohr [Paul Siebeck], 3rd edn, 1933). Bultmann (see for instance *Primitive Christianity in its Contemporary Setting* [London: Thames & Hudson; New York: Meridian, 1955], p. 162) never doubted that Gnosticism was a pre-Christian movement and a significant contributor to Christian theology. E. Haenchen ('Gab es eine vorchristliche Gnosis?', *ZTK* 49 [1952], pp. 316-49; repr. in *Gott und Mensch: Gesammelte Aufsätze* [Tübingen: Mohr (Paul Siebeck), 1965] pp. 265-98) believes that there was a 'Simonian' pre-Christian Gnosticism, so-called in honor of Simon Magus.

ably older. Bultmann's views, however, never won general acceptance.[1]
Indeed, they have been abandoned by many of his pupils.[2]

1.   Not only did Bultmann's theory face serious chronological difficulties (in that
most of the Mandaean materials date from the sixth, seventh and eighth centuries),
the *Odes of Solomon*, whose author probably had knowledge of the Johannine tradition and many important Christian elements, may not be Gnostic at all; cf.
J.H. Charlesworth, 'The Odes of Solomon—Not Gnostic', *CBQ* 31 (1969), pp. 357-
69. H. Lietzmann ('Ein Beitrag zur Mandäerfrage', *Sitzungsberichte der Preussischen
Akademie der Wissenschaft: Phil.-Hist. Klasse* 17 (1930), pp. 595-608) identified
the presence of Syrian Christian liturgy in the Mandaean texts, while F.C. Burkitt
(*Church and Gnosis* [Cambridge: Cambridge University Press, 1932]) found
evidence that the Mandaeans had knowledge of the Peshitta. Moreover, Mandaean
scholars think that the Mandaean writings directly borrowed from the Fourth Gospel;
cf. E.M. Yamauchi, *Pre-Christian Gnosticism: A Survey of the Proposed Evidences*
(Grand Rapids: Baker, 2nd edn, 1983), pp. 117-42; *idem*, 'Jewish Gnosticism? The
Prologue of John, Mandaean Parallels, and the Trimorphic Protennoia', in R. van
den Broek and M.J. Vermaseren (eds.), *Studies in Gnosticism and Hellenistic
Religions* (EPRO, 91; Leiden: Brill, 1981), pp. 467-97. G. MacRae (*NCE*, VI,
p. 523) concluded that 'Mandaeism may safely be regarded as a late form of Gnostic
religion, perhaps originating in the 5th century AD'. Moreover, K. Rudolph (*Die
Mandäer*, I [FRLANT, 56; 2 vols.; Göttingen: Vandenhoeck & Ruprecht, 1960–61],
pp. 9 n. 3, 65-80) has shown that there is no direct connection between the
Mandaeans and John the Baptist and that the Baptist was not viewed as a savior
figure. E.M. Yamauchi (*Gnostic Ethics and Mandaean Origins* [HTS, 24;
Cambridge, MA: Harvard University Press, 1970]) has questioned the assumption
that the Mandaeans had adopted Gnostic teachings prior to the end of the first
century. He also questions (cf. *Pre-Christian Gnosticism*, pp. 135-40) the claims
that some have made that the Mandaeans were an offshoot of Judaism. He doubts
this because Mandaeans were opposed to circumcision, did not observe the Sabbath,
and showed little familiarity with the Old Testament.
2.   For an early defection, see G. Bornkamm, 'Der Paraklet im Johannes-
Evangelium', in E. Wolf (ed.), *Festschrift Rudolf Bultmann zum 65. Geburtstag
überreicht* (Stuttgart: Kohlhammer, 1949), pp. 12-35; revised and repr. in
G. Bornkamm, *Geschichte und Glaube*, III (GA; 3 vols.; Munich: Chr. Kaiser
Verlag, 1968), pp. 68-89. E. Käsemann ('The Structure and Purpose of the Prologue
to John's Gospel', in *New Testament Questions of Today* [London: SCM Press;
Philadelphia: Fortress Press, 1969], p. 150) states: 'The pre-Christian character of the
hymn is more than problematical, the Aramaic original incredible, the alleged Baptist
hymn a pure hypothesis'. Similarly, E. Haenchen ('Probleme des johanneischen
"Prologs"', *ZTK* 60 [1963], pp. 305-34, and *John 1: A Commentary on the Gospel
of John Chapters 1–6* [Hermeneia; Philadelphia: Fortress Press, 1984], pp. 34-37)
concluded that the hymn was neither Aramaic nor Gnostic, but a Christianized
version of a Jewish wisdom hymn, and that whereas in the Jewish context it was in

In the recently published Festschrift in honor of James M. Robinson
the question of the Johannine Prologue's relationship to Gnosticism
has once again been raised. To be sure, Gnosticism's relationship to

praise of Torah, in Christian circles it was in praise of Christ. Even W. Schmithals
('Der Prolog des Johannesevangeliums', *ZNW* 70 [1979], pp. 16-43), who thinks
that Gnosticism lies behind much of the New Testament, no longer believes that the
hymn lying behind the Prologue of the Fourth Gospel was Gnostic. The discovery
that Mani (216–275 CE) had been influenced by Elchasaites and not Mandaeans, as
had previously been assumed, dealt a serious blow to Bultmann's theory. It has, in
the words of G. Quispel, 'destroyed this beautiful story'; cf. Yamauchi, 'Jewish
Gnosticism?', p. 474. Years earlier H.E.W. Turner (*The Pattern of Christian Truth*
[London: Mowbrays, 1954], p. 113) had commented: 'The attempt to derive the
Fourth Gospel from Mandaean sources is already a curiosity of scholarship'.

However, Bultmann's hypothesis did not expire without a struggle. J.M. Robinson
('The Johannine Trajectory', in J.M. Robinson and H. Koester, *Trajectories through
Early Christianity* [Philadelphia: Fortress Press, 1971], pp. 232-68, esp. pp. 252-
66), citing a small, select number of studies, largely out of date and superseded, tried
to argue that a consensus had begun to form in support of the basic thrust of
Bultmann's interpretation. Thanks to the Dead Sea Scrolls and the Nag Hammadi
codices, we are able, says Robinson, to perceive a 'gnosticizing trajectory...on which
the Gospel of John has its history-of-religions location ('Johannine Trajectory',
p. 266). This conclusion, we are asked to believe, points to the 'growing edge' of
Johannine research. It appears, however, that Robinson's expectations have not been
realized. Although several recognized Johannine scholars (such as C.K. Barrett,
R. Schnackenburg and D.M. Smith) continue to discuss the possibility of pre-
Christian gnosticizing tendencies which the Fourth Evangelist may have adopted or
opposed, virtually everyone has abandoned the Gnostic redeemer hypothesis. See
K.-W. Tröger, 'Ja oder Nein zur Welt: War der Evangelist Johannes Christ oder
Gnostiker?', *Theologische Versuche* 7 (1976), pp. 61-77. Nonetheless, a curious
atavism should be noted. K. Rudolph (*Gnosis: The Nature and History of Gnosticism* [San Francisco: Harper & Row, 1983], pp. 149, 382 n. 48) has commented
recently that the theory of the Gnostic hymn underlying the Prologue 'has been
shown *beyond a doubt* by R. Bultmann' (my emphasis). This is hardly the case.
Perusal of Rudolph's bibliography and Robinson's footnotes reveals a very selective
cadre of scholars. Only among these hand-picked studies does one find a
'consensus' supportive of Bultmann's hypothesis. A broader and more inclusive
survey reveals, quite to the contrary, that a consensus has indeed emerged, namely,
that the Gnostic redeemer hypothesis is improbable and unhelpful. R. Kysar's
survey (*The Fourth Evangelist and His Gospel: An Examination of Contemporary
Scholarship* [Minneapolis: Augsburg, 1975] 111) reveals a trend quite different from
that described by Robinson. Kysar reports: 'The bulk of research published in the

the Fourth Gospel had never ceased to be an item of ongoing discussion,[1] but the recent publication of the Coptic Gnostic codices from Nag Hammadi has in some quarters generated new interest in Bultmann's original hypothesis. Gesine Robinson (formerly Gesine Schenke) has returned to the *Trimorphic Protennoia* (NHC XIII, *1*) as offering the most relevant theological background against which one should understand the Prologue.[2] For twenty years this question has been discussed, with conclusions ranging from the view that the *Trimorphic Protennoia* made use of the Prologue[3] to various suggestions that the Prologue, if

recent past has found more reason to locate the author of the Prologue in a Jewish-rabbinic setting than any other, and one would have to say that a clear direction of that kind is discernible. The proponents of some sort of non-Jewish setting have not been overwhelmed, but the gnostic hypothesis for the background of the logos concept appears less tenable in the light both of the stronger evidence for an Old Testament-Jewish milieu and the effective refutations of arguments for a gnostic influence'.

1.   L. Schottroff, *Der Glaubende und die feindliche Welt: Beobachtungen zum gnostischen Dualismus und seiner Bedeutung für Paulus und das Johannesevangelium* (WMANT, 37; Neukirchen–Vluyn: Neukirchener Verlag, 1970); J.-M. Sevrin, 'Le quatrième évangile et le gnosticisme: questions de méthode', in J.-D. Kaestli *et al.* (eds.), *La communauté johannique et son histoire: La trajectoire de l'évangile de Jean aux deux premiers siècles* (MB; Geneva: Labor & Fides, 1990), pp. 251-68.

One of the most provocative points of discussion was raised by E. Käsemann (*Jesu letzter Wille nach Johannes 17* [Tübingen: Mohr (Paul Siebeck), 1966]) who argued that the Fourth Gospel was Gnosticizing and docetic. This conclusion has been widely criticized; see W.A. Meeks, review of *Jesu letzter Wille nach Johannes 17*, by E. Käsemann, *USQR* 24 (1969), p. 420; E. Schweizer, 'Jesus der Zeuge Gottes: Zum Problem des Doketismus im Johannesevangelium', in A.S. Geyser *et al.* (eds.), *Studies in John* (NovTSup, 24; Leiden: Brill, 1970), pp. 161-68; G. Richter, 'Die Fleischwerdung des Logos im Johannes-Evangelium', *NovT* 13 (1971), 81-126; 14 (1972), pp. 257-76; and especially M.M. Thompson, *The Humanity of Jesus in the Fourth Gospel* (Philadelphia: Fortress Press, 1988), and U. Schnelle, *Antidocetic Christology in the Gospel of John* (Minneapolis: Fortress Press, 1992).

2.   G. Robinson, 'The Trimorphic Protennoia and the Prologue of the Fourth Gospel', in Goehring *et al.* (eds.), *Gnosticism and the Early Christian World*, pp. 37-50.

3.   Y. Janssens, 'Une source gnostique du Prologue?', in M. de Jonge (ed.), *L'Evangile de Jean: Sources, rédaction, théologie* (BETL, 44; Leuven: Leuven University Press, 1977), pp. 355-58; P. Hofrichter, *Im Anfang war der 'Johannesprolog': Das urchristliche Logosbekenntnis—Die Basis neutestamentlicher und gnostischer Theologie* (Regensburg: Pustet, 1986), pp. 215-21. Neither of these views is compelling. Janssens is certainly right to object to the conclusions reached

not dependent upon the *Trimorphic Protennoia* itself, is at least dependent upon the tradition lying behind it.[1] I have argued that the Prologue of John and the *Trimorphic Protennoia* represent independent expressions of Jewish sapiential traditions, that neither is dependent on the other, and that writings such as the *Trimorphic Protennoia* document gnosticizing proclivities within some streams of these sapiential traditions.[2] My argument was based on the observation of the extensive common vocabulary, particularly in the section of the *Trimorphic Protennoia* concerning the 'Word'.[3] But my conclusion, which G. Robinson cites with approval,[4] falls short of supporting some of her other assumptions and conclusions.

I believe there is a fundamental methodological problem in appealing to this tractate from Nag Hammadi in order to reach the conclusion that G. Robinson has. If there were no other parallels to the

---

by those mentioned in the following note, but the way she frames the alternatives lacks sophistication. On the other hand, Hofrichter's position is undermined by claiming too much. He argues that the original hymn underlying the Prologue is the ultimate source for all of early Christology.

    1.   H.-M. Schenke, 'Die neutestamentliche Christologie und der gnostische Erlöser', in K.-W. Tröger (ed.), *Gnosis und Neues Testament: Studien aus Religionswissenschaft und Theologie* (Berlin: Evangelische Verlagsanstalt, 1973), pp. 205-29. Schenke comments: 'but especially the gnostic redeemer scheme, through whose connection with the bare idea of pre-existence, the pre-existence christology (which underlies Johannine theology) first becomes firm as a real conception' (p. 207). See also G. Schenke (now G. Robinson), 'Die dreigestaltige Protennoia', *TLZ* 99 (1974) cols. 731-46, esp. 733-34; C. Colpe, 'Heidnische, jüdische und christliche Überlieferung in den Schriften aus Nag Hammadi, III', *JAC* 17 (1974), pp. 109-25, esp. pp. 122-24; J.M. Robinson, 'Gnosticism and the New Testament', in B. Aland (ed.), *Gnosis* (Göttingen: Vandenhoeck & Ruprecht, 1978), pp. 125-43, esp. pp. 128-31; *idem*, 'The Prologue of the Gospel of John and the Trimorphic Protennoia', in P.J. Achtemeier (ed.), *Society of Biblical Literature, 1978, Abstracts* (Missoula, MT: Scholars Press, 1978), p. 29; *idem*, 'Sethians and Johannine Thought: The *Trimorphic Protennoia* and the Prologue of the Gospel of John', in B. Layton (ed.), *The Rediscovery of Gnosticism: Proceedings of the International Conference on Gnosticism at Yale, New Haven, Connecticut, March 28-31, 1978; Volume Two: Sethian Gnosticism* (NumSup, 41; Leiden: Brill, 1981), pp. 643-62, esp. pp. 660-62.

    2.   C.A. Evans, 'On the Prologue of John and the *Trimorphic Protennoia*', *NTS* 27 (1981), pp. 395-401, esp. pp. 398-99.

    3.   Evans, 'On the Prologue of John', p. 397.

    4.   G. Robinson, 'The Trimorphic Protennoia', pp. 45-46.

language and ideas of the Johannine Prologue, then perhaps a carefully qualified appeal to the *Trimorphic Protennoia* could be justified. But when parallels can be adduced, most of which antedate the Johannine Prologue, and many of which are much closer in vocabulary, theme and provenance than those found in Gnostic writings, appeal to late Gnostic sources is problematic at best.[1]

This study compares the parallels between the Johannine Prologue and the *Trimorphic Protennoia* (and other 'Gnostic' sources) on the one hand, and various biblical and rabbinic sources on the other. The purpose of the study is threefold: (1) to offer a critique of the methods presupposed and articulated by certain scholars of Gnosticism who believe that Gnostic sources, principally Coptic and Mandaean, provide the best literary and theological context against which the Fourth Gospel, particularly its Prologue (1.1-18), should be viewed; (2) to offer a more compelling alternative background interpretation of the Prologue (and the Gospel as well); and (3) to propose criteria for making comparative use of materials whose composition post-dates the New Testament period.

A Proposed Method

The problem of method quickly becomes apparent. Several traditions that will be examined derive from sources that postdate the Fourth Gospel. The question of chronology is a difficulty not only for those who appeal to Gnostic sources, but also for those who appeal to certain Jewish sources, such as rabbinic writings and the targums. Scholars of Gnosticism utilize Coptic and Mandaean sources that range from the second to the seventh centuries, while scholars of Judaica attempt to exploit materials that derive from a similar span of time. The utilization of these sources is not necessarily improper, but this chronological fact necessitates careful controls. Without controls such comparative work is in danger of being discredited by serious anachronisms.

There are at least four criteria that should be considered in evaluating the potential relevance of concepts found in a document that postdates the New Testament writing in question. First, is there

1. The difficulty is analogous to the problems faced by New Testament interpreters who make use of rabbinic and targumic sources. These later sources can be used, but careful qualification is required. The criteria that are developed below attempt to provide the necessary qualification.

antecedent documentation, that is, is there external (as opposed to internal) evidence that the later source reflects traditions that probably existed in one form or another in the first century or earlier? Secondly, is there evidence of *contamination*, that is, are there indications that the later source has been influenced by the New Testament (or the Fourth Gospel) itself? If there are, then the 'parallels' may be no more than echoes of the New Testament, thus rendering the utilization of the later source much more problematic, though not necessarily rendering it useless. Thirdly, the *provenance* of the respective documents must also be taken into account. That is to say, is it likely that the later document contains traditions that were part of the milieu of the New Testament writer or the traditions he utilized? Finally, the degree of *coherence* between the New Testament passage and the proposed parallel must be considered. Is the parallel merely formal, perhaps even coincidental, or does it point to a genuine and meaningful relationship of language and conceptuality?

The first criterion speaks directly to the chronological problem. If components of a late tradition can be found in documents that are contemporaneous with or prior to the New Testament, then the proposed parallel with the New Testament writing has a stronger claim to legitimacy. What is hinted at here and there in early sources (which are often fragmentary, such as many of the Dead Sea Scrolls and Pseudepigrapha) may be more fully preserved, even if further developed, in later sources. The parallel with the New Testament may on this reckoning prove to be one more early witness to the concept preserved in the later document. The second criterion faces up to the possibility that close parallels may in fact be the result of New Testament ideas having found their way into the later document, either directly or indirectly through second- and third-hand acquaintance. This criterion is very important in view of the syncretistic nature of Gnosticism. The third criterion addresses the problem of proximity. It does little good, for example, to show that certain traditions in a given post-New Testament document might reach back to the first century, only to be unable to place them in a geographic (or social or religious) location from which the New Testament document in question, or its antecedent tradition, could have originated. The fourth criterion quite rightly concerns itself with the meaning of the putative parallel. Is the parallel meaningful? (Although this sometimes may be forgotten, this is the real reason for searching for backgrounds and sources of biblical passages.) Does the parallel in the later document actually clarify its New Testament counterpart, and vice versa? Ultimately there should be an exegetical 'payoff'.

Testing the Method

Virtually every commentary and scholarly study makes use of documents which were written after the New Testament period. Very often used are targumic and rabbinic parallels, probably because it is assumed that what the rabbis said and believed in the second through sixth centuries was probably fairly consistent with the views of the Jewish religious teachers and interpreters of the first century. Such an assumption, however, is very questionable. Nevertheless, many biblical interpreters assume that this is the case, and so extract numerous 'parallels' from sources like Paul Billerbeck's *Kommentar zum Neuen Testament aus Talmud und Midrasch*. To be sure, many of the items found in this resource are helpful, but unless contextual and chronological questions are carefully considered exegesis is in danger of becoming eisegesis.[1] Generalized statements about what 'the rabbis' said, or what the practices and beliefs of 'the old synagogue' were, can be very misleading. As the size of Billerbeck's work demonstrates, there is little in the New Testament that does not 'parallel' something that one rabbi or another said at one time or another in the first five or six centuries of the Common Era. But how much of this material is relevant? How much of it actually sheds light on ideas held by people in the first century? In this connection the criticisms of Jacob Neusner are apposite. He has rightly argued that the traditions contained in the rabbinic compendia must be sifted and analyzed. Some of the material, he contends, can be shown to derive from the first century, but much of it cannot.[2]

1.   See P.S. Alexander, 'Rabbinic Judaism and the New Testament', *ZNW* 74 (1983), pp. 237-46. Alexander comments: 'Many New Testament scholars are still guilty of massive and sustained anachronism in their use of Rabbinic sources' (p. 244).

2.   See J. Neusner, *Rabbinic Traditions about the Pharisees before 70* (3 vols.; Leiden: Brill, 1971). For an example of treating the problem of the relevance of these materials for New Testament interpretation, see Neusner's 'The Use of the Later Rabbinic Evidence for the Study of Paul', in W.S. Green (ed.), *Approaches to Ancient Judaism II* (BJS, 9; Chico, CA: Scholars Press, 1980), pp. 43-63.

Study of the targums must be approached in the same manner. Two extremes should be avoided: either the assumption, on the one hand, that the targums are too late to be of use for New Testament interpretation because they contain traditions obviously dating to the early Middle Ages, or, on the other, that virtually everything in the targums that seems to parallel New Testament ideas may be used. Recently Bruce Chilton has attempted to work out criteria for assessing times and places of origin of the traditions contained in the *Targum of Isaiah*.[1] In my judgment his criteria are on the right track and the principles that he has thus far set forth should prove fruitful when applied not only to the other targums but to much of the rabbinic material as well.

To test the four criteria that have been proposed above, let us draw on examples from Chilton's work, where he has attempted by an appeal to the *Targum of Isaiah* to clarify certain aspects of Jesus' teaching and preaching.[2] The challenge that Chilton faces is precisely the problem that concerns this book: how to determine what, if anything, from a document that is appreciably later than the New Testament may clarify some saying or interpretation found in the New Testament. In this case Chilton hopes to show that there are readings in the *Targum of Isaiah* that approximate interpretive distinctives found in Jesus' teaching. If Chilton is successful, he will in effect have forged a link of several centuries between Jesus and a document that in its earliest form was not formally put into writing until some two or three centuries after the time of Jesus and even then was subject to generations of redaction and embellishment.

Chilton has proposed two basic criteria, although they are cross-referenced with other historical criteria in a variety of ways. His first criterion concerns diction: is there *dictional coherence* between something that Jesus said and the wording found in the *Targum of Isaiah*? The second criterion concerns theme: is there *thematic coherence* between the perspective or emphasis of Jesus and that found in the *Targum of Isaiah*? His examples clarify how these criteria work.

There are three clear examples of dictional coherence between

1. B.D. Chilton, *The Glory of Israel: The Theology and Provenence of the Isaiah Targum* (JSOTSup, 23; Sheffield: JSOT Press, 1983); *idem, The Isaiah Targum* (ArBib, 11; Wilmington, DE: Michael Glazier, 1987).
2. B.D. Chilton, *A Galilean Rabbi and His Bible: Jesus' Use of the Interpreted Scripture of His Time* (GNS, 8; Wilmington, DE: Michael Glazier, 1984).

sayings of Jesus and readings found in the *Targum of Isaiah*. A fourth
example from *Targum Pseudo-Jonathan* will also be considered.
1. The paraphrase of Isa. 6.9-10 in Mk 4.12 concludes with 'and *it be
forgiven* them'. Only the *Targum of Isaiah* reads this way.[1] The
Hebrew and the LXX read 'heal'. Perceiving this dictional coherence,
Chilton rightly suspects that the *Targum of Isaiah* has preserved an
interpretation that in an earlier form was known to Jesus and his contemporaries.[2] The well known criterion of dissimilarity argues for the
authenticity of this strange saying, for the tendencies in both Jewish[3]
and Christian[4] circles were to understand this Isaianic passage in a
way significantly different from the way it appears to be understood
in the Markan tradition. 2. The saying, 'All those grasping a sword by
a sword will perish' (Mt. 26.52), coheres dictionally with *Targ. Isa.*
50.11: 'Behold, all you who kindle a fire, who grasp a sword! Go, fall
in the fire which you kindled and on the sword which you grasped!'
Chilton observes that the items that the targum has added to the
Hebrew text are the very items that lie behind Jesus' statement.[5]
3. Jesus' saying on Gehenna (Mk 9.47-48), where he quotes part of
Isa. 66.24, again reflects targumic diction. This verse in the Hebrew
and the LXX says nothing about Gehenna, but it does in the Targum:
'...will not die and their fire shall not be quenched, and the wicked
shall be judged in Gehenna...'[6] The verse is alluded to twice in the
Apocrypha (Jdt. 16.17; Sir. 7.17), where it seems to be moving
beyond temporal punishment (which appears to be the primary thrust
of Hebrew Isaiah) toward eschatological judgment. But the implicit
association of Gehenna with Isa. 66.24 is distinctly targumic. And, of
course, the targumic paraphrase is explicitly eschatological, as is
Jesus' saying. 4. Chilton and others think that the distinctive reading

1.   The Peshitta also reads this way, but it is dependent upon the Targum (and
the LXX in other places); cf. C.A. Evans, *To See and Not Perceive: Isaiah 6.9-10 in
Early Jewish and Christian Interpretation* (JSOTSup, 64; Sheffield: JSOT Press,
1989), pp. 77-80, 195 (for the notes).
2.   Chilton, *A Galilean Rabbi and His Bible*, , pp. 90-98.
3.   See *Mek.* on Exod. 19.2 (*Bahodeš* §1); *b. Roš Haš.* 17b; *b. Meg.* 17b; *y. Ber.*
2.3; *T. d. Eliyy.* 16 (§82-83); *Gen. R.* 81.6 (on Gen. 42.1).
4.   See Mt. 13.11b-17; Lk. 8.10; Acts 28.26-27; Jn 12.40. The latter is an exception, serving the Fourth Evangelist's distinctive scriptural apologetic.
5.   Chilton, *A Galilean Rabbi and His Bible*, pp. 98-101.
6.   Chilton, *Isaiah Targum*, p. 128; *A Galilean Rabbi and His Bible*, pp. 101-
107.

found in *Targ. Ps.-J.* Lev. 22.28 ('My people, children of Israel, as our Father is merciful in heaven, so shall you be merciful on earth') lies behind Jesus' statement in Lk 6.36: 'Become merciful just as your Father is merciful'.[1] Matthew (5.48) reads 'Father in heaven'. Although it is unnecessary to claim that Jesus has actually quoted the Targum, as has actually been suggested,[2] or even less plausibly that the Targum has quoted him,[3] the parallel demands explanation. The most probable one is that the Targum has preserved a saying that circulated in first-century Palestine (cf. *y. Ber.* 5.3; *y. Meg.* 4.9), a saying which Jesus was remembered to have uttered himself.

The much-discussed parable of the Wicked Vineyard Tenants (Mk 12.1-12 par.) appears to offer a clear example of thematic coherence between the *Targum of Isaiah* and the teaching of Jesus. The parable is based on Isaiah's Song of the Vineyard (Isa. 5.1-7), as the dozen or so words in the opening lines of the Markan parable clearly indicate. But Isaiah's parable was directed against the 'house of Israel' and the 'men of Judah' (cf. Isa. 5.7). In contrast, Jesus' parable is directed against the 'ruling priests, scribes, and elders' (cf. Mk 11.27), who evidently readily perceived that the parable had been told 'against them' and not against the general populace (cf. Mk 12.12). Why was this parable so understood, when it is obviously based on a prophetic parable that spoke to the nation as a whole? Chilton and others have rightly pointed to the *Targum of Isaiah*, which in place of 'tower' and 'wine vat' reads 'sanctuary' and 'altar' (cf. Isa. and *Targ. Isa.* 5.2),[4] institutions which will be destroyed (cf. Isa. 5.5 and *Targ. Isa.* 5.5). The *Targum of Isaiah* has significantly shifted the thrust of the prophetic indictment against the priestly establishment. Jesus' parable seems to

1. Chilton, *A Galilean Rabbi and His Bible*, 44; cf. M. McNamara, *The New Testament and the Palestinian Targum to the Pentateuch* (AnBib, 27; Rome: Pontifical Biblical Institute, 1966), pp. 133-38; *idem, Targum and Testament* (Grand Rapids: Eerdmans, 1972), pp. 118-19; R. Le Déaut, *The Message of the New Testament and the Aramaic Bible* (SubBib, 5; Rome: Pontifical Biblical Institute, 1982), p. 31; *idem*, 'Targumic Literature and New Testament Interpretation', *BTB* 4 (1974), pp. 243-89, esp. p. 246.

2. A.T. Olmstead, 'Could an Aramaic Gospel be Written?', *JNES* 1 (1942), pp. 41-75, esp. p. 64.

3. See M. Black, *An Aramaic Approach to the Gospels and Acts* (Oxford: Clarendon Press, 3rd edn, 1967), p. 181.

4. This allegorizing interpretation appears also in the Tosefta (cf. *t. Me'il.* 1.16; *t. Suk.* 3.15).

reflect this orientation: the problem does not lie with the vineyard; it lies with the caretakers of the vineyard.[1] A few of these components appear outside of the New Testament and the *Targum of Isaiah*. In *1 En.* 89.66-67 the Temple is referred to as a 'tower'. Its (first) destruction is referred to, but without any apparent allusion to Isaiah 5. This Enochic tradition appears in *Barn.* 16.1-5, where it is applied to the second destruction, but without reference to either Isaiah 5 or Mark 12. Thus the coherence between *Targum of Isaiah* 5 and Mark 12 is distinctive and probably cannot be explained away as coincidence.

Even the much-disputed quotation of Ps. 118.22-23 may receive some clarification from the Targum. Although Chilton suspects that the citation of Ps. 118.22-23 derives from the church and not from Jesus, Klyne Snodgrass has argued plausibly that its presence is due to a play on words between 'the stone' (*haeben*) and 'the son' (*haben*), which probably explains the reading in *Targ. Ps.* 118.22: 'The son which the builders rejected...'[2] This kind of wordplay is old and is witnessed in the New Testament (cf. Mt. 3.9 par.: 'from these stones God is able to raise up children [which in Aramaic originally could have been "sons"] to Abraham'; cf. Lk. 19.40). The quotation was assimilated to the better-known Greek version, since it was used by Christians for apologetic and christological purposes (cf. Acts 4.11; 1 Pet. 2.4, 7) and possibly because second-generation Christians were unaware of the original Aramaic wordplay.

In sum, Chilton has made a good case for regarding as relevant for New Testament interpretation the above examples of targumic dictional and thematic coherence. The four criteria delineated at the beginning of the second section of this chapter complement and to some extent confirm his examples and his principles of coherence. The first criterion called for corroboration from antecedent traditions. The obvious advantage that the targums have here is that they are paraphrases of *Scripture*, the very Scripture that was available in the New Testament period. Obviously, much of the paraphrasing now found in the extant targums is post-New Testament and is not helpful. But there is evidence that this paraphrasing activity was well under-

---

1. Chilton, *A Galilean Rabbi and His Bible*, pp. 111-14.
2. K.R. Snodgrass, *The Parable of the Wicked Tenants: An Inquiry into Parable Interpretation* (WUNT, 27; Tübingen: Mohr [Paul Siebeck], 1983), p. 111; C.A. Evans, 'On the Vineyard Parables of Isaiah 5 and Mark 12', *BZ* 28 (1984), pp. 82-86, esp. p. 85.

way before 70 CE. The discovery of fragments of first-century targums offers conclusive proof (cf. 4QtgLev; 4QtgJob; 11QtgJob). There are instances where targumic readings, as well as interpretive traditions, have their roots in older traditions. For example, readings thought to be distinctively targumic have been found at Qumran.[1] These considerations remove the objections that otherwise could legitimately be leveled against making comparisons with the targums in the first place.

The second criterion requires us to look for evidence of contamination. With regard to Chilton's examples, is there any indication that the *Targum of Isaiah*'s parallels are in fact owing to Christian influences? Has the *Targum of Isaiah* anywhere quoted or alluded to the New Testament or to Christian ideas? Here and there in the rabbinic writings (particularly the Gemara) criticisms of and reactions to Christian teaching may be found.[2] The tendency, and it appears to

---

1. See W.H. Brownlee, 'The Habakkuk Midrash and the Targum of Jonathan', *JJS* 7 (1956), pp. 169-86.

2. The clearest examples include the following. Some rabbis expressed the hope that they will 'not have a son or a disciple who burns his food in public [that is, teaches heresy], like Jesus the Nazarene' (*b. Sanh.* 103a; *b. Ber.* 17a-b). 'One of the disciples of Jesus...told me, "Thus did Jesus the Nazarene teach me: 'For of the hire of a harlot has she gathered them, and to the hire of a harlot shall they return' [cf. Deut 23.18]"' (*b. 'Abod. Zar.* 16b-17a; *t. Ḥul.* 2.24 ['...Jesus ben Pantera...']; cf. *Eccl. R.* 1.8 §3; *Yal. Šim.* on Mic. 1 and Prov. 5.8). 'He [a judge] said to them: "I looked at the end of the book, in which it is written, 'I am not come to take away the Law of Moses and I am not come to add to the Law of Moses' [cf. Mt. 5.17], and it is written, 'Where there is a son, a daughter does not inherit' [cf. Num. 27.8]." She said to him: "Let your light shine forth as a lamp" [cf. Mt. 5.16]. Rabbi Gamaliel said to her: "The ass came and kicked the lamp over"' (*b. Šab.* 116b). From the same tradition we find a proverbial statement that probably sums up very well the rabbinic view of Jesus' teaching: 'Since the day that you were exiled from your land [that is, the destruction of Jerusalem in 70 CE] the Law of Moses has been abrogated, and the law of the *euangelion* has been given' (*b. Šab.* 116a). In fact, by playing on the Greek word *euangelion*, some rabbis referred to it as the *'awen-gillayon* ('falsehood of the scroll') or the *'awon-gillayon* ('perversion of the scroll'). Most offensive to the rabbis was Jesus' claim to be God and Son of Man (cf. Mk 14.61-62; Jn 19.7), who would ascend to heaven (cf. Jn 20.17). Rabbi Abbahu (late third, early fourth century) is reported to have said: 'If a man says to you, "I am God", he is a liar; [or] "I am the son of man", in the end he will regret it; [or] "I will go up to heaven"—he that says it will not perform it' (*y. Ta'an.* 2.1). Again from Abbahu: '[God] says..."I am the first"—I have no father; "I am the last"—I have no son' (*Exod. R.* 29.5 [on Exod. 20.2]). Similarly Rabbi Aha (fourth century) declares: 'There is One that is alone, and he has not a second; indeed, he has neither son nor

be consistent, is to *avoid* Christian teachings and interpretations, not to
adopt them. Aquila's rescension of the LXX is an example of this concern. But if the targums were all that we had to go on, we would not
possess a clue that the New Testament or Christianity ever existed. If
there has been any 'contamination', it has been negative only, that is,
avoidance or countering of Christian ideas.[1] The most likely example
of Jewish avoidance of Christian teaching in the targums is the possible muting of passages that Christians, and probably first-century non-
Christian Jews, regarded as messianic. 'Messiah' as a name or title
never appears in the *Targum of Ezekiel*, although many of its passages
could have been easily exploited in a messianic sense.[2] More surprising, Psalm 2 and 2 Samuel 7 are not interpreted as messianic. Both of
these passages were associated with messianic ideas in the first
century[3] and yet neither is treated messianically in the Targum. It is
impossible to say for certain, but given their prominence in the New
Testament[4] and Church Fathers,[5] there is the distinct possibility that

---

brother—but: "Hear O Israel, the Lord our God, the Lord is One"' (*Deut. R.* 2.33
[on Deut. 6.4]). 'There was a man, the son of a woman, who would rise up and seek
to make himself God, and cause the entire world to err...If he says that he is God, he
lies; and in the future he will cause to err—that he departs and returns in the end. He
says, but will not do...Alas, who shall live of that people that listens to that man who
makes himself God?' (*Yal. Šim.* on Num. 23.7). Elsewhere we are told that Moses
warns Israel not to expect 'another Moses' who will 'arise and bring another Law
from heaven' (*Deut. R.* 8.6 [on Deut. 30.11-12]; cf. Rom. 10.6-8). The rabbis pre-
dict that 'the "servant" [i.e., Jesus] will bow down to the [real] Messiah' (*b. Sanh.*
61b). Lying behind this statement is the Christian view of Jesus as the Lord's Servant.

　　1.　　J. Bowker (*The Targums and Rabbinic Literature* [Cambridge: Cambridge
University Press, 1969] xi) comments: 'The Targums...frequently represent the
other side of the Christian-Jewish debate. Christians tended to base their arguments
against Judaism on verses of Scripture, and the Targum-interpretation of those
verses was often deliberately designed to exclude the Christian argument'.

　　2.　　See S.H. Levey, *The Messiah: An Aramaic Interpretation: The Messianic
Exegesis of the Targum* (MHUC, 2; Cincinnati: Hebrew Union College/Jewish Institute of Religion, 1974), pp. 78-87. The avoidance of explicit reference to 'Messiah'
could also have been to avoid provoking the Roman government.

　　3.　　See 4QFlor 1.1-13, 18-19; 4QpsDan ar^a 1.9; 2.1-2; 1QSa 2.11-12.

　　4.　　On Ps. 2.1-2 cf. Acts 4.25-26; on Ps. 2.7 cf. Mk 1.11 par.; Acts 13.33; Heb.
1.5; 5.5; on 2 Sam. 7.2-16 cf. Lk. 1.32-33; Acts 2.30; 7.45-46; 13.23; Rom. 1.3-4;
Heb. 1.5.

　　5.　　For a few examples from the early Fathers, see *1 Clem.* 36.4; Justin Martyr,
Dialogue with Trypho 88, 103, 118, 122.

their non-messianic presentation in the Targum was conscious and deliberate.[1] In view of these tendencies and in view of the absence of any positive indication of Christian influence in the targumic passages examined above, the criterion of contamination has not disqualified Chilton's parallels or his results.

The third criterion called for a provenance shared by the documents that offer the parallels. Here Chilton's parallels enjoy solid support. The Gospel tradition is unanimous in reporting that Jesus regularly preached in the synagogues of Galilee (Mk 1.21, 39; 3.1; 6.2 par.; Jn 6.59; 18.20). The synagogue, of course, was the very place in which the targums evolved and grew. One should recall that the earliest description of what went on in the synagogue is found in Lk. 4.16-30. On that occasion Jesus read and interpreted Isaiah (Lk. 4.18-19; cf. Isa. 61.1-2)! In view of this observation it is only natural that one should expect to find points of coherence between Jesus' teachings, particularly his interpretation of Scripture, and some of the distinctive readings, traditions and interpretations preserved in the targums.

The fourth criterion required the parallels to be meaningful and clarifying. Here again Chilton's results appear very promising. Peculiar readings (such as the paraphrase of Isa. 6.9-10 in Mk 4.12) and interpretations that are not in alignment with the Hebrew or Greek versions of Scripture (such as the allusion to Isa. 5.1-7 in the parable of the Wicked Vineyard Tenants) receive helpful clarification when compared to the *Targum of Isaiah*.

It is evident that Chilton's method is efficacious. Potential objections regarding time and place have been answered satisfactorily. The value of the results is impressive. In short, Chilton has in at least the instances reviewed above convincingly bridged the gap between the first-century Gospels and a document that was committed to writing probably not earlier than the third century and which subsequently was edited and embellished by succeeding generations of meturgemanim. His method reflects the rigorous controls necessary, if relatively late documents are to be utilized effectively for New Testament interpretation.

Outside of the Prologue itself the Johannine passages that Bultmann thought were particularly illuminated by comparison with Mandaean sources were the Good Shepherd and True Vine discourses. Even Siegfried Schulz, who has serious reservations about most of the

1. Levey (*The Messiah: An Aramaic Interpretation*, pp. 37, cf. 105, 152 n. 10) thinks that this may have been the case.

alleged Mandaic parallels, regards the Good Shepherd and True Vine discourses as the strongest examples of Mandaean influence.[1] These discourses and the Mandaean parallels that Bultmann and others have proposed afford us another opportunity to test our criteria. With them firmly in mind, let us examine the various parallels that have been adduced and compare them, by way of contrast, to the parallels found in the Old Testament and in early Jewish interpretation.

The Good Shepherd Discourse

Bultmann was fully aware of the many Old Testament parallels to John 10. The notes in his commentary are rich with pertinent details.[2] Moses and David are shepherds *par excellence* (Isa. 63.11; Ps. 77.21 [Moses]; Ps. 78.70-72). The former prays that God will provide a leader, lest Israel become 'like sheep which have no shepherd' (Num. 27.17; cf. Jer. 3.15).[3] The latter becomes the type of the Messiah who is to come, who will shepherd Israel. Unlike the evil shepherds who have neglected and exploited the sheep (Ezek. 34.1-10; cf. Isa. 56.11; Jer. 25.34-38; Zech. 11.4-14) one like David will arise who will feed the flock and be its shepherd (Ezek. 34.23) and king (Ezek. 37.24). Ezekiel's hope probably echoes Jeremiah's prophecy that the day will come when God will replace the wicked shepherds with caring ones (Jer. 23.1-4), one of whom, as the context seems to indicate, will be 'David a righteous branch' (Jer. 23.5). The prophet Micah also used similar language to express his hope for the appearance of a Davidic king (Mic. 5.1-3 [5.2-4e]). Probably reflecting the second century BCE *1 En.* 89.10–90.39, employing the imagery of sheep and shepherds (including good ones and bad ones), offers an allegorical account of the history of Israel. In the first century BCE the author of the *Psalms of Solomon* anticipated the appearance of the 'Lord Messiah' (17.32; 18.7) who 'will gather a holy people' (17.26), 'purge Jerusalem' (17.30), rule as a 'righteous king' (17.32), 'expose officials and drive out sinners' (17.36), and who 'faithfully and righteously shepherding

---

1. S. Schulz, *Komposition und Herkunft der johanneischen Reden* (BWANT, 5; Stuttgart: Kohlhammer, 1960), pp. 90-131.

2. Bultmann, *Gospel of John*, pp. 364-67. He rightly comments: 'It is so common in the OT that the comparison is not normally given at length, but is reduced to allusions and metaphors' (pp. 364-65).

3. According to LXX Num. 27.18, in response to Moses' prayer, the people tell Moses to 'take Jesus ['Ιησοῦς] to yourself...a man who has the Spirit in him'.

the Lord's flock, will not let any of them stumble in their pasture' (17.40). Moreover, God himself is described as Israel's shepherd: 'For he is our God and we are the people of his pasture, the sheep of his land' (Ps. 95.7; cf. Gen. 48.15; Pss. 23.1; 77.21; 78.52; 79.13; 80.1; 100.3; Isa. 40.11; 49.9-10; 63.14; Mic. 2.12; 4.6-8; Zech. 11.15-17).[1] The description of God as shepherd could have significance for the Johannine image, when it is remembered that in the Prologue the *logos* had been identified as God. Elsewhere in the New Testament the sheep/shepherd imagery is found (Jn 21.15-17; Acts 20.28; Heb. 13.20; 1 Pet. 5.2-4; Rev. 12.5; 19.15). The imagery continues on into the early Church Fathers (*1 Clem.* 16.1; 44.3; 54.2; 57.2; *Ign. Phld.* 2.1-2). It is important to note too that in the synoptic tradition the sheep/shepherd imagery is used in reference to Jesus (Mk 6.34 par., alluding to Num. 27.17). In one instance a saying of Jesus implies that he is the Shepherd (Mk 14.27, alluding to Zech. 13.7), while in another he calls his followers a 'little flock' (Lk. 12.32). The Parable of the Lost Sheep (Mt. 18.10-14; Lk. 15.3-7) is, of course, well known.[2]

Not only does this imagery clearly lie behind behind the Good Shepherd discourse, and to an extent Bultmann agreed that it did, but some of the aforementioned Old Testament passages contribute key words and phrases, as is seen in the following parallels:

Septuagint	*Fourth Gospel*
'who shall lead them out (ἐξάξει αὐτούς)' (Num. 27.17b)	'He…leads them out (ἐξάγει αὐτά)' (10.3c)
'I shall lead them out (ἐξάξω αὐτούς)' (Ezek. 34.13)	
'who shall go out before them' (Num. 27.17a)	'He goes before them' (10.4b)

---

1. For further discussion, see J. Beutler, 'Der alttestamentlich-jüdische Hintergrund der Hirtenrede in Johannes 10', in J. Beutler and R.T. Fortna (eds.), *The Shepherd Discourse of John 10 and its Context* (SNTSMS, 67; Cambridge: Cambridge University Press, 1991), pp. 18-32, 144-47.

2. J.A.T. Robinson ('The Parable of the Shepherd [John 10.1-5]', *ZNW* 46 [1955], pp. 233-40; repr. in *Twelve New Testament Studies* [SBT, 34; London: SCM Press, 1962], pp. 67-75) suggested that Jn 10.1-5 might represent a reworked synoptic-like parable. But few have followed him.

'at his word they shall go out (ἐξελεύσονται), and at his word they shall come in (εἰσελεύσονται)' (Num. 27.21b)

'and will go in (εἰσελεύσεται) and out (ἐξελεύσεται)' (10.9b)

'they shall feed in a good pasture (νομῇ)' (Ezek. 34.14a)

'he will find pasture [νομήν]' (10.9b)

'I shall set them in their pasture (νομήν)' (Jer. 23.3b)

'you kill, and you do not feed the sheep' (Ezek. 34.3)

'that he should steal, kill, and destroy' (10.10a)

'And there will not be a synagogue of the Lord as sheep (πρόβατα) for whom there is no shepherd (ποιμήν)' (Num. 27.17b)

'I am the Good Shepherd (ποιμήν)...in behalf of his sheep (πρόβατα)' (10.11)

'You have scattered my sheep (διεσκορπίσατε τὰ πρόβατά μου)' (Jer 23.2)
'(the flock) which is scattered (ἐσκορπισμένον)' (Zech 11.16)

'the wolf...scatters (σκορπίζει) them'[1] (10.12c)

'my sheep were scattered...they became meat to all the wild beasts of the field' (Ezek. 34.5)

'and they shall know (γνώσονται) that I am the Lord' (Ezek. 34.30)

'I know (γινώσκω) my sheep and my (sheep) know (γινώσκουσι) me' (10.14b)

'who shall...bring them in (εἰσάξει)...that all the synagogue of the people of Israel may hearken to (εἰσακούσωσιν) him' (Num. 27.17a, 20b)

"I must bring (ἀγαγεῖν) them also, and they will heed (ἀκούσουσιν) my voice' (10.16b)

'there shall be one shepherd (ποιμὴν εἷς)' (Ezek. 37.24)

'there shall be one flock, one shepherd (εἷς ποιμήν)' (10.16c)

---

1. Cf. *4 Ezra* 5.18: 'that you may not forsake us, like a shepherd who leaves his flock in the power of savage wolves'. *4 Ezra* was composed at about the same time as the Fourth Gospel.

'I will shepherd the sheep (ποιμανῶ τὰ πρόβατα)' (Zech. 11.4, 7)

'Shepherd my sheep (ποίμαινε τὰ πρόβατά μου)' (21.16)

'the shepherds do not feed (ἐβόσκησαν) my sheep (τὰ πρόβατά μου)' (Ezek 34.8; cf. 34.3)

'Feed my sheep (βόσκε τὰ πρόβατά μου)' (21.17)

Messianic interpretation of the above passages was not limited to early Christians. They are understood messianically in non-Christian Jewish sources as well. Some of these passages are paraphrased messianically in the *Targum of the Prophets*. As mentioned above, the title 'Messiah' does not occur in the *Targum of Ezekiel*, but Samson Levey thinks that both shepherd passages (chs. 34 and 37) are meant to be understood in a messianic sense.[1] Both passages are clearly eschatological and the figure of the Davidic king is emphasized. Jeremiah's passage on the replacement of the corrupt shepherds is interpreted in a messianic sense. The 'shepherds' of the Hebrew text (Jer. 23.4) become in the Targum 'leaders' and the 'righteous branch' of David (23.5) becomes 'a righteous Messiah'. This king will gather the scattered flock (23.2, 8). The Aramaic paraphrase of Mic. 5.1-3 is also explicitly messianic: 'And you, O Bethlehem Ephrath...from you shall come forth before Me the Messiah, to exercise dominion over Israel, he whose name was mentioned from before, from the days of creation'. This paraphrase is not only messianic, but it is the one passage in the targums where the pre-existence of the Messiah is hinted at,[2] an aspect that certainly coheres with Johannine Christology.[3] The Aramaic paraphrase of Mic. 2.12-13 should also be noted, where Israel (likened to a flock of sheep) is gathered into a fold and is led by a king who will destroy Israel's enemies.[4]

1. Levey, *The Messiah: An Aramaic Interpretation*, pp. 80-84.
2. In *b. Pes.* 54a the name of the Messiah is one of seven things that existed prior to creation. A saying in *Pes. R.* 33.6 seems to go further: 'You find that at the very beginning of the creation of the world, the King Messiah had already come into being, for he existed in God's thought even before the world was created...Where is proof that the King Messiah existed from the beginning of God's creation of the world? The proof is in the verse, "And the Spirit of God moved" [Gen. 1.2], words which identify the King Messiah, of whom it is said, "And the Spirit of the Lord shall rest upon him" [Isa. 11.1]'. But this tradition is quite late.
3. Levey, *The Messiah: An Aramaic Interpretation*, 93.
4. So G. Reim, 'Targum und Johannesevangelium', *BZ* 27 (1983), pp. 1-13, esp. pp. 9-10.

These Old Testament passages provide all of the essential imagery and vocabulary for the Good Shepherd discourse, with the exception of the Shepherd's laying down of his life (10.17-18), which undoubtedly reflects a widespread Christian interpretation of the fact of Jesus' death on the cross. It is hardly a Johannine distinctive (cf. Rom. 5.6-8), but may ultimately derive from Isaiah 53 (cf. Jn 1.29: 'Behold the Lamb of God who takes away the sin of the world'; Isa. 53.7, 12: 'he was led as a sheep to the slaughter, and as a lamb...he poured out his soul to death...he bore the sin of many') and possibly Zech. 13.7 (cf. Mk 14.27: 'I shall strike the shepherd, and the sheep will be scattered'). In contrast to other shepherds who exploit and oppress the sheep, or hirelings who flee at the first sign of danger, the Good Shepherd (or 'Model Shepherd', as Raymond Brown translates[1]) protects and cares for the sheep. If it is necessary to imagine what 'thieves and robbers' (Jn 10.1) may have conjured up in the minds of late first-century Jews and Christians, the ruling priests, who in targumic tradition likely originating in the first century are called 'thieves' who 'stole their ways',[2] and the would-be messiahs who led various

1.   R.E. Brown, *The Gospel according to John*, I (AB, 29, 29a; 2 vols.; Garden City, NY: Doubleday, 1966–70), pp. 384, 386.

2.   The epithet 'thieves' is found in *Targ. Jer.* 7.9, while the phrase 'stole their ways' comes from *Targ. Jer.* 23.11, reflecting criticism of the first-century CE ruling priesthood. (Note that this reference to the 'scribe and priest' who 'have stolen' occurs in the passage that complains of the bad shepherds.) These criticisms are amply attested by several first-century and early second-century sources, for example, *T. Mos.* 6.6; Josephus, *Ant.* 20.8.8 §181; 20.9.2 §206-207; *2 Bar.* 10.8; *4 Bar.* 4.4-5. For similar accusations in the targumim of priestly theft and robbery, see *Targ. 1 Sam.* 2.17, 29; *Targ. Jer.* 6.13; 8.10. These accusations are found in the rabbinic writings as well; cf. *t. Men.* 13.18-22; *t. Soṭ* 14.5-6; *t. Zeb.* 11.16-17; *y. Ma'as. Š.* 5.15; *b. Pes.* 57a; *Sifre Deut.* §357 (on 34.1, 3). On one occasion Rabbi Simeon ben Gamaliel (c. 10–80 CE) protested the exorbitant charge for doves (*m. Ker.* 1.7), the poor man's sacrifice (cf. Lev. 5.7; 12.8). In what are probably traditions dating back to the first (or even second) century BCE, some of the Dead Sea Scrolls accuse the priestly establishment of theft and robbery; cf. 1QpHab 8.12; 9.5; 10.1; 12.10; 4QpNah 1.11. A few commentators think that 'thieves' and 'robbers' recall Mk 11.17: 'you have made [the Temple] a cave of robbers'; cf. R.H. Strachan, *The Fourth Gospel: Its Significance and Environment* (London: SCM Press, 3rd edn, 1941), pp. 224-25; G.R. Beasley-Murray, *John* (WBC, 36; Dallas: Word Books, 1987), p. 170; R. Schnackenburg, *The Gospel according to St John*. I. *Introduction and Commentary on Chapters 1–4* (repr.; New York: Crossroad, 1987

insurrections against Rome (or against the Herodian dynasty), whom Josephus regularly calls 'robbers',[1] would be likely candidates (and certainly better ones than Bultmann's suggested Hellenistic saviors[2]). Both groups would have been viewed by early Christians as opponents, the former group because of its opposition to Jesus, his apostles, and the early church, and the latter group because as kingly (and in some cases probably messianic) claimants they would have rivaled the Christian proclamation of Jesus as Israel's king and Messiah.[3]

These parallels are such that one would think that it is hardly necessary to look elsewhere. But Bultmann, believing that some important ingredients are missing from the Old Testament imagery, argued that the Johannine Good Shepherd is ultimately based on the idea of the Good Shepherd in Mandaean sources. Herein, he thinks, lies the true inspiration behind the Johannine discourse. The Old Testament details are no more than secondary influences. But Bultmann's parallels are very disappointing.[4] Not only can he find no parallel to Jn 10.14 ('I know my sheep, and my sheep know me'), the one detail that one should expect in a Gnostic source, Bultmann can find no parallel to the shepherd's laying down of his life (Jn 10.17-18), the one important

[1980]), p. 291. Brown (*Gospel according to John*, I, p. 393) thinks the Pharisees and Sadducees are in view.

1. Josephus regularly calls the insurrections and kingly claimants 'bandits' (λησταί); cf. *War* 2.17.8 §434; *Ant.* 17.10.8 §285. Recall that one such kingly aspirant was none other than Athronges the Judean shepherd; cf. *Ant.* 17.10.7 §278-284. Some commentators think that the Fourth Evangelist's λησταί refer to these men; cf. B.F. Westcott, *The Gospel according to St John* (London: Macmillan, 1881), p. 153; J.N. Sanders and B.A. Mastin, *A Commentary on the Gospel according to John* (HNTC; New York: Harper, 1968), p. 249; C.K. Barrett, *The Gospel according to St John* (London: SPCK; Philadelphia: Westminster Press, 2nd edn, 1978), p. 371; D.A. Carson, *The Gospel according to John* (Grand Rapids: Eerdmans, 1991), p. 385; R. Schnackenburg, *The Gospel according to St John. II. Commentary on Chapters 5–12* (repr.; New York: Crossroad, 1987 [1980]), p. 291.

2. Bultmann, *Gospel of John*, pp. 371-72 (see the notes).

3. Evidently during the second revolt against Rome, Simon ben Kosiba (who may have been proclaimed Messiah by Rabbi Aqiba; cf. *y. Ta'an.* 4.5) required Christians to renounce Jesus as the Messiah; cf. Justin Martyr, *Apology* 31.6. According to Eusebius (*Ecclesiastical History* 4.6.2) Simon 'claimed to be a luminary who had come down from heaven to enlighten the miserable with wonders'. There is also rabbinic tradition to the effect that Simon performed signs, but died because of arrogance and blasphemy; cf. *b. Git.* 57a-b; *Lam. R.* 2.2 §4.

4. Bultmann, *Gospel of John*, pp. 367-69.

detail (possibly) not paralleled in the Old Testament shepherd/sheep passages. Bultmann's parallels are not helpful, for they simply fill in no blanks. Indeed, the Mandaean picture of the boat, the flood, the drowning of some of the sheep, and the recruitment of a messenger to watch over tens of thousands of sheep strikes me as a secondary jumble of images far removed from the much simpler picture found in the Old Testament and in John 10. The only close parallels (for example, 'Like a good shepherd who leads his sheep to their fold'; 'no wolf jumps into our fold'; and 'no thief penetrates into the fold') may very well be allusions to John (cf. 10.1, 12). The Mandaean *Book of John* also says that the Shepherd carries his sheep 'on his shoulders', something the Johannine Good Shepherd does not do, but something that the shepherd of Jesus' parable of the Lost Sheep (Lk. 15.3-7)[1] does! We probably have here an allusion to this very parable.[2] Another

---

1.   Compare Lk. 15.5: 'And when he has found it, he lays it on his shoulders, rejoicing'. The parable of the Lost Sheep was popular in Gnostic circles. A version of it appears in the *Gospel of Thomas*: 'The Kingdom is like a shepherd who had a hundred sheep. One of them went astray, the biggest one. He left the ninety-nine and sought for that one sheep until he found it. When he had [thus] exerted himself, he said to the sheep, "I love you more than the ninety-nine"' (50.22-27 = log. §107). Note that here, as well as in the *Book of John* (cf. 44.27) the shepherd says that he 'loves' the sheep. A version of the parable also appears in the *Gospel of Truth*: 'He is the shepherd who left behind the ninety-nine sheep which had not strayed. He went searching for the one which had strayed. He rejoiced when he found it. For 99 is a number on the left hand which holds it. But when the one is found, the entire sum passes over to the right [hand]' (NHC I, 31.35–32.9). Both of these versions have been allegorized, implying that the lost sheep is superior to the ninety-nine.

The detail of the shepherd placing the lost sheep on his shoulder parallels a rabbinic parable: 'Moses was tested by God through sheep. Our rabbis said that when Moses our teacher, peace be upon him, was tending the flock of Jethro in the wilderness, a little kid escaped from him. He ran after it until it reached a shady place. When it reached the shady place, there appeared to view a pool of water and the kid stopped to drink. When Moses reached it, he said: "I did not know that you ran away because of thirst; you must be weary". So he placed the kid on his shoulder and walked away. Thereupon God said: "Because thou hast mercy in leading the flock of a mortal, thou wilt assuredly tend my flock Israel"' (*Exod. R.* 2.2 [on Exod. 3.1]); trans. S.M. Lehrman, 'Exodus', in H. Freedman and M. Simon (eds.), *Midrash Rabbah*, III (10 vols.; London and New York: Soncino, 1983), p. 49.

2.   See Yamauchi, *Pre-Christian Gnosticism*, p. 27, who notes that recently the *Book of John* has come to be viewed as a collection of late traditions. The *Right Ginza* also likely draws upon the New Testament, especially the Fourth Gospel; cf. H. Odeberg, *The Fourth Gospel: Interpreted in its Relation to Contemporaneous*

point that should be made is that Bultmann's parallels are gathered from scattered passages in the *Ginza* and the *Book of John*. The picture of the 'Good Shepherd' that he has constructed from these materials looks more like a pastiche whose diverse components have been put together on the basis of the blueprint provided by the Gospel of John.[1]

The Mandaean parallels do not fare well when evaluated by the four criteria for the assessment of post-New Testament documents. These parallels fail the first criterion, for there is no objective evidence of Mandaean traditions early enough to have influenced the Fourth Evangelist or his community. By way of contrast, the Old Testament parallels that have been adduced obviously antedate the Fourth Gospel. The Mandaean parallels probably do not meet the second criterion either. Since these writings quote from and allude to New Testament writings and ideas, and since the parallels put forth by Bultmann appear to be reminiscences of passages from John itself, we may have a problem with contamination. In short, the Mandaean 'parallels' may not be parallels at all, but allusions. The third criterion, which addresses proximity, is also problematic. The origin of Mandaeism remains obscure. Where did this movement originate? Was it in the vicinity of the Johannine community? And again, thinking of the chronological problem, did this movement exist early enough for the Johannine community to have become acquainted with its ideas? The Mandaean parallels fare rather better when evaluated by the fourth criterion. Their picture of the Good Shepherd is similar to that of the Johannine discourse. Their respective functions are similar. One problem is that the Mandaean Good Shepherd is very much a composite. But in any case, if the priority and independence of the Mandaean parallels cannot be established, then their relevance, regardless of similarity, is called into question. Their thematic coherence, after all, may be due more to their dependence on the New Testament (and on the Old Testament, one of the New Testament's sources).

The contrast with the relevance of the Old Testament parallels is stark. Whereas there is no proof whatsoever that the Mandaean

Religious Currents in Palestine and in the Hellenistic-Oriental World (repr.; Amsterdam: Grüner; Chicago: Argonaut, 1968 [1929]), p. 163.

1. Bultmann (*Gospel of John*, pp. 369-70) also points to Poimandres (the 'Shepherd Man') of the Hermetic literature. This parallel is hardly more helpful than those found in the Mandaean writings; cf. Schnackenburg, *Gospel according to St John*, II, p. 295. This material will be evaluated in the following chapter.

parallels derive from a tradition that is prior to the Johannine Good
Shepherd discourse, the Old Testament parallels had been in circulation for centuries. Whereas the Mandaean traditions derive from a
relatively unknown provenance, the Old Testament was the book used
by Jews and Christians alike. The Fourth Evangelist's extensive use of
the Old Testament and his familiarity with Jewish exegesis will be
considered in Chapter 5 below. Judaism, the Old Testament and the
Fourth Gospel intersect at a common locus: the synagogue. The Old
Testament parallels, moreover, account for virtually all of the major
elements in the Johannine discourse. The one element for which they
might not account (that is, the death of the Shepherd) is not found in
the Mandaean sources either. Finally, the Old Testament sheep/
shepherd imagery is unified and coherent. Ezekiel 34 alone offers a
nearly complete picture.[1] One must forage through the Mandaean
sources to construct a similar picture, and even then important items
are missing and the closest parallels may in fact be echoes of the
Fourth Gospel itself. For these reasons most commentators see no
point in pursuing the Mandaean parallels further.[2]

1. This point is in large part conceded by J.D. Turner ('The History of Religions
Background of John 10', in Beutler and Fortna [eds.], *The Shepherd Discourse of
John 10*, pp. 33-52, 147-50 [notes]), a recognized scholar of Gnosticism. In his
conclusions Turner points out that the 'image of the shepherd was widespread in
antiquity' and 'lent itself aptly to designate a figure mediating between' heaven and
earth (p. 49). Thus it would seem quite precarious to argue that the vague and disparate sheep/shepherd allusions in late documents attest specific ideas in a given
document (such as the Fourth Gospel) originating from an earlier period.

2. So Barrett, *Gospel according to St John*, p. 374; Brown, *Gospel according to
John*, I, pp. 397-98; Carson, *Gospel according to John*, pp. 381-82; B. Lindars, *The
Gospel of John* (NCB; London: Marshall, Morgan & Scott; Grand Rapids: Eerdmans,
1972), pp. 353-54; Schnackenburg, *Gospel according to St John*, II, p. 295; H. Thyen,
'Johannes 10 im Kontext des vierten Evangeliums', in Beutler and Fortna (eds.), *The
Shepherd Discourse of John 10*, pp. 116-34, 163-68 (notes), esp. pp. 124, 129-31.
K.M. Fischer ('Der johanneische Christus und der gnostische Erlöser: Überlegungen
auf Grund von Joh 10', in K.-W. Tröger [ed.], *Gnosis und Neues Testament:
Studien aus Religionswissenschaft und Theologie* [Gütersloh: Gerd Mohn; Berlin:
Evangelische Verlagsanstalt, 1973], pp. 245-67) attempts to salvage Bultmann's
interpretation by collecting scattered references in the Nag Hammadi Codices. But
his results suffer from the same shortcomings. A composite assembled from documents of uncertain chronology and provenance, documents which also draw upon
the New Testament, hardly provide the interpreter with a better point of reference.

The True Vine Discourse

The statements 'I am the true [or genuine] vine, and my Father is the vinedresser' (Jn 15.1) and 'I am the vine, you are the branches' (15.6) echo several Old Testament passages, mostly from the prophets. Best known is Isaiah's Song of the Vineyard (5.1-7), in which the prophet complains that God's carefully chosen and nurtured vine has produced worthless grapes. Therefore, the vineyard will be judged. In the later, eschatological part of the book of Isaiah the vineyard will be redeemed: 'In that day there shall be a good vineyard and a desire to begin (a song) for it' (LXX Isa. 27.2). Alluding to Isaiah's older passage, God complains through Jeremiah: 'I planted a fruit-bearing vine, altogether true [or genuine]. How have you turned into a foreign and bitter vine?' (LXX Jer. 2.22). God complains further: 'Many shepherds have destroyed my vineyard...it is made a complete ruin' (LXX Jer. 12.10-11a). Several important parallels are found in Ezekiel. God asks the prophet: 'of all the branches that are among the trees of the forest, what shall be made of the wood of the vine...It is only given to the fire to be consumed; the fire consumes that which is yearly pruned from it' (LXX Ezek. 15.2-4). Later Ezekiel tells the 'parable' (17.2) of the eagle that plants a 'vine' which sends forth 'branches' and 'bears fruit' (17.7-8). But because the vine has provoked God (17.12), its shoots 'shall be dried up' (17.9). Similar metaphors are found in Gen. 49.22; Ezek. 19.10-14; Hos. 10.1-2; Ps. 128.3. An intriguing passage is found in Psalm 80 (LXX 79), portions of which read as follows:

8	You have transplanted a vine out of Egypt.
	You have cast out the heathen, and planted it.
11	It sent forth its branches to the sea,
	and its shoots to the river.
12	Why have you broken down its hedge,
	while all who pass by the way pick it?
13	The boar out of the woods has laid it waste,
	and the wild beast has devoured it.
14	O God of hosts, turn, we pray.
	Look on us from heaven, and behold and visit this vine;
15	and restore what your right hand has planted;
	and look on the son of man
	whom you strengthened for yourself (vv. 9-16 in the MT).

This passage not only offers the characteristic description of a vine well cared for which then suffers judgment for its faithlessness, it adds the element of restoration. That the restoration is to come through the (or a) 'son of man' is certainly very interesting.[1] Had this text read this way in the first century, and there is some textual uncertainty,[2] early Christians would have found the passage very suggestive.[3] Finally, there are two remaining passages that may be of importance. Wisdom likens herself to a tree whose 'branches are glorious and graceful' and to a 'vine' whose 'blossoms became glorious and abundant fruit' (Sir. 24.16-17). Sirach 24 parallels the Fourth Gospel at several points, including the Prologue, and will be further considered later. *2 Baruch* (late first century CE) likens God's 'Messiah' to a 'vine' (39.7). Finally, another observation regarding Ezekiel 17 could be made. After judgment upon the faithless vine (17.11-21), God promises to plant the twig of a cedar upon a high mountain 'to bear fruit' (17.22-23a). The cedar's 'branches will be restored' (17.23b). This eschatological passage is exploited in the Targum, which messianizes it by replacing the cedar with 'a child from the kingdom of the house of David' whom God 'will anoint and establish' (*Targ. Ezek.* 17.22). The fact that Ezek. 17.22-23 has in all probability contributed to the parable of the Mustard Seed (Mk 4.30-32), a parable concerned with the kingdom of God, could be significant.

These passages provide all the essential ingredients for the True Vine discourse. The people of Israel are identified as a vine (or vineyard), which may or may not be fruitful. Although expected to be fruitful, it often is not. When fruitless, it is judged and its shoots dry up and its branches are burned. In one passage restoration may come through a 'son of man'. Wisdom and even the Messiah are likened to a vine.

As in the Good Shepherd discourse, not only does the Johannine True Vine imagery derive from the Old Testament, but virtually all of the significant vocabulary does as well. Consider the following phrases:

---

1. See Carson, *Gospel according to John*, pp. 513-14.
2. See Brown, *Gospel according to John*, II, pp. 670-71.
3. See C.H. Dodd, *The Interpretation of the Fourth Gospel* (Cambridge: Cambridge University Press, 1953), pp. 410-12.

Septuagint	*John 15*
'I planted a fruit-bearing (καρποφόρον) vine (ἄμπελον), altogether true (ἀληθινήν)' (Jer. 2.21)	'I am the vine (ἡ ἄμπελος) the true one (ἡ ἀληθινή)' (v. 1)
'the vine (ἡ ἄμπελος)... sent forth her branches (κλήματα)... to bear fruit (φέρειν καρπόν)' (Ezek. 17.7-8) 'Israel is a vine (ἄμπελος) with excellent branches (εὐκληματοῦσα), her fruit (καρπός) is abundant: according to the multitude of her fruits (καρπῶν) she has multiplied [her] altars' (Hos. 10.1)	'every branch (κλῆμα) that bears fruit (καρπὸν φέρον)' (v. 2)
'fire consumes its yearly pruning (κάθαρσιν)' (Ezek. 15.4)	'he prunes (καθαίρει) (every fruit-bearing branch)' (v. 2); 'you are clean (καθαροί)' (v. 3)
'[the vine's] branches (κλήματα)' (Ezek. 17.7)	'you are the branches (κλήματα)' (v. 5)
'the multitude of her fruits (καρπῶν)' (Hos. 10.1)	'the one who abides in me... bears much fruit (καρπόν)' (v. 5)
'her early shoots shall be dried up (ξηρανθήσεται)' (Ezek. 17.9)	'as the branch and it is dried up (ἐξηράνθη)' (v. 6)
'the vine's (ἀμπέλου)... branches (κλημάτων)... [are] given to the fire (πυρί) to be consumed' (Ezek. 15.2-4) 'the east wind dried up (ἐξήρανε) her choice [branches]... fire (πῦρ) consumed her' (Ezek. 19.12)	'they are cast into the fire (εἰς τὸ πῦρ) and burned' (v. 6)

Similar imagery is employed in the Synoptic Gospels. Jesus himself likens Israel to a vineyard and its religious leaders to vinedressers (Mk 12.1-9 par.). Although the parable is clearly based on Isaiah's Song of the Vineyard (Isa. 5.1-7, esp. vv. 1-2), Jesus modifies its thrust by impugning the vinedressers, not the vineyard. Of course, this theme is not without precedent, when one recalls that Jeremiah accused the shepherds of allowing the vineyard to go to wrack and ruin (Jer. 12.10-11). The parable of the Mustard Seed (Mk 4.30-32) probably draws on Ezek. 17.22-23: 'it puts forth large branches, so that "the birds of the air can make nests in its shade"' (Mk 4.32). Thus the kingdom of God is likened to a fruitful plant whose branches are so great that they afford shelter. Other parables reflect Old Testament vineyard imagery and themes. One is reminded of the fruitless fig tree planted in a vineyard: 'If it bears fruit next year, well and good; but if not, you can cut it down' (Lk. 13.6-9). 'Are grapes gathered from thorns...So, every sound tree bears good fruit, but the bad tree bears evil fruit' (Mt. 7.16-17 par.). Recall also the parable of the Vineyard Laborers (Mt. 20.1-15).

Later rabbinic interpretations and allegories offer instructive parallels. In a midrash on Ps. 80.9-11 ('You transplanted a vine out of Egypt' [= LXX 79.8-10]) Israel is likened to a vine (*Lev. R.* 36.2 [on Lev. 26.42]). The keeper (God) stands over the vine (cf. Jn 15.1: 'I am the vine, and my Father is the Vinedresser'). The more the vine is cared for, the more it improves (cf. Jn 15.2: 'he prunes it that it might bear more fruit'). From this vine a single branch will appear that will rule over the whole world (Joseph, Solomon, and Mordecai are cited as examples). Within the vine there are clusters of grapes (scholars) and raisins (masters of Scripture, Mishnah, Talmud and Haggadah), although there are fruitless leaves (the ignorant and lowly). Trampled down in this world, in the world to come the vine will triumph over all other kingdoms ('first its fruit is trampled...then it is set on the king's table'; cf. Jn 15.16: 'that your fruit should remain'). Israel the vine is sustained by the merit of the Torah and the patriarchs. In the Targum, Ps. 80.14-17 (vv. 15-18 in the MT and Targum) is paraphrased messianically: 'O God of hosts, turn now, look down from heaven and see, and remember this vine in mercy, and the stock which Thy right hand has planted and upon the King Messiah whom Thou hast made strong for Thyself' (vv. 14-15).[1] Another midrash is based on Gen. 49.10 ('and in the vine were three branches') where the vine and the branches are variously explained (*b. Ḥul.* 92a). According to Rabbi Eliezer the vine is the world and the three branches are the patriarchs Abraham, Isaac and Jacob. Rabbi Joshua understood the vine as Torah and the branches as Moses, Aaron and Miriam. Rabbi Eleazar the Modiite interpreted the vine to refer to Jerusalem, while the branches referred to the Temple, the King (Messiah) and the High Priest. Rabbi Jeremiah ben Abba thought that the budding of the vine was an exhortation to Israel to be fruitful.

---

1. Translated in Levey, *The Messiah: An Aramaic Interpretation*, p. 119. See also Reim, 'Targum und Johannesevangelium', p. 9.

It cannot be said that any one of these interpretations lies behind (or has been influenced by) the Johannine discourse, but their style is certainly similar. Whereas Jesus calls himself the vine and his disciples branches, with fruitful ones abiding in him and fruitless ones not, the rabbis similarly suggested that the vine and branches were various institutions, nations, or individuals (some fruitful, some not). Put into the third person ('Messiah is the True Vine, and his disciples are the branches') the Johannine interpretation of the vine could be placed into the midrashim above and scarcely be thought of as out of place. Of course, with the comparison placed in the first person we have Jesus cast into the role of the self-predicating Wisdom and *logos*.

Another point should be mentioned. As Martin Hengel has recently argued, the True Vine discourse probably relates to the wine miracle at Cana (Jn 2.1-11).[1] In other words, by turning the water into wine Jesus illustrates that he is indeed the 'True Vine'. The wine miracle, which was the 'beginning of the signs' (Jn 2.11), may have been intended to recall Gen. 49.10-12 (which in the targums is paraphrased messianically): Messiah's robes will drip with wine. The wine miracle may also be part of the midrashic tradition associated with Moses: 'Moses said to Jethro: "In the waters of this well which God has given us we can taste of old wine, the taste of new wine…"'…Moses said to Jethro: "God is going to give us six good portions: the land of Israel, the future world, the new world, the kingdom of David, and the institution of the priests and Levites"' (*Mek.* on Exod. 18.9 [*Amalek* §3]).[2] Thus, at yet another point the True Wine discourse appears to suggest a context against the background of Jewish messianic ideas, ideas with which the Fourth Evangelist was familiar.

In sum, we have here all of the antecedents necessary to explain the origin and context of the Johannine True Vine discourse. The relevant imagery and vocabulary are almost ubiquitous in the Scriptures that the Johannine community shared with the synagogue. This imagery, taken up and applied by Jesus, circulated in early Christian traditions. The discourse found in the Fourth Gospel is distinctive, to be sure, but

1. M. Hengel, 'The Wine Miracle at Cana', in L.D. Hurst and N.T. Wright (eds.), *The Glory of Christ in the New Testament: Studies in Christology* (Oxford: Clarendon Press, 1987), pp. 83-112, esp. pp. 99-102.
2. Translation based on J.Z. Lauterbach, *Mekilta de-Rabbi Ishmael*, II (3 vols.; Philadelphia: Jewish Publication Society, 1933), pp. 174-75. See also Hengel, 'Wine Miracle', p. 111.

there is nothing about it that is inexplicable. Obviously there are no problems of chronology or provenance. The meaning of the vine/vineyard imagery of the Old Testament clarifies the Johannine discourse. The exegete is not left wondering what this discourse is talking about. One should think that it is hardly necessary to go off investigating other backgrounds, especially ones that are remote in time and place. But that is what Bultmann and a few others have done.

In this instance Bultmann does not examine the Old Testament backgrounds nearly as thoroughly as he did those lying behind the Good Shepherd discourse. Misreading the Johannine True Vine discourse (placing emphasis on the 'life' that the Revealer offers, when in fact the word 'life' does not occur in the passage and does not seem to be at issue),[1] he finds, relying primarily on the dissertation of his student Eduard Schweizer,[2] the Mandaean tree of life concept the true background against which John 15 should be understood. Like the parallels to the Good Shepherd proffered above, the parallels to the True Vine are of dubious value. Even the two most frequently quoted parallels, when understood in context, remind us more of typical wisdom language than of Johannine Christology: 'I am a gentle vine... and the great (Life) [= God] was my planter' (*Ginza* 301.11-14; cf. Jn 15.1); 'We are a vine, the vine of life, a tree on which there is no lie, the tree of praise, from the odor of which each man receives life' (*Ginza* 59.39–60.2; cf. Jn 15.5).[3] All of these self-predicates are

1. Reading Bultmann's discussion (*Gospel of John*, pp. 529-31) of the passage is very illuminating. He starts out discussing the meaning of the vine, two or three sentences later substitutes 'tree' for 'vine', and soon begins to talk about the significance of the 'tree of life' myth underlying the Johannine discourse. Then he notes that the tree of life myth plays a prominent role in Mandaean literature, thus pointing once again to the importance of this literature for the interpretation of the Fourth Gospel. The circularity of this reasoning is obvious.

2. E. Schweizer, *Ego Eimi: Die religionsgeschichtliche Herkunft und theologische Bedeutung der johanneischen Bildreden, zugleich ein Beitrag zur Quellenfrage des vierten Evangeliums* (FRLANT, 38; Göttingen: Vandenhoeck & Ruprecht, 1939), pp. 39-41. Schweizer has since largely abandoned his position; cf. *Ego Eimi* (Göttingen: Vandenhoeck & Ruprecht, 2nd edn, 1968), pp. 3-4; *idem*, 'The Concept of the Church in the Gospel and Epistles of St. John', in A.J.B. Higgins (ed.), *New Testament Essays: Studies in Memory of T.W. Manson* (Manchester: Manchester University Press, 1959), pp. 230-45, esp. pp. 233-234; *idem*, *Neotestamentica* (Zürich: Zwingli-Verlag, 1963), pp. 77-78, 260 n. 22.

3. R. Schnackenburg, *The Gospel according to St John*. III. *Commentary on*

reminiscent of what Old Testament Wisdom claims of herself: 'I grew
tall like a cedar in Lebanon...I grew tall like a palm tree in Engedi...
Like a cassia and camel's thorn I gave forth aroma, and like choice
myrrh I spread a pleasant odor...Like a vine I cause loveliness to bud,
and my blossoms became glorious and abundant fruit' (Sir. 24.13-
17);[1] 'She [Wisdom] is a tree of life to those who lay hold of her'
(Prov. 3.18).[2] Reference to the 'tree of life' is not uncommon in Old
Testament wisdom (cf. Prov. 11.30; 13.12; 15.4). The image has its
roots in the ancient creation account (cf. Gen. 2.9; 3.24). The origin
of Wisdom's association with the tree of life is not hard to deduce.
Wisdom's presence at creation (cf. Prov. 8.22-31) and her giving of
life to those who find her (cf. Prov. 8.35) made such an association all
but inevitable (cf. Prov. 3.18-20; Wis. 10.1-2). Remember too that
the vine was an important symbol for Israel.[3]

Moreover, the tree of life image in late antiquity was widespread,
represented in many cultures and languages. This makes it dangerous
to propose direct lines of influence, unless these lines are clearly
visible.[4] Paradise's tree of life gave rise to a variety of apocalyptic
and revelatory images. We find it frequently in apocalyptic literature,
both Jewish and Christian (cf. Rev. 22.2; *1 En.* 24–25, 30–32
[fragrant trees 'of wisdom']; *2 En.* 8; *3 En.* 5; 2 Esd. 2.12; *4 Bar.* 9.3,
16). The tree of life also inspired Gnostic allegories and interpretations, which, like much of the wisdom tradition, were usually based
on the Genesis account. The 'Tree of Eden' bears 'grapes of the vine'
in a passage some think may represent a Gnostic interpolation (*Apoc.
Abr.* 23.6-12; a similar Gnostic interpretation appears in *3 Bar.* 4.8:

Chapters 13–21 (repr.; New York: Crossroad, 1987 [1982]), p. 105.

1.   Bultmann (*Gospel of John*, p. 530 n. 5) notes that the Mandaean tree of life is
represented as a vine and as various types of trees. This is precisely the case in the
Old Testament wisdom traditions.

2.   For further discussion, see G. Ziener, 'Weisheitsbuch und Johannesevangelium', *Bib* 38 (1957), pp. 396-418.

3.   The vines and clusters of grapes were symbols of Israel's election (Num.
13.23-24; Deut. 1.25). Isaiah's Song of the Vineyard (Isa. 5.1-7) was probably
uttered on the occasion of the vintage celebration, which recalled the gift of the
Promised Land. The most prominent images of this symbol were the golden vines
and grape clusters that hung over the Temple gates. For a description, see Josephus,
War 5.5.4 §210; *Ant.* 15.11.3 §395; cf. Tacitus, *Hist.* 5.5. Vines and grapes were
commonly engraved on Jewish coinage.

4.   Carson, *Gospel according to John*, p. 513.

'the tree was the vine').[1] The *Apocryphon of John* says the tree of life
was placed in the garden in a grove of poisonous trees (NHC II,
21.16–22.2), while according to the *Gospel of Philip* Joseph the
carpenter planted a garden of trees, which included the tree of life and
the very tree from which he fashioned the cross (NHC II, 73.8-19).[2]
In the *Hypostasis of the Archons* (or *Reality of the Rulers*) we are told
that Eve (the 'mother of the living') is herself the tree of life (NHC II,
89.11-30). Epiphanius refers to a similar Gnostic allegorical interpretation (*Against Heresies* 26.5.1). In view of these interpretive
traditions, some of which can be dated to the second century, if not
late first, I think it is precarious to argue that the tree of life imagery
found in the late Mandaean sources is the principal element underlying
the True Vine discourse in the Fourth Gospel.

But perhaps even more problematic is the observation that the
Mandaean image says nothing about abiding and bearing fruit, which
are the main points of the Johannine discourse. Had Jesus said, 'I am
the tree of life', Bultmann's parallels might be worth taking a little
more seriously (although even this statement seems quite clearly to
derive from Old Testament wisdom and speculative traditions). As the
facts stand, it is hard to understand why the Mandaean parallels are
appealed to at all. Few have taken Bultmann's position,[3] arguing
instead that the Old Testament and early Jewish exegesis offer the
proper backdrop.[4] Schnackenburg is quite correct when he says that

1.   See R. Rubinkiewicz, 'Apocalypse of Abraham', in J.H. Charlesworth (ed.),
The Old Testament Apocrypha, I (2 vols.; Garden City, NY: Doubleday, 1983–85),
p. 684; H.E. Gaylord, '3 (Greek Apocalypse of) Baruch', in Charlesworth (ed.),
Apocrypha, I, pp. 666-67. The identification of the tree in the garden as a vine
appears in some early rabbis; cf. *b. Sanh.* 70a (R. Meir); *Gen. R.* 15.7 (on Gen. 2.9)
(R. Judah ben Ilai).
2.   The association of the cross with the trees of paradise is probably dependent
upon early Christian allegory. See the similar allegory in *Ign. Trall.* 11.1-2.
3.   For a cautious exception, see Schulz, *Komposition und Herkunft*, pp. 114-17.
4.   Barrett, *Gospel according to St John*, pp. 470-71; Beasley-Murray, *John*,
pp. 271-72; Brown, *Gospel according to John*, II, pp. 669-72; Carson, *Gospel
according to John*, pp. 511-14; Dodd, *Interpretation of the Fourth Gospel*, pp. 136-
37; E.C. Hoskyns, *The Fourth Gospel*, II (ed. F.N. Davey; 2 vols.; London: Faber
& Faber, 1940), pp. 559-60; Schnackenburg, *The Gospel according to St John*, III,
pp. 104-107. See especially R. Borig, *Der wahre Weinstock: Untersuchungen zu Jo
15,1-10* (SANT, 16; Munich: Kösel, 1967), pp. 79-128. For discussion of the comparison between Jesus and Israel as the vine, see A. Jaubert, 'L'image de la vigne

these parallels 'show the very different origin and meaning of the Mandaean image of the vine'.[1] Haenchen appropriately adds that 'the Fourth Gospel is not interested in the principal aim of Gnosticism, "rest" (ἀνάπαυσις), the final rest and passivity'.[2] It is hardly surprising therefore that contemporary commentators find little in the Mandaean sources that is helpful.

But bearing fruit is the main point of some of the Old Testament parallels surveyed above. The closest verbal parallel to the opening verse of the Johannine discourse ('I am the True Vine') is the statement in Jer. 2.21 ('I planted a fruit-bearing vine, altogether true').[3] Through his prophet God complains that Israel has not been fruitful (cf. Isa. 5.2, 4). The vine has not borne good fruit, only bad. This is the common complaint of the Old Testament prophets. But according to wisdom tradition (for example, Sir. 24.17) Wisdom is a fruitful vine. Wisdom becomes the antidote, as it were. Clearly this is the idea that lies behind the Fourth Gospel's True Vine discourse. Jesus, as God's wisdom, is the True Vine and by abiding in him (as opposed to a fruitless vine) one can bear fruit. In contrast to the false and failed vine, Jesus has produced the fruit that God has all along sought in Israel, but never found.

Assessment

The analysis offered above demonstrates the problem of using Mandaean sources for the interpretation of the Fourth Gospel. The Mandaean parallels simply do not meet the criteria that have been outlined for the determination of the validity of parallels found in post-New Testament documents. A second problem has also been revealed in that in the two discourses that have been examined, appeal to late sources was hardly necessary. To be sure, the Mandaean

(Jean 15)', in F. Christ (ed.), *Oikonomia: Heilsgeschichte als Thema der Theologie* (Hamburg: Reich, 1967), pp. 93-99.

1. Schnackenburg, *The Gospel according to St John*, III, p. 105.

2. E. Haenchen, *John 2: A Commentary on the Gospel of John Chapters 7–21* (Hermeneia; Philadelphia: Fortress Press, 1984), p. 131.

3. Assuming that 'vine' is the original reading (some versions and Fathers read ἀμπελῶν, 'vineyard'), it is then likely that Jer. 2.21 is in view; however, as it reads in the LXX (ἄμπελον...ἀληθινήν), not in the Hebrew (שֹׂרֵק, 'choice vine'), it is in contrast to LXX Isa. 5.2 which transliterates σωρήκ.

sources testify to the popularity of the shepherd/sheep and vine/tree imagery of late antiquity, but there is nothing about their forms of this imagery that compels us to conclude that they contain traditions that explain Johannine Christology better than the similar imagery found in Old Testament writings known to the Johannine community.

What remains to be seen is whether other Gnostic sources can meet our criteria and meaningfully clarify Johannine Christology. This question is addressed in the following chapter.

Chapter 2

GNOSTIC AND HERMETIC PARALLELS

After a masterful and illuminating survey of the Old Testament and Jewish Wisdom parallels that underlie the Johannine Prologue Rudolf Bultmann states: 'the Logos speculation of the Prologue of John derives from wisdom speculation present in Jewish sources'.[1] But because he could not account for the shift from Wisdom to *logos*, even after (a brief) consideration of Philo's concept of *logos* as a 'second God',[2] Bultmann felt it necessary to turn to the Mandaean myth of the Primal Man as it had recently been formulated by Richard Reitzenstein and others.[3] Although viewed by scholars for a few years as having promise, serious objections eventually were raised. Reitzenstein's

---

1. R. Bultmann, 'The History of Religions Background of the Prologue to the Gospel of John', in J. Ashton (ed.), *The Interpretation of John* (London: SPCK; Philadelphia: Fortress Press, 1986), p. 27.

2. Bultmann ('History of Religions Background', p. 33 n. 1) specifically rejected the view of J.R. Harris (*The Origin of the Prologue to St. John's Gospel* [Cambridge: Cambridge University Press, 1917]), who just a few years before the appearance of Bultmann's essay had concluded that the Prologue presents Jesus as God's Wisdom personified and that all elements are derived from the Old Testament.

3. R. Reitzenstein, *Das iranische Erlösungsmysterium* (Bonn: Marcus & Weber, 1921); cf. R. Reitzenstein and H.H. Schaeder, *Studien zum antiken Synkretismus aus Iran und Griechenland* (repr.; Darmstadt: Wissenschaftliche Buchgesellschaft, 1965 [1926]). Bultmann was also influenced by M. Lidzbarski, *Das Johannesbuch der Mandäer* (2 vols.; repr.; Giessen: Töpelmann, 1966 [1905–15]); ET of portions in G. Meade, *The Gnostic John the Baptizer* (London: Watkins, 1924); *idem, Mandäische Liturgien* (Berlin: Weidmann, repr.; 1962 [1920]); *idem, Ginza: Der Schatz order das grosse Buch der Mandäer* (QR, 13; Göttingen: Vandenhoeck & Ruprecht; Leipzig: Hinrichs, 1925). See also Bultmann's more detailed assessment of the value of the Mandaean materials in 'Die Bedeutung der neuerschlossenen mandäischen und manichäischen Quellen', pp. 55-104. Bultmann draws heavily upon these materials in his commentary on John.

construct was recognized as artificial and in places simply inaccurate.[1] The gap that he sensed existed between Old Testament–Jewish Wisdom traditions and the Johannine *logos* was exaggerated and his rejection of Philo's *logos* ideas too hasty.[2] And, of course, the chronological problem had not been overcome.[3] Hellenistic Jewish mysticism, perhaps with gnosticizing tendencies, appeared to many to be the more prudent approach, rather than Bultmann's speculative construct.[4]

1.   Dodd, *Interpretation of the Fourth Gospel*, p. 128; R.P. Casey, 'Gnosis, Gnosticism and the New Testament', in W.D. Davies and D. Daube (eds.), *The Background of the New Testament and its Eschatology* (Cambridge: Cambridge University Press, 1956), pp. 52-80, esp. p. 54; C. Colpe, *Die religionsgeschichtliche Schule: Darstellung und Kritik ihres Bildes vom gnostischen Erlösermythus* (FRLANT, 60; Göttingen: Vandenhoeck & Ruprecht, 1961), pp. 10-57; *idem*, 'New Testament and Gnostic Christology', in J. Neusner (ed.), *Religions in Antiquity* (NumSup, 14; Leiden: Brill, 1968), pp. 227-43, esp. pp. 235-37; R.N. Frye, 'Reitzenstein and Qumrân Revisited by an Iranian', *HTR* 55 (1962), pp. 261-68.

2.   Barrett, *Gospel according to St John*, pp. 152-54; Brown, *Gospel according to John*, I, pp. 519-24; Carson, *Gospel according to John*, pp. 114-17; Lindars, *Gospel of John*, pp. 77, 80-82; Schnackenburg, *Gospel according to St John*, I, pp. 229-32; P. Borgen, 'God's Agent in the Fourth Gospel', in Neusner (ed.), *Religions in Antiquity*, pp. 137-48; repr. in Ashton (ed.), *The Interpretation of John*, pp. 67-78, esp. p. 75; *idem*, 'Observations on the Targumic Character of the Prologue of John', *NTS* 16 (1970), pp. 288-95, esp. p. 290; J.D.G. Dunn, *Christology in the Making: An Inquiry into the Origins of the Doctrine of the Incarnation* (London: SCM Press, 1980), pp. 239-44.

3.   Hoskyns, *Fourth Gospel*, I, pp. 140-41; Dodd, *Interpretation of the Fourth Gospel*, p. 130; Casey, 'Gnosis', p. 55; R.M. Grant, *Gnosticism: A Sourcebook of Heretical Writings from the Early Christian Period* (New York: Harper & Brothers, 1961), p. 14.

4.   The number of scholars who view the Johannine Prologue as Gnostic or based on Gnostic sources is dwindling; pace D. Deeks, 'The Prologue of St. John's Gospel', *BTB* 6 (1976), pp. 62-78. See H. Schlier, '"Im Anfang war das Wort" im Prolog des Johannesevangeliums', *Wort und Wahrheit* 9 (1954), pp. 169-80; repr. as 'Im Anfang war das Wort: Zum Prolog des Johannesevangeliums', in *Die Zeit der Kirche: Exegetische Aufsätze und Vorträge* (Freiburg: Herder, 5th edn, 1972), pp. 274-86; R. Schnackenburg, 'Logos-Hymnus und johanneischen Prolog', *BZ* 1 (1957), pp. 69-109; *idem*, 'Und das Wort ist Fleisch geworden', *IKZ* 8 (1979), pp. 1-9; W. Eltester, 'Der Logos und sein Prophet: Fragen zur heutigen Erklärung des johanneischen Prologs', in U. Eickelberg *et al.* (eds.), *Apophoreta* (BZNW, 30; Berlin: Töpelmann, 1964), pp. 109-34; P.H. Langkammer, 'Zur Herkunft des Logostitels im Johannesprolog', *BZ* 9 (1965), pp. 91-94; H. Ridderbos, 'The Structure and Scope of the Prologue to the Gospel of John', *NovT* 8 (1966), pp. 180-201; C. Demke, 'Der sogennante Logos-Hymnus im johannischen Prolog', *ZNW* 58

However, the discovery and eventual publication of the Coptic Gnostic Codices discovered at Nag Hammadi sparked new interest in the problem and has led some to think that Bultmann's theory might have been right, but had suffered from lack of adequate documentation.[1] Coptic Gnosticism, it is supposed, may supply the missing evidence, and, along with other expressions of Gnosticism, may provide the closest parallels to Johannine thought.

This chapter will consider three sources that have been and continue to be viewed as important witnesses to significant components of Johannine Christology. The first source is Coptic Gnosticism, particularly the *Trimorphic Protennoia* from Nag Hammadi. The second source is the Syriac *Odes of Solomon*, a document some have thought to be Gnostic (and on which Bultmann drew heavily in his interpretation of the Johannine Prologue). As we shall see, this is highly debatable. The third source is the *Corpus Hermeticum*, particularly tractates I and XIII.

Coptic Gnosticism

Trimorphic Protennoia

The *Trimorphic Protennoia* ('First Thought in Three Forms') is the only surviving tractate from NHC XIII. The extant MS dates from the

(1967), pp. 45-68; E. Fascher, 'Christologie und Gnosis im vierten Evangelium', *TLZ* 93 (1968) cols. 721-30; J.C. O'Neill, 'The Prologue to St John's Gospel', *JTS* 20 (1969), pp. 41-52; K. Wengst, *Christologische Formeln und Lieder im Urchristentums* (SNT, 7; Gütersloh: Gerd Mohn, 1972), pp. 200-208; H. Zimmermann, 'Christushymnus und johanneischer Prolog', in J. Gnilka (ed.), *Neues Testament und Kirche* (Freiburg: Herder, 1974), pp. 249-65; I. de la Potterie, 'Structure du Prologue de Saint Jean', *NTS* 30 (1984), pp. 354-81; Sevrin, 'Le quatrième évangile et le gnosticisme: questions de méthode', pp. 251-68. Although some of the above studies allow for Gnostic influences of one sort or another (with 'Gnostic' broadly defined), there is little support for arguments that see a Gnostic myth underlying the Prologue.

1. See Robinson, 'The Johannine Trajectory', pp. 264-66. Holding forth along the same lines, H. Koester (*Introduction to the New Testament*, II [2 vols.; New York: deGruyter, 1982], pp. 178-98, 214-16; *idem*, 'Les discours d'adieu de l'évangile de Jean: leur trajectoire au premier et au deuxième siècle', in Kaestli *et al.* [eds.], *La communauté johannique*, pp. 269-80) continues to argue that Gnosticism is pre-Christian and that a Gnostic interpretation of Jesus' words lay at the beginning of Johannine theology.

mid-fourth century CE. John Turner dates its composition, like that of the *Apocryphon of John* (NHC II, *1*; III, *1*; IV, *1*; BG8502, 2), to the middle of the second second century CE.[1] The tractate receives its name from the fact that it treats three aspects of the invisible spirit's 'first thought': the Barbelo aeon, Life (*zoe*), and Word (*logos*). It is the last aspect that offers some of the most important parallels to Johannine thought. Another important feature is that *Protennoia* speaks in the first person, frequently saying, 'I am', for example, 'I am Protennoia' (35.1), 'I am the Life' (35.12), 'I am Voice' (35.32; 36.14; 42.4), 'I am the Word' (for example, 46.5, 14), and 'I am the Light' (47.28-29). Some of these self-predicates parallel those of the Fourth Gospel.

On the basis of his study of the *Trimorphic Protennoia*, Carsten Colpe listed the following parallels (which he described as 'stupendous'):[2]

Prologue of John	Trimorphic Protennoia
1 'In the beginning was the Word... this one	'[I] am...[the first-]born among those who [came
2 was in the beginning with God'	to be, she who exists] before the All' (35.1-6).
3 'All things came to be through him'	'it is through me that the All took shape' (38.12-13).
4 'in him was life'	'I am the life of my Epinoia' (35.12-13).
5 'the light shines in the darkness'	'I shone down [upon the darkness]' (36.5).

1. J.D. Turner, 'Trimorphic Protennoia', in J.M. Robinson (ed.), *The Nag Hammadi Library in English* (Leiden: Brill; San Francisco: Harper & Row, rev. edn, 1988), pp. 511, 513.

2. C. Colpe, 'Heidnische, jüdische und christliche Überlieferung in den Schriften aus Nag Hammadi, III', *JAC* 17 (1974), pp. 109-25, esp. p. 123. He calls the parallels 'stupendous' on p. 122. J.M. Robinson ('Gnosticism and the New Testament', pp. 129-30) also cites them. Translations of the Coptic are taken from Turner, 'Trimorphic Protennoia', pp. 513-22. See also B. Layton, *The Gnostic Scriptures* (Garden City, NY: Doubleday, 1987), pp. 89-100. For a critical edition of the Coptic text, see C.W. Hedrick (ed.), *Nag Hammadi Codices XI, XII, XIII* (NHS, 28; Leiden: Brill, 1990). For a critical commentary, see Y. Janssens, *La Protennoia Trimorphe* (Bibliothèque copte de Nag Hammadi: Section 'Textes' 4; Québec: Laval University Press, 1978).

7 'This one came for a witness, in order that he should witness concerning the light, in order that all should believe through him.'

'Then the Son... that is, the Word who originated through that Voice... revealed the everlasting things and all the unknowns were known' (37.3-9).

9 'He was the true light which enlightens every person.'

'[I] am the light that illumines the All' (47.28-29).

10 'He was in the world, and the world came into being through him, and the world did not know him.'

'Then the perfect Son revealed himself to his aeons who originated through him' (38.16-18); 'those who watch over their dwelling places did not recognize me' (50.15-16).

11 'He came to his own things, and his own people did not receive him.'

'Indeed all these I explained to those who are mine, who are the Sons of the Light' (41.15-16); 'I hid myself within them until I revealed myself to my [brethren]. And none of them (the Powers) knew me, [although] it is I who work in them' (47.22-25).

12 'But as many as received him, he gave to them authority to become children of God.'

'He taught unrepeatable doctrines to all those who became Sons of the Light' (37.18-20); 'to the Sons of the Light, alone, that is, the ordinances of the Father. These are the glories that are higher than every glory, that is, [the Five] Seals complete by virtue of Intellect' (49.25-28).

14 'And the Word became flesh and dwelt among us, and we beheld his glory, glory as of the only begotten of the Father, full of grace and truth.'

'The third time I revealed myself to them in their tents as Word... And I wore everyone's garment' (47.13-17); 'and (he) stood in the glory with which he glorified himself. They blessed the Perfect Son, the Christ' (38.20-22).

16 'Of his fulness we all received.'

'It (the Word) is a hidden Light, bearing a Fruit of Life, pouring forth a Living Water from the... immeasurable Spring' (46.16-19).

| 18 | 'No one has ever seen God; the only begotten God who exists in the bosom of the Father has made him known.' | 'It is invisible' (36.30); 'I am the thought of the Father and through me proceeded [the] Voice, that is, the knowledge of the everlasting things. I exist as Thought for the [All]—being joined to the unknowable and incomprehensible Thought—I revealed myself' (36.17-23). |

Colpe's parallels are drawn from the entire text of the *Trimorphic Protennoia*. Impressed with these parallels, and in an attempt to underscore the extent and concentration of the verbal and conceptual similarities, twelve years ago I offered the following parallels between the Prologue and slightly less than two pages of the Coptic text:[1]

Prologue of John		*Trimorphic Protennoia*
1	beginning	46.10 beginning
	word	46.5, 14, 16, 30; 47.15 word
	with God	46.20-21 offspring of God
3	through him all things became	46.24-25 the source of the All, the root of the entire Aeon; 47.10 a foundation for the All
4	life	46.17 life; 46.17 living water
	light	46.11, 16, 24 light
5	darkness	46.32 darkness
9	illuminates every man coming into the world	46.32 illumine those who dwell in darkness
10	know	46.35; 47.19 know
11	he came to his own, but his own did not receive him	46.31 it was sent; 47.18-19 they did not know the one who empowers me
12	to them he gave power to be children of God	47.10-11 I empowered them

1. Evans, 'On the Prologue of John', p. 397. By restricting the parallels to two pages of the Coptic text I felt that the comparison with the prologue, itself only about a page in length, was more realistic.

14	the Word became flesh	47.15-16 as the Word and I revealed myself in the likeness of their shape
	and dwelt (σκηνοῦν) among us	47.13-18 I revealed myself to them in their tents [Greek loan word: σκηνή] as the Word
	glory	46.19, 27 glory
16	fullness	46.11-30 [fullness=list of attributes]
18	that one revealed him	46.33-35 I will reveal to you my mysteries since you are my fellow brethren

As impressive as these parallels are, serious questions remain as to the relationship between John's Prologue and the *Trimorphic Protennoia*. Here we may look to the criteria delineated above in Chapter 1. First, there is no solid evidence that a Jewish Gnostic redeemer myth existed early enough to have had any influence on the Fourth Gospel or any other writings of the New Testament.[1] Robinson and his colleagues, of course, are convinced that such a myth did exist and that it predated Christianity. The problem, however, is that the putative evidence for such a pre-Christian myth derives from documents such as the *Trimorphic Protennoia*. But dating the tradition underlying the *Trimorphic Protennoia* is largely determined by conclusions as to its relationship to John and the New Testament. The circularity of the problem is obvious. In short, the *Trimorphic Protennoia* does not meet the criterion of antecedent documentation. This does not necessarily disqualify it as a potentially helpful source, but it does measurably increase the burden of proof for those who wish to argue that it contains ideas that antedate the Fourth Gospel.

Secondly, there are the obvious allusions to Christianity and to other writings of the New Testament. This fact could mean that much of the thought of the tractate, and not just the extant text, has been influenced

1. As has been ably pointed out recently by C.H. Talbert, 'The Myth of a Descending–Ascending Redeemer in Mediterranean Antiquity', *NTS* 22 (1976), pp. 418-40; and earlier by Colpe, *Die religionsgeschichtliche Schule*, pp. 39-40, 50-51. Pace K. Rudolph ('Problems of a History of the Development of the Mandaean Religion', *History of Religions* 8 [1969], pp. 210-35, esp. pp. 210-11), who believes that the evidence is more than sufficient, and whom Robinson ('The Johannine Trajectory', p. 264 n. 56) cites with full approval, there is no objective evidence that such a myth as reconstructed by Reitzenstein, Bultmann or Rudolph existed in the first century CE, or if it did, that it is the presupposition of Johannine Christology.

by Christian ideas and even by the New Testament writings.[1] Gnostic
scholars are, of course, aware of these allusions, but tend to regard
many of them as secondary Christianizing.[2] It must be admitted that
this could very well be the case in some instances, but many of these
obvious Christian allusions cannot be explained away so readily. (These
allusions and possible influences will be further examined below.)
Some Gnostic scholars believe that some of the most impressive parallels
are part of the original form of the text and possibly point to a
redeemer myth that Christianity, in this case the Johannine community,
later adopted and adapted.[3] Nevertheless, the burden of proof
rests heavily on those who maintain that the *Trimorphic Protennoia*
has not been significantly influenced by distinctively Christian ideas.[4]

1.   See R.M. Wilson, 'The *Trimorphic Protennoia*', in M. Krause (ed.), *Gnosis
and Gnosticism* (NHS, 8; Leiden: Brill, 1977), pp. 50-54, esp. p. 54.
2.   J.M. Robinson, 'Gnosticism and the New Testament', p. 129. At this point
Robinson sharply disagrees with Wilson, for the latter thinks that in some instances
apparently non-Christian Gnostic texts may have been Christian originally but have
gone through a process of de-Christianization, as Gnostic groups became increasingly
alienated from the 'Great Church'.
3.   See the discussion in J.M. Robinson, 'The Prologue of John and the
Trimorphic Protennoia', p. 29; *idem*, 'Sethians and Johannine Thought', p. 665; and
G. Robinson, 'The Trimorphic Protennoia', pp. 42-45. Turner ('Trimorphic
Protennoia', pp. 512-13) has concluded that the *Trimorphic Protennoia* went through
three stages of development. 1. 'There was the original triad of the aretalogical self-
predications of Protennoia as Voice, Speech, and Word that were probably built up
out of the Jewish wisdom tradition [for example, *1 En.* 42, Sir. 24, Wis. 7–8, and
Philo] and maybe out of *The Apocryphon of John*'s similar Pronoia aretalogy itself
sometime during the first century C.E.; there is little here that seems specifically
gnostic or Christian'. 2. 'This was supplemented...by various narrative doctrinal
passages based upon traditional Barbeloite [Gnostic] theogonic materials similar to
those of *The Apocryphon of John*'. 3. The 'last stage of composition seems to have
involved a deliberately polemical incorporation of Christian, specifically Johannine
Christian, materials into the aretalogical portion of the third subtractate [i.e., the
Word]'.
4.   Years ago W. Bousset (*KYRIOS CHRISTOS: Geschichte des Christusglaubens von den Anfängen des Christentums bis Irenaeus* [Göttingen: Vandenhoeck & Ruprecht, 5th edn, 1965], pp. 305-306; ET *KYRIOS CHRISTOS: A History
of the Belief in Christ from the Beginnings of Christianity to Irenaeus* [Nashville:
Abingdon Press, 1970], pp. 388-90) had observed that the figure of *logos* remained
foreign to Gnosticism until introduced into Valentianism under the influence of the
Johannine writings. He regarded its appearance in Barbeloite Gnosticism (such as
seen in the *Apocryphon of John* [cf. BG 8502, 2]) as late and syncretistic. Bousset, of

Thus, it is far from clear that the strictures arising out of the criterion of contamination have been met.

Thirdly, no one has been able to identify the provenance of the *Trimorphic Protennoia*. Did it derive from the world shared by the Johannine community or by this community's ideological ancestors? Some scholars assume that it did, but this is simply an assumption. The problem once again is one of circularity. Since it is argued that the *Trimorphic Protennoia* presupposes the redeemer myth presupposed by the Fourth Gospel, the two documents must share a common background. But if the protasis of this statement is faulty, then the apodosis is completely without force. Although the *Trimorphic Protennoia* has not necessarily failed to meet the criterion of provenance, there is no objective evidence that it has met it.

Does Qumran suggest that the *Trimorphic Protennoia* could be part of a gnosticizing Jewish world? Bultmann and others thought that the discovery of the Dead Sea Scrolls, with their dualism and emphasis on knowledge and wisdom, provided the 'missing link' between Old Testament Judaism and gnosticizing Christianity. He states: 'While a pre-Christian gnosticizing Judaism could hitherto only be deduced out of later sources, the existence of such is now testified by the manuscripts recently discovered in Palestine (that is, Qumran)'.[1] The relevance of the Scrolls for Johannine studies can scarcely be doubted.[2]

---

course, had no opportunity to analyze the function of *logos* in the *Trimorphic Protennoia*. Nevertheless, Bousset's conclusion with regard to Valentianian Gnosticism may very well apply to the Barbeloite *Trimorphic Protennoia*.

1. R. Bultmann, *Theology of the New Testament*, II (2 vols.; New York: Charles Scribner's Sons, 1951–55), p. 13 (and note). Robinson ('Johannine Trajectory', p. 265) concurs with O. Cullmann's assertion that the existence of pre-Christian Gnosticism 'is especially confirmed by...the discovery of the scrolls from Qumran'.

2. H. Braun (*Qumran und das Neue Testament*, I [2 vols.; Tübingen: Mohr (Paul Siebeck), 1966], p. 98) concluded that Johannine dualism can be understood against a Palestinian backdrop. For a delineation of the parallels between Qumran and the Fourth Gospel, see Braun, *Qumran*, II, pp. 135-44. After identifying eleven significant parallels between the Fourth Gospel and 1QS 3.13–4.26, J.H. Charlesworth ('A Critical Comparison of the Dualism in 1QS 3.13–4.26 and the "Dualism" Contained in the Gospel of John', in J.H. Charlesworth [ed.], *John and the Dead Sea Scrolls* [repr.; New York: Crossroad, 1990 (1972)], pp. 104) concludes that 'John probably borrowed some of his dualistic terminology and mythology from 1QS'. This subject will be taken up and discussed further in Chapter 5.

But do they provide evidence of first-century Palestinian Gnosticism? Some scholars think they do.[1] The following emphases found in the Scrolls are often cited as evidence: (1) dualism; (2) elitism; (3) revelatory exegesis; and (4) social separatism. Other scholars, however, have noted that there are significant points of differences between Qumran and Gnosticism.[2] 1. In Qumran there is no split in the Godhead, hence there is no demiurge.[3] God is the God of the Old Testament and the Jewish people. 2. In Qumran there is no concept of the 'divine spark'. Qumranian elitism has to do with morality, having a heart for God, much in the way it is understood in the Old Testament. 3. At Qumran

1. According to C.K. Barrett, *The Gospel of John and Judaism* (London: SPCK; Philadelphia: Fortress Press, 1975), p. 56: 'Thus, it is not to be denied that the scrolls show a decided interest in "knowledge" and in apparently dualistic pairs such as light and darkness. This interest confirms the conjecture already made, that is, that Hellenistic and Gnostic ways of thinking had already penetrated Palestine'. See also *idem*, 'The Theological Vocabulary of the Fourth Gospel and of the Gospel of Truth', in W. Klassen and G.F. Snyder (eds.), *Current Issues in New Testament Interpretation* (New York: Harper & Row; London: SCM Press, 1962), pp. 210-23. K.G. Kuhn ('Die in Palästina gefundenen hebräischen Texte und das Neue Testament', *ZTK* 47 [1950], pp. 192-211) agrees that 'the gnostic "concept of knowledge" is present' (p. 203) in the Scrolls and that therefore it is appropriate to speak of a 'preliminary form of gnostic thought' (p. 204), but in a later study ('Johannesevangelium und Qumrantexte', in A.N. Wilder *et al.* (eds.), *Neotestamentica et Patristica* [NovTSup, 6; Leiden: Brill, 1962], pp. 111-22, esp. pp. 117-21) he identifies several important differences between Johannine and Qumranian thought and that of Gnosticism. Other scholars who think that the Scrolls document early Jewish Gnosticism include K. Rudolph, 'War der Verfasser der Oden Salomos ein "Qumran-Christ"? Ein Beitrag zur Diskussion um die Anfänge der Gnosis', *RevQ* 4 (1964), pp. 523-55; K. Schubert, 'Der Sektenkanon von En-Feschcha und die Anfänge der jüdischen Gnosis', *TLZ* 78 (1953) cols. 495-506; and W. Schmithals, 'Introduction', in Bultmann, *Gospel of John*, p. 8. B. Reicke ('Traces of Gnosticism in the Dead Sea Scrolls?', *NTS* 1 [1954], pp. 137-41) is more cautious, suggesting that Qumran represents 'a stage on the way to Jewish-Hellenistic speculations' that bridge 'the gap between Jewish Apocalyptic and Gnosticism' (p. 141).

2. H. Ringgren, 'Qumran and Gnosticism', in U. Bianchi (ed.), *Le Origini dello Gnosticismo* (NumSup, 12; Leiden: Brill, 1967), pp. 379-84; M. Mansoor, 'The Nature of Gnosticism in Qumran', in Bianchi (ed.), *Le Origini dello Gnosticismo*, pp. 389-400; M. Black, *The Scrolls and Christian Origins* (New York: Charles Scribner's Sons, 1961); W.S. LaSor, *The Dead Sea Scrolls and the New Testament* (Grand Rapids: Eerdmans, 1972), pp. 89-91.

3. 1QS 3.15-18, part of the well-known dualism passage, expressly affirms that 'the God of knowledge' created all that there is.

it is *righteousness* (which entailed strict obedience to the Law, as the sectaries interpreted it) and not *gnosis* that is the crucial ingredient for salvation. 4. In Qumran there is no cosmic dualism. Matter is not considered evil. Qumranian dualism is ethical. 5. Important Gnostic terms such as 'sleep', 'intoxication' and 'awakening' are not found in Qumran. 6. Qumranian terminology as 'knowledge' (דעת), 'wisdom' (חכמה), 'understanding' (בינה or שׂכל), and 'mystery' (רז) indicate that at most some members of the community may have thought of them-selves as sages.[1] What we have here is a wisdom tradition more akin to Old Testament wisdom than to a form of Jewish Gnosticism. 7. Finally, there is no Gnostic myth of a divine redeemer in the literature of Qumran. Indeed, Qumranian eschatology is remarkably reserved when it comes to speculations about heavenly agents of redemption and restoration. Only in a very few places is there reference to an 'anointed' one. How important his role will be is not made clear. There certainly is no idea of some sort of heavenly agent who will descend and impart knowledge. Even the revered Teacher of Righteousness (or Right Teacher) is human and nothing more. George MacRae, who was sympathetic to much of what Robinson has tried to advance, concluded that the 'Scrolls do not contain Gnostic ideas, although they do belong to the broader movement of apocalyptic Judaism which may well have been a forerunner of Gnosticism'.[2] MacRae is probably correct. In view of its syncretistic nature, many ideas can legitimately be identified as 'forerunners' of Gnosticism.

Fourthly, to demonstrate that the *Trimorphic Protennoia* actually contains a redeemer myth that lies behind the Johannine Prologue (and the Gospel as a whole) it would be helpful, although not essential, to

1. C. Romaniuk, 'Le thème de la sagesse dans les documents de Qumran', *RevQ* 15 (1978), pp. 429-35; R.E. Brown, *The Semitic Background of 'Mystery' in the New Testament* (Philadelphia: Fortress Press, 1968). Qumran's emphasis on knowledge is hardly evidence of Gnosticism; cf. B. Reicke, 'Da'at and Gnosis in Intertestamental Literature', in E.E. Ellis and M. Wilcox (eds.), *Neotestamentica et Semitica* (Edinburgh: T. & T. Clark, 1969), pp. 245-55. Reicke here seems a little more reserved than he was in the older study cited above ('Traces of Gnosticism in the Dead Sea Scrolls?'). He finds that 'knowledge' was very common in the intertes-tamental literature, especially in Wisdom writings. 'This should be a caution-sign to those who talk uncritically of a general Gnostic background of primitive Christianity' ('Da'at and Gnosis', p. 245).

2. G.W. MacRae, 'Gnosticism and New Testament Studies', *Bible Today* 38 (1968), p. 2629.

show how the former clarifies the meaning of the latter. But we encounter two difficulties here. First, if it was indeed based on the Gnostic redeemer myth documented by the *Trimorphic Protennoia*, the Johannine Prologue made use of only one element of the myth (that is, the *logos*'s dwelling on earth). This presents us with a difficulty. By way of illustration, it would be like arguing that Jude made use of 2 Peter, rather than the reverse. As is well known, a major reason that interpreters have universally concluded that 2 Peter made use of Jude is because what is tightly and succinctly argued in the latter is spread out and altered in the former. Most of Jude is found in 2 Peter, but the reverse cannot be said. If Jude had made use of 2 Peter, then why was so much of 2 Peter left out? To apply this question to the issue at hand, if the Johannine Prologue presupposes the myth found in the *Trimorphic Protennoia*, why has only part of it been adopted?

The second problem that I see is that J.M. Robinson and his supporters believe that the Prologue's relationship to the *Trimorphic Protennoia* clarifies the theology of the Prologue (and so meets our fourth criterion). According to Robinson, 'the *Trimorphic Protennoia* would not itself be the long-sought "source" of the Johannine prologue, but would through its own pre-Christian Jewish background provide the *best available access* [my emphasis] to the background of the Johannine prologue'.[1] To this adds G. Robinson: '[The] *Trimorphic Protennoia*...provides the *natural context* [my emphasis] for the Fourth Gospel...[What is important is *Protennoia*'s] basic substance, which is no doubt pre-Christian, if not perhaps in a chronological sense, at least in terms of the history of tradition'.[2] Citing this recent study with approval, Jack Sanders asserts that her 'essay makes it clear that the Nag Hammadi literature, and the *Trimorphic Protennoia* in particular, is of *prime importance* [my emphasis] for an adequate understanding of the christological expressions in the Johannine prologue'.[3] These are remarkable claims, and they are essentially the same views expressed a few years earlier by Robinson's German colleagues: 'The light falls more from the *Protennoia* to the Prologue

    1.   J.M. Robinson, 'The Prologue of the Gospel of John', p. 29.
    2.   G. Robinson, 'The Trimorphic Protennoia', p. 45.
    3.   J.T. Sanders, 'Nag Hammadi, Odes of Solomon, and NT Christological Hymns', in Goehring *et al.* (eds.), *Gnosticism and the Early Christian World*, p. 53.

of John than vice versa'.[1] But does this relationship, as Robinson and
the Berliner Arbeitskreis have described it, significantly clarify
Jn 1.1-18?[2] I do not think that it does. As will be shown in Chapters 3
and 4, the Old Testament and Jewish wisdom–exegetical traditions,
which are not open to the objections raised against the late Gnostic
sources, are sufficient to clarify the Johannine background.

For James Robinson perhaps the most compelling argument for
viewing the *Trimorphic Protennoia* as relatively independent of New
Testament Christology and therefore as a potentially early witness to
the concepts that went into New Testament, particularly Johannine,
Christology is the presence in this sole surviving tractate of Codex
XIII of a concentration of the vocabulary and imagery found in the
Johannine Prologue. Early on this feature was observed by Carsten
Colpe: 'What is disparate there [that is, in Wisdom traditions], stands
together here [that is, in the *Protennoia*], even though not in the
sequence of the Prologue. This would seem to be unique up to the present'.[3] Robinson believes that this concentration testifies to the
'trajectory of the spirit of Late Antiquity' that provides the 'background of the Johannine Prologue'.[4] He raised this point again at the
1978 Yale Conference on Gnosticism. In the discussion following the
presentation of his paper he made the following statement:

> Professors Colpe and [Alexander] Böhlig both have vacillated in deciding
> whether the background of the two texts is already Gnostic or still Jewish
> Wisdom. Admittedly one can't use the *Trimorphic Protennoia* to estab-
> lish the Gnostic origin of the Johannine prologue. But Professor Wilson
> is understating the evidence when he speaks of both texts as simply going
> back to Jewish Wisdom literature. Given the mass of Jewish literature
> available, why do we find the only concentrated cluster of parallels to the

---

1. See G. Schenke, 'Die dreigestaltige Protennoia', col. 733.

2. In view of the parallels adduced above it is still possible, of course, that the
Trimorphic Protennoia contains an essentially independent version of a redeemer
myth that coincides closely with the incarnational theology of the Johannine Prologue. I am inclined to think that this is probable and that the *Trimorphic Protennoia*
documents this myth with significant Christian, even specifically Johannine,
influences.

3. Colpe, 'Heidnische, jüdische und christliche Überlieferung', p. 122.
J.M. Robinson cites this statement approvingly in 'Gnosticism and the New
Testament', p. 129.

4. J.M. Robinson, 'Gnosticism and the New Testament', p. 131.

prologue in one text, *Trimorphic Protennoia*? We must try to use this fact in a more pointed fashion. I agree that the background is Jewish Wisdom literature. But these two texts shared in the same converging force that drew out from Jewish Wisdom a unique concentration.[1]

By way of reply, two points should be made. First, I think that the significance of the 'unique concentration' in the *Trimorphic Protennoia* has been exaggerated. In my judgment the concentration of parallels that one finds in Sirach 24 is equally impressive, perhaps even more so (see Chapter 3). Colpe's point about the 'disparate' parallels in Jewish Wisdom is in a certain sense misleading. The most significant Jewish Wisdom parallels can be found in two or three books (that is, Proverbs, Sirach, and Wisdom of Solomon), which in the first century were contained within a single book (or collection of scrolls) known as the Septuagint. Secondly, the relationship of the *Trimorphic Protennoia* to the Gospel of John, as well as to several New Testament writings, is very problematic. Robinson prefers to believe that this Nag Hammadi tractate is essentially independent, with at best some minor secondary Christianizing.[2] But when one observes what appear to be allusions to Johannine passages and phrases and to other other New Testament writings, such as Colossians and even synoptic tradition, one begins to wonder if this remarkable 'concentration' is not as independent as Robinson hopes.[3] This question relates directly to the problem of contamination and the difficulty of knowing when a 'parallel' is a true parallel or no more than an allusion to an antecedent text or tradition.

The criterion of contamination is a problem for much of the Nag Hammadi library. Many of the tractates quote, allude to, or appear to be influenced by the writings of the New Testament. Several examples will serve to underscore the magnitude of this problem. The *Trimorphic Protennoia* is but one of many of these writings that betrays knowledge of Jn 1.1, 14, 18. The *Prayer of the Apostle Paul* (I, *1*) speaks of the 'First-born of the Pleroma [that is, fullness] of grace'[4]

---

1. J.M. Robinson, 'Sethians and Johannine Thought', p. 666.
2. J.M. Robinson, 'Sethians and Johannine Thought', pp. 653-62.
3. According to M. Hengel (*The Johannine Question* [London: SCM Press; Philadelphia: Trinity Press International, 1989], pp. 113, 213 n. 47) the *Trimorphic Protennoia* 'is a relatively late mixed product of a great variety of influences, including Jewish wisdom speculation, but also the Gospels, above all John'; 'The Valentinian features are obvious'.
4. Translations are from J.M. Robinson (ed.), *The Nag Hammadi Library in*

(A 23-24; cf. Jn 1.14c), which 'was formed in the beginning' (A 32-33; cf. Jn 1.1a).[1] According to the *Apocryphon of James* (I, 2) the Lord says to James: 'I came down to dwell with you [pl.] so that you [pl.] in turn might dwell with me...I have made my abode in the houses that could receive me at the time of my descent' (9.2-8; cf. Jn 1.14b). According to the *Gospel of Truth* (I, 3) the Father contemplates his Word, then sends it forth, and by so doing has revealed his bosom (23.19-22, 33-35; 24.9-10; cf. Jn 1.1, 14, 18).[2] 'When the Word appeared...it became a body' (*Gos. Truth* 26.4-8),[3] for 'he [the Son] came by means of fleshly form' (*Gos. Truth* 31.4-6). The *Treatise on the Resurrection* (I, 4) adds that the Son of God, who was also the Son of Man, came to restore the Pleroma, through whom come grace and truth (43.36–45.13; cf. Jn 1.14).[4] According to the *Tripartite Tractate* (I, 5) the redeemer is 'an only Son' (57.19, 21; cf. Jn 1.18), who has 'existed from the beginning' (*Tri. Trac.* 57.35; cf. Jn 1.1), who gives light to those who have taken his name (*Tri. Trac.* 62.33-35; cf. Jn 1.5, 9, 12), who is the '*logos*' (*Tri. Trac.* 75.22; cf. Jn 1.1), who 'gave glory to the Father' (*Tri. Trac.* 76.3-6; 77.11-13; cf. Jn 1.14b; 17.5), and who 'came into being in flesh' (*Tri. Trac.* 113.38; cf. Jn 1.14). The Savior, we are told, received his flesh from this *logos* (*Tri. Trac.* 114.7-10; cf. Jn 1.14).[5] 'About the [one] who appeared in flesh they believed without any doubt that he is the Son of the unknown God, who was not previously spoken of and who could not be seen' (*Tri. Trac.* 133.16-21; cf. Jn 1.12, 14, 18).[6] According to the *Apocryphon of John* (II, 1) the divine mother gave birth to 'an only-begotten child', an 'only-begotten one of the Father' (*Ap. John*

English. Layton (*Gnostic Scriptures*, 305) also detects an allusion at A 23-24 to Jn 1.14.

1. Note also the clear allusion in A 26-29 to 1 Cor. 2.9.

2. Layton (*Gnostic Scriptures*, 257) also detects an allusion at *Gos. Truth* 24.9-10 to Jn 1.18.

3. Layton (*Gnostic Scriptures*, 257) also detects an allusion to Jn 1.14.

4. Note also the clear allusion in *Treat. Res.* 115.9-11 ('he had let himself be conceived and born as an infant, in body and soul') to the Gospel infancy tradition.

5. Note also the clear allusion in *Tri. Trac.* 45.14-15 ('the Savior swallowed up death...he put aside the world which is perishing [and] transformed [himself] into an imperishable Aeon') to 1 Cor. 15.53-54.

6. Note also the clear allusion in *Tri. Trac.* 133.30–134.1 ('and when he was in the tomb as a dead man the [angels] thought that he was alive, [receiving] life from the one who had died') to the Gospel Easter tradition.

Word and Glory

6.15-18; cf. Jn 1.14, 18). 'And the [W]ord followed the will. For because of the [W]ord, Christ the divine Autogenes created everything' (*Ap. John* 7.9-11; cf. Jn 1.1-3).[1]

The *Gospel of Thomas* (II, 2) also alludes to the Johannine Prologue: 'Jesus said, "I took my place in the midst of the world, and I appeared to them in flesh. I found all of them intoxicated; I found none of them thirsty' (38.21-24 [log. §28]; cf. Jn 1.14; 4.13-15; 6.35; 7.37). The *Gospel of Thomas* contains many other allusions to the Fourth Gospel.[2] The *Gospel of Philip* (NHC II, 3) contains allusions to the Fourth Gospel: 'the Logos emanated from there [that is, heaven]' (58.33; cf. John 1.1).[3] *On the Origin of the World* (II, 5) says that the

---

1. Note also the clear allusion in *Ap. John* 14.21-24 ('the image of the invisible one who is the Father of the all [and] through whom everything came into being, the first Man. For he revealed his likeness in a human form') to Col. 1.15-17; Phil. 2.7-8.

2. Note the following: *Gos. Thom.* 32.12-14 (log. §1) // Jn 8.51-52; *Gos. Thom.* 35.5-7 (log. §13) // Jn 4.10-14; 7.38; *Gos. Thom.* 35.10-14 (log. §13) // Jn 8.59 and 10.31; *Gos. Thom.* 38.4-5 (log. §24) // Jn 14.4-5; *Gos. Thom.* 38.20 (log. §27) // Jn 14.9; *Gos. Thom.* 39.55-57 (log. §31) // Jn 4.44; *Gos. Thom.* 39.27-29 (log. §37) // Jn 14.22; 1 Jn 3.2; *Gos. Thom.* 40.2-7 (log. §38) // Jn 7.33-34, 36; *Gos. Thom.* 41.31–42.1 (log. §50) // Jn 12.36; *Gos. Thom.* 42.3-4 (log. §50) // Jn 6.57; *Gos. Thom.* 43.28-30 (log. §61) // Jn 6.37, 39; 17.2, 6, 9; *Gos. Thom.* 45.25-29 (log. §69) // Jn 4.23-24; 17.17, 19); *Gos. Thom.* 45.34-35 (log. §71) // Jn 2.19; *Gos. Thom.* 46.11-13 (log. §75) // Jn 3.29; *Gos. Thom.* 46.23-24 (log. §77) // Jn 8.12; 9.5; *Gos. Thom.* 48.20-21 (log. §91) // Jn 6.30; *Gos. Thom.* 50.12-13 (log. §104) // Jn 8.46; *Gos. Thom.* 50.16-18 (log. §105) // Jn 8.41; *Gos. Thom.* 50.28-30 (log. §108) // Jn 4.14; 7.37; 14.20-21; 1 Jn 3.2.

The *Dialogue of the Savior* (III, 5), which is similar to the *Gospel of Thomas*, comprises 104 sayings that purport to be conversations between Jesus and a few of his disciples (Matthew, Judas and Mary). This Johannine-like document contains numerous allusions to the New Testament. The *Gospel of Philip* (II, 3) also draws upon the Fourth Gospel and several New Testament writings: 'Before Christ came there was no bread in the world...but when Christ came, the perfect man, he brought bread from heaven in order that man might be nourished' (55.6-13; cf. Jn 6.31-33). Here one can hardly claim that John has made use of a Gnostic image. On the contrary, he has quoted the Old Testament (cf. Ps. 78.24) and has interpreted it in a way that closely resembles early rabbinic interpretation. See Borgen, *Bread from Heaven*. Elsewhere there are explicit quotations of New Testament passages: *Gos. Phil.* 55.34 (cf. Mt. 16.17); 56.32-34 (1 Cor. 15.50); 57.4-5 (Jn 6.53); 72.34–73.1 (Mt. 3.15); 77.18, 24 (Jn 8.34); 77.25-26 (1 Cor. 8.1); 78.11 (1 Pet. 4.8); 83.12-13 (Mt. 3.10; Lk. 3.9); 85.29-31 (Mt. 15.13).

3. Note the clear allusions in *Gos. Phil.* 53.2 (cf. Jn 10.17); 57.3 (cf. Jn 6.53);

logos was sent to proclaim the unknown (125.14-19; cf. Jn 1.1, 14), with Mk 4.22 par. quoted. In the *Second Treatise of the Great Seth* (VII, 2) the revealer (probably assumed to be Seth, as the title of the work implies; cf. *Treat. Seth* 70.11-12) identifies himself as Christ (65.18), the Son of Man (65.19; 69.21-22), and as Jesus (69.21), who tells his disciples: 'You do not know it because the fleshly cloud overshadows you. But I alone am the friend of Sophia. I have been in the bosom of the father from the beginning' (70.1-6; cf. Jn 1.1, 18). The *Teaching of Silvanus* (VII, 4) contains a cluster of predicates that in part derives from the Fourth Gospel: 'For the Tree of Life is Christ. He is Wisdom. For he is Wisdom; he is also the Word. He is the Life, the Power, and the Door. He is the Light, the Angel, and the Good Shepherd' (106.21-28; 113.11-16; cf. Jn 1.1; 10.7, 9, 11, 14; 8.12; 9.5; 11.25; 14.6). The opening verses of the Prologue are echoed elsewhere: 'the divine Word is God' (*Teach. Silv.* 111.5; cf. Jn 1.1c); 'the things which have come into being through the Word, who is the Son as the image of the Father' (115.17-19; cf. Jn 1.3). Similarly, the *Letter of Peter to Philip* (VIII, 2) has Jesus Christ (134.17) explain the 'pleroma' (fullness) to his disciples: 'I am the one who was sent down in the body because of the seed which had fallen away. And I came down in their mortal mold...And I spoke with him who belongs to me, and he harkened to me...And I gave him authority' (136.16-26; cf. Jn 1.11-12, 14).[1] According to *Melchizedek* (IX, 1) Jesus

58.14 ('Do not despise the lamb, for without it one cannot see the door'; cf. Jn 10.7); 61.8 (cf. Jn 8.44); 77.15-21 (cf. Jn 8.32, 34); 84.7-9 (cf. Jn 8.32). There are several other references to New Testament writings.

1. The *Letter of Peter to Philip* contains several clear allusions to the New Testament. The document as a whole 'shares important features with the part of the first (Petrine) section of the Acts of the Apostles (chapters 1-12)' (M.M. Meyer, 'The Letter of Peter to Philip', in Robinson [ed.], *The Nag Hammadi Library*, p. 431). Meyer ('Peter to Philip', p. 432) has further observed that the second revelatory answer (136.16–137.4) resembles the Johannine Prologue. The apostles are filled with the Spirit and are enabled to heal and to preach (140.2-13), which recalls Pentecost (Acts 2–3). Meyer ('Peter to Philip', p. 432) observes similarities with the Johannine account of 'Pentecost' (Jn 20.19-23). He also comments: 'Likewise, the description of the resurrected Christ as a light and a voice [*Ep. Pet. Phil.* 134.9-14; 135.3-4; 137.17-19; 138.11-13, 21-22] represents a primitive way of depicting the appearances of the risen Lord [Mk 9.2-8 par.; 2 Pet. 1.16-19; Acts 9.1-9; 22.4-11; 26.9-18; 1 Cor. 15; Rev. 1.12-16], but among Gnostic Christians such theophanic descriptions were particularly appreciated' ('Peter to Philip', p. 433).

Christ, the Son of God (cf. 1.3) 'is unfleshly though he has come in the flesh' (5.6-7; cf. Jn 1.14). The *Testimony of Truth* (IX, *3*) combines synoptic and Johannine tradition: 'The [Holy] Spirit [came] down upon him [as a] dove [...] accept for ourselves that [he] was born of a virgin [and] he took flesh' (39.26-31; cf. Mk 1.10; Mt. 1.18-25; Jn 1.14). The *Interpretation of Knowledge* (XI, *1*), which alludes to and interprets New Testament passages throughout,[1] probably echoes the Johannine Prologue when it says: '[It is the] shape [that] exists in the presence [of the Father], the [W]ord and the height' (*Interp. Know.* 10.23-25; cf. Jn 1.1, 18). Later we are told that the Son 'appeared as flesh' (*Interp. Know.* 12.18; cf. Jn 1.14). Johannine language is probably echoed when the *Valentinian Exposition* (XI, *2*) speaks of the revelation of the Father and the thought called the 'Monogenes' (*Val. Exp.* 23.31–24.39; 28.22-25; 40.34-35; cf. Jn 1.18). The references to 'Word' may also be Johannine (29.27, 30; 30.31).

With regard to the *Trimorphic Protennoia* (XIII, *1*), there are several apparent allusions to the Fourth Gospel: 'I will reveal myself to those who have heard my mysteries, that is, the Sons of the Light' (40.36–41.1; 42.16; 49.25; cf. Jn 12.35-36); 'I revealed myself to them [in] their tents (σκηνή) as the Word' (47.14-15; cf. Jn 1.14); 'I am the Light' (47.29-30; cf. Jn 8.12; 9.5); 'I gave to them from the Living Water' (48.7; 46.17; cf. Jn 4.10-11); 'the spring of the Water of Life' (48.20-21; 37.3; 41.23; cf. Jn 4.14; 7.38); 'I abide in them and they also abide in me' (50.11-12; cf. Jn 15.5); 'I established him in the dwelling places (μονή) of his Father' (50.14-15; cf. Jn 14.2). There are also allusions to various other New Testament passages: 'I...am the first-born...before the All' (35.4-6; cf. Col. 1.15); 'image of the Invisible Spirit' (38.11; cf. Col. 1.15); 'it is through me that the All took shape' (38.12; Col. 1.16); 'the times are cut short and the days have been shortened' (44.16; cf. Mk 13.20); 'our time has been fulfilled' (44.17; cf. Lk. 21.24); 'the weeping of our destruction has approached us' (44.17-18; cf. Lk. 19.41, 44); 'He...has stripped off the garments of ignorance and put on a shining Light' (49.30-32; cf. Col. 3.9-10). These are by no means obvious examples of secondary Christianization.

Allusions to the Johannine ideas of Word and its incarnation fall outside of the two pages of the Coptic text (that is, pp. 46-47)

---

1. See *Interp. Know.* 9.28-29 (cf. Mt. 23.9); 9.30 (cf. Mt. 5.14); 9.33-34 (cf. Mt. 16.26); 17.14-21 (cf. 1 Cor. 12.12, 14-25); 21.32-33 (cf. Jas 1.12; 1 Pet. 5.4).

tabulated above. The Son is 'the Word who originated through that Voice; who proceeded from the height... who is a Light... and revealed himself to those who dwell in darkness... and taught unrepeatable doctrines to all those who became Sons of the Light' (*Trim. Prot.* 37.4-20; 40.29–41.1, 16; cf. Jn 1.1, 4-5, 9, 12). Elsewhere Jesus is called 'the Perfect Son, the Christ, the only-begotten God' (38.22-23; cf. 39.6-7, 12-13) which probably echoes Jn 1.18 (μονογενὴς θεός, which is read by $\mathfrak{P}^{66,75}$ א B C* L 33). What is important to observe is that the idea of incarnation seems to be the point that the *Trimorphic Protennoia* has borrowed from Johannine (and Christian) thought.[1] Almost everything else is typical of wisdom mythology. Even the emphasis on 'Word' may owe in part to Johannine influence.[2]

As potentially independent witnesses of New Testament ideas, most of the Nag Hammadi materials, as well as the apocryphal Gospels such as the *Gospel of Peter* or the *Secret Gospel of Mark*, are problematic. These writings simply do not meet the second criterion (the criterion of contamination) outlined above in Chapter 1. Although in recent years several scholars, such as Robinson and Koester, have argued or, as is often the case, assumed that Nag Hammadi contains independent and even pre-synoptic and pre-Johannine traditions,[3] many scholars remain unconvinced, and for good reason.[4] For example, the oft

---

1. In a recent study S. Pétrement (*Le Dieu séparé: Les origines du gnosticisme* [Paris: Cerf, 1984]) has concluded that Gnosticism grew out of Christianity and that the ideas of the demiurge, Redeemer and salvation through *gnosis* are developments of Christian ideas (esp. those of Paul and the Fourth Gospel).

2. The Johannine Prologue was a favorite passage in Gnostic exegesis; cf. E. Pagels, *The Johannine Gospel in Gnostic Exegesis: Heracleon's Commentary on John* (SBLMS, 17; Nashville: Abingdon Press, 1973), pp. 1-50; Layton, *Gnostic Scriptures*, pp. 276-302; J.-D. Kaestli, 'L'exégèse valentinienne du quatrième évangile', in *idem et al.* (eds.), *La communauté johannique*, pp. 323-50. See especially Irenaeus, *Adv. Her.* 1.8.5; Epiphanius, *Adv. Her.* 33.3.6. Both of these fathers criticize aspects of Ptolemy's interpretation of the Prologue. See also the possible allusion in Ignatius, *Eph.* 6.2–7.2. Janssens ('Une source gnostique du Prologue?', p. 358) rightly observes that 'c'est précisément dans les passages "chrétiens" que la "parenté" avec le Prologue johannique est la plus marquée!'

3. See H. Koester, 'Apocryphal and Canonical Gospels', *HTR* 73 (1980), pp. 105-30, esp. pp. 112-19; J.M. Robinson, 'The Johannine Trajectory', pp. 232-68; and, with respect to the Synoptics, see J.D. Crossan, *Four Other Gospels: Shadows on the Contours of Canon* (Minneapolis: Winston, 1985).

4. See C.M. Tuckett, *Nag Hammadi and the Gospel Tradition* (Studies of the New Testament and its World; Edinburgh: T. & T. Clark, 1986); J.P. Meier, *A*

asserted claim that the *Gospel of Thomas* contains primitive, pre-synoptic tradition is highly questionable. Quoting from or alluding to more than half of the books of the New Testament (Matthew, Mark, Luke, John, Acts, Romans, 1–2 Corinthians, Galatians, Ephesians, Colossians, 1 Thessalonians, 1 Timothy, Hebrews, 1 John, Revelation), the *Gospel of Thomas* appears to comprise hardly more than a pastiche of New Testament and apocryphal materials which have been interpreted, often allegorically, in such a way as to advance second-century Gnostic ideas. Moreover, the traditions contained in the *Gospel of Thomas* hardly reflect a setting that predates the writings of the New Testament.[1] The most telling factor against seeing the *Gospel of Thomas* as containing early and independent material lies in the fact that not only does it contain material that has been identified as special to Matthew ('M') and to Luke ('L'), which Koester and others gratuitously assign to Q, but it also has features characteristic of Matthean and Lukan redaction. In view of these considerations, and there are others, any attempt to deduce pre-synoptic and pre-Johannine forms of tradition from the *Gospel of Thomas* would be speculative and precarious.[2]

With respect to the hypothesized redeemer myth the problem is similar. Although in a few instances one can argue plausibly that this or that New Testament parallel could be a secondary Christianizing interpolation, in most cases involving the parallels surveyed above this is not likely. The whole point of the document is the idea that Jesus is the *logos* or Son (or both) who has descended from heaven and assumed a body of flesh. Removal of these Christian details would seriously disrupt the flow and logic of the document in question. In some cases apart from these details there simply would be no

Marginal Jew: Rethinking the Historical Jesus (ABRL; Garden City, NY: Doubleday, 1991), pp. 123-39, 159-62 nn. 108-24.

1. For studies that express this view, see H.E.W. Turner, 'The Gospel of Thomas: Its History, Transmission and Sources', in H. Montefiore and H.E.W. Turner, *Thomas and the Evangelists* (SBT, 35; London: SCM Press, 1962), pp. 11-39; R.E. Brown, 'The Gospel of Thomas and St John's Gospel', *NTS* 9 (1963), pp. 155-77; W. Schrage, *Das Verhältnis des Thomas-Evangeliums zur synoptischen Tradition und zu den koptischen Evangelienübersetzungen* (BZNW, 29; Berlin: Töpelmann, 1964); C.M. Tuckett, 'Thomas and the Synoptics', *NovT* 30 (1988), pp. 132-57.

2. See Meier, *A Marginal Jew*, pp. 134-39, 162-66 nn. 125-46. At this point I retract the opinion that I expressed in 'Current Issues', p. 125 n. 38.

document. When it is remembered, moreover, that no redeemer myth from the first century (or earlier) can actually be documented, the hypothesis that Johannine (and Pauline) Christology reflects such a myth is hardly more than a guess. Such a hypothesis should be discarded if there are patterns and parallels that are known to antedate the Johannine Gospel that can account for the essential components of Johannine Christology.

It will be argued below that in fact there are other parallels, largely ignored or minimized by Robinson and his supporters, which not only do not suffer from difficulties of chronology and uncertain provenance, but adequately clarify the meaning of the Johannine Prologue. Before moving on to these parallels it will be necessary to treat another 'Gnostic' source that seems to have a close relationship to some of the distinctive ideas in the Fourth Gospel.

Syrian Gnosticism

Odes of Solomon

The relationship of the *Odes of Solomon* to the Prologue of the Fourth Gospel presents special problems of its own. J.H. Charlesworth and others[1] do not see the *Odes* as Gnostic (as Bultmann and others[2] have thought). Nor do Charlesworth and others see the relationship of the *Odes* and the Prologue in terms of direct dependence of one upon the other.[3] Rather, as they argue, these materials constitute independent

---

1. Charlesworth, 'The Odes of Solomon—Not Gnostic'. M. Testuz ([ed.], *Papyrus Bodmer VII-IX* [Cologne and Geneva: Bibliothèque Bodmer, 1959]) thought that the *Odes* were produced at Qumran. Similarly, J. Carmignac, 'Les affinités qumrâniennes de la onzième Ode de Salomon', *RevQ* 3 (1961), pp. 71-102; *idem*, 'Un Qumrânien converti au Christianisme: l'auteur des Odes de Salomon', in H. Bardtke (ed.), *Qumran-Probleme* (Berlin: Akademie Verlag, 1963), pp. 75-108. J.A. Emerton ('Notes on some Passages in the Odes of Solomon', *JTS* 28 [1977], pp. 507-19) and Charlesworth have concluded that the *Odes* is a Christian work.

2. H. Gunkel, 'Die Oden Salomos', *ZNW* 11 (1910), pp. 291-328; *idem*, 'Die Oden Salomos', *Deutsche Rundschau* 154 (1913), pp. 25-47; H.-M. Schenke, 'Die zweite Schrift des Codex Jung und die Oden Salomos', in *Die Herkunft des sogenannten Evangelium Veritatis* (Göttingen: Vandenhoeck & Ruprecht, 1959), pp. 26-29; Rudolph, 'War der Verfasser der Oden Salomos ein "Qumran-Christ"?', pp. 523-55; Koester, *Introduction*, II, pp. 216-18.

3. J.H. Charlesworth and R.A. Culpepper, 'The Odes of Solomon and the Gospel of John', *CBQ* 35 (1973), pp. 298-322.

literary expressions of a common milieu. Similarly Sanders has argued
that the *Odes* 'give evidence of parallel development and are not
dependent on the Gospel of John'.[1] (This conclusion will be questioned
below.) He further concludes that the *Odes*, the *Trimorphic Protennoia*
and the Johannine Prologue derive from a common milieu.[2]

Listed below are some of the most significant parallels:[3]

Prologue of John		*Odes of Solomon*
1	'In the beginning was the Word.'	'He was before anything came to be' (16.18).
3	'All things were made through him, and without him nothing was made that has come into being.'	'By him the generations spoke to one another, and those that were silent acquired speech... And they were stimulated by the Word [*masc.*]' (12.8, 10). 'And there is nothing outside of the Lord, because he was before anything came to be. And the worlds are by his Word [*fem.*]' (16.18-19; cf. 32.2).
4a	'In him was life'	'The generations... were stimulated by the Word [*masc.*]' (12.8, 10).
4b	'and the life was the light of people.'	'The Lord directed my mouth by his Word [*fem.*], and has opened my heart by his Light. And he has caused to dwell in me his immortal life' (10.1-2). 'Light dawned from the Word [*fem.*]' (41.14). 'The mouth of the Lord is the true Word [*masc.*], and the door of his light' (12.3).

1.   Sanders, 'Nag Hammadi, Odes of Solomon', p. 56.
2.   Sanders, 'Nag Hammadi, Odes of Solomon', p. 59.
3.   I follow Sanders ('Nag Hammadi, Odes of Solomon', pp. 54-55) and
E.M. Yamauchi ('Jewish Gnosticism? The Prologue of John, Mandaean Parallels,
and the Trimorphic Protennoia', in van den Broek and Vermaseren [eds.], *Studies in
Gnosticism and Hellenistic Religions*, pp. 467-97, esp. p. 477), though not without
some modifications. The translation of the *Odes* comes from J.H. Charlesworth,
'Odes of Solomon', in *idem* (ed.), *The Old Testament Pseudepigrapha*, II (2 vols.;
Garden City, NY: Doubleday, 1983–85), pp. 725-71. For the Syriac text, see
J.H. Charlesworth, *The Odes of Solomon* (SBLTT: Pseudepigrapha Series, 7;
Missoula, MT: Scholars Press, 1978).

5	'The light shines in the darkness, and the darkness did not overcome it.'	'Let not light be conquered by darkness, nor let truth flee from falsehood' (18.6). 'I stripped off darkness and put on light' (21.3).
9	'He was the true light.'	'I was the Son of Man, I was named the light, the Son of God' (36.3).
10	'The world did not know him.'	'They were rejected because the truth was not with them' (24.12).
11	'He came to his own.'	'He has allowed him to appear to them that are his own; in order that they may recognize him that made them' (7.12). 'I turn not my face from my own, because I know them' (8.12).
12	'as many as received him'	'He became like me that I might receive him' (7.4).
	'He gave them power to be children of God.'	'Blessed are they who by means of him have recognized everything' (12.13). 'I will be with those who love me' (42.4).
14	'The Word became flesh and dwelt among us... full of grace and truth.'	'For the dwelling place of the Word [*masc.*] is man, and his truth is love' (12.12).

Of the above parallels Bultmann only mentions those found in *Odes* 7 and 12.[1] In addition to these he treats *Odes* 24 and 33.[2] The first *Ode* says that 'the Lord declared his way, and spread out his grace. And those who recognized it knew his holiness' (24.13-14).[3] Bultmann supposes that this approximates Jn 1.12: 'As many as received him, to them he gave authority to become children of God, to those who believe in his name'. The latter *Ode* describes the descent of 'Grace' (33.1) who, as the 'perfect Virgin' (33.5), calls out to men and women to 'come' (33.6) and 'abandon the ways of that Corruptor... and I will enter into you, and bring you forth from destruction' (33.7-8). Grace goes on to say: 'Hear me and be saved, for I am proclaiming unto you

1. Bultmann, *Gospel of John*, pp. 14-15. In n. 3 on p. 14 Bultmann examines some formal features in *Odes* 6 and 30.
2. Bultmann, *Gospel of John*, pp. 14 n. 3, 14-15.
3. Trans. from Charlesworth, 'Odes of Solomon', p. 757.

the grace of God' (33.10).[1] 'The parallels,' Bultmann tells us, 'show
that, taken as a whole, the Prologue is the hymn of a community
which gratefully reveres the secret of the revelation that has been
given to it'.[2] Where one finds reverence for secrecy in the Johannine
Prologue I am at a loss to say.

In my judgment these parallels should be assessed in about the same
way as those drawn from the *Trimorphic Protennoia* above. They do
not appear to be particularly Johannine except in the most general
way. They are reminiscent of typical Wisdom language. The *Odes*
probably derive from the same broad milieu from which emerged
both the *Trimorphic Protennoia* and the Prologue of John. The principal idea that a hypostatic being called 'Word' came from heaven and
enlightened those who would receive him or her is common to all
three (although in the *Odes* 'word' appears both in the masculine, *ptgm*,
and in the feminine, *mlt'*, with somewhat distinct functions[3]). Indeed,
these ideas are hardly more than logical extensions of ideas current in
Jewish Wisdom speculation two or three centuries before the Common
Era.[4] What the Johannine Prologue alone articulates is the explicit
statement that the *logos* became 'flesh' (σάρξ). (*Protennoia* comes
close when it says that the Word revealed himself 'in their tents'.) It is
the lack of this concept in the *Odes*,[5] as well as parallels with the
polemical portions of 1 John, that has recently led James Brownson to
conclude that the community that produced the *Odes* was probably the
community that broke from the Johannine church over differences in
Christology and soteriology.[6] If Brownson's conclusion is correct,
then obviously the relationship of the *Odes* with the Johannine
Prologue is cast into a very different light. In any case, it is doubtful
that we shall find in the *Odes* an earlier or logically prior expression

1.   Trans. from Charlesworth, 'Odes of Solomon', pp. 763-64.

2.   Bultmann, *Gospel of John*, p. 15.

3.   For a discussion of the differences and their importance, see Sanders, 'Nag
Hammadi, Odes of Solomon', pp. 56-58.

4.   Summarizing recent findings, J.H. Charlesworth ('Qumran, John and the
Odes of Solomon', in *idem* [ed.], *John and the Dead Sea Scrolls*, p. 135) concludes
that the 'discussion shows that we are no longer justified in speaking about the Odes
and John as if they were late and gnostic'.

5.   See Charlesworth and Culpepper, 'The Odes of Solomon and the Gospel of
John', p. 310.

6.   J. Brownson, 'The Odes of Solomon and the Johannine Tradition', *JSP* 2
(1988), pp. 49-69.

of the heavenly redeemer idea now found in the Fourth Gospel.

The criterion of contamination must again be invoked, not only because many of the parallels tabulated above are indications of possible familiarity with the Johannine tradition, but also because there are indications throughout of general familiarity with many important Christian traditions and beliefs. *Ode* 7 may allude to the heavenly voice that spoke at the baptism and transfiguration (v. 15; cf. Mk 1.11; 9.7 par.). *Ode* 19 presents a poetic description of the virgin birth (see vv. 6-11; cf. Mt. 1.18-25; Lk. 1.26-38; 2.4-7), complete with the divine triad (Father, Son, Holy Spirit; cf. v. 2; Mt. 28.19) that eventually would constitute the Christian Trinity. *Ode* 29 alludes to the Lukan portrait of the infancy: 'And I gave praise to the Most High, because he has magnified his servant and the sons of his maid-servant' (v. 11; cf. Lk. 1.35, 38, 46-48). *Ode* 24 offers a poetic and interpretive description of Jesus' baptism. The allusions are unmistakable: 'The dove fluttered over the head of our Lord Messiah' (v. 1; cf. Mk 1.10). His 'submersion' (v. 7) is then interpreted allegorically. *Ode* 39 is probably an allegorical depiction of Jesus walking on the water: 'Raging rivers [are like] the power of the Lord' (v. 1); 'the Lord has bridged them by his word, and he walked and crossed them on foot. And his footsteps were standing firm on the waters' (vv. 9-10; cf. Mk 6.48-51). The exodus crossing is also drawn upon: 'On this side and that the waves were lifted up, but the footsteps of our Lord Messiah were standing firm' (v. 11; cf. Exod. 14.21-22). Several odes contain allusions to the Passion and other details found in the Gospels, including some of the lament Psalms cited by the evangelists: 'you were despised' (8.5; cf. Isa. 53.3); 'the upright cross' (27.3); 'they surrounded me like mad dogs' (28.14; cf. Ps. 22.16); 'in vain did they cast lots against me' (28.18; cf. Ps. 22.18b; Mk 15.24 par.); 'And they condemned me when I stood up, me who had not been condemned' (31.8; cf. Ps. 94.21); 'they divided my spoil' (31.9; cf. Ps. 22.18a; Mk 15.24 par.); 'I endured and held my peace and was silent' (31.10; cf. Isa. 53.7; Acts 8.32-33). *Ode* 42 describes the resurrection: 'I arose and am with them, and will speak by their mouths' (v. 6); 'Sheol saw me and was shattered, and Death ejected me and many with me' (v. 11; cf. Ps. 16.10; Mt. 27.52-53; Acts 2.27); 'I have been vinegar and bitterness to [Death]' (v. 12; cf. Ps. 69.21; Mk 15.36 par.); 'those who had died ran toward me; and they cried out and said, "Son of God, have pity on us...and bring us out from the chains of darkness"'

(vv. 15-16; cf. Mk 5.4, 7-8; 1 Pet. 3.19; 2 Pet. 2.4).

There is no clear indication that these Christian allusions are embellishments or interpolations. Evidently, these allusions constitute part of the original form of the tradition. In view of their presence, it would seem precarious indeed to argue that lying behind the *Odes of Solomon* is an independent and pre-Johannine redeemer myth. The only pre-Johannine mythology present is the Wisdom mythology well represented in the Old Testament and intertestamental writings. Everything else appears to represent very imaginative Christian allegory, poetry and mysticism, which do not, in my judgment, constitute Gnosticism.

Corpus Hermeticum

In his classic study of the Fourth Gospel C.H. Dodd was persuaded that the Hermetic writings offered several important parallels.[1] Here are those that appear to be the most promising:

Corpus Hermeticum	*Johannine Writings*
'I am that light (τὸ φῶς)... your God (ὁ σὸς θεός)' (1.6)	'I am the light (τὸ φῶς) of the world' (Jn 8.12) 'God is light (ὁ θεὸς φῶς)' (1 Jn 1.5)
'This one remains in darkness (μένει ἐν τῷ σκότει) deceived' (1.19)	'in order that every one who believes in me should not remain in darkness (ἐν τῇ σκοτίᾳ μείνῃ)' (Jn 12.46)
'if you learn that God is of life and light... then you will advance again into life (εἰς ζωήν)' (1.21)	'he has passed out of death into life (εἰς τὴν ζωήν)' (Jn 5.24)
'They ascend to the Father' (1.26)	'I ascend to my Father' (Jn 20.17)
'Holy God the Father' (1.31)	'Holy Father' (Jn 17.11)
'I shall enlighten (φωτίσω) my brothers who are in ignorance' (1.32)	'the true light which enlightens (φωτίζει) every human being' (Jn 1.9)

---

1.   Dodd, *Interpretation of the Fourth Gospel*, pp. 34-35, 50-51. Koester (*Introduction*, I, pp. 388-89) describes the Hermetic writings as a 'pagan Gnosticism' which 'attempts a reconciliation of Gnosticism and philosophy'. Two Hermetic tractates are among the writings of Nag Hammadi (cf. *The Discourse on the Eighth and Ninth* [NHC VI, *6*] and *Asclepius 21-29* [NHC VI, *8*).

'I believe (πιστεύω) and I bear witness (μαρτυρῶ)' (1.32)

'he came for a witness (μαρτυρίαν) ... that all should believe (πιστεύσωσιν) through him' (Jn 1.7)

'I advance unto life and light (ζωὴν καὶ φῶς)' (1.32)

'he will have the light of life (φῶς τῆς ζωῆς)' (Jn 8.12)

'your human being wishes to sanctify with you (συναγιάζειν)' (1.32)

'I sanctify (ἁγιάζω) myself in order that they might be sanctified (ἡγιασμένοι)' (Jn 17.19)

'none can be saved before regeneration' (13.1)

'except one be born again, he cannot see the Kingdom of God' (Jn 3.4)

'of such mothers (μήτρας) a human is born (ἐγεννήθη)' (13.1)

'one is not able to enter the womb of his mother (μητρός) a second time and be born (γεννηθῆναι), is he?' (Jn 3.4)

'The true seed (σπορά) is good' (13.2)

'His seed (σπέρμα) abides forever' (1 Jn 3.9)

'this generation is not taught (διδάσκεται), but whenever it will, it will be reminded (ἀναμιμνήσκεται) by God' (13.2)

'that One will teach (διδάξει) you all things and will remind (ὑπομνήσει) you of all things' (Jn 14.26)

'I was begotten (ἐγεννήθην) by the Mind' (13.3)

'that which is begotten (γεγεννημένος) by the Spirit' (Jn 3.8)

'not with these eyes I am now beheld (θεωροῦμαι)' (13.3)

'the world no longer beholds (θεωρεῖ) me, but you shall behold (θεωρεῖτε) me' (Jn 14.19)

'the begetting (γένεσιν) by God' (13.6)

'they are begotten (ἐγεννήθησαν) of God' (Jn 1.13)

'cleanse (κάθαραι) yourself' (13.7)

'He cleanses (καθαίρει) every one bearing fruit' (Jn 15.2)

'knowledge of God (γνῶσις θεοῦ) came to us' (13.8)

'that they should know (γινώσκωσιν) you, the only true God (θεόν)' (Jn 17.3)

'knowledge of joy (χαρᾶς) came to us; the pain (λύπη) of this arrival shall flee' (13.8)

'your pain (λύπη) will become joy (χαράν)' (Jn 16.20)

'no longer no punishment of darkness came upon you' (13.9)

'lest darkness overcome you' (Jn 12.35; cf. Jn 1.5)

'a child of that One (ἑνός)' (13.14)	'We have one (ἕνα) Father, God' (Jn 8.41)
'I rejoice in the joy (χαρᾷ) of my mind' (13.18)	'in order that my joy (χαρά) might be in you' (Jn 15.11)
'The Powers which are in me...complete your will (θέλημα)' (13.19)	'in order that I should do the will (θέλημα) of the One who sent me' (Jn 4.34)
'Light, enlighten (φώτιζε φῶς)!' (13.19)	'the true light (φῶς) which enlightens (φωτίζει)' (Jn 1.9)
'The mind shepherds (ποιμαίνει)' (13.19)	'I am the Good Shepherd (ποιμήν)' (Jn 10.11)

Dodd concludes that the Hermetic writings and the Fourth Gospel shared a 'common background of thought' and that comparison is useful for mutual illumination: 'It seems clear that as a whole they represent a type of religious thought akin to one side of Johannine thought, without any substantial borrowing on the one part or the other'.[1] Dodd could be right, but when all is said and done, very little is actually gained. At best we have the Fourth Evangelist attempting to communicate Christian doctrine in a manner that would be understood and appreciated by the kind of people who would have been familiar with the concepts and language of the Hermetic writings.[2] Beyond the concept of regeneration (cf. Jn 3), there is little here that sheds important light on Johannine theology, and virtually nothing that clarifies his Christology.

We are once again faced with the problems raised by the criteria of antecedent tradition and contamination. With regard to the former, there is no clear evidence that the language and concepts of the *Hermetica* that parallel the Fourth Gospel existed in a 'Hermetic stream' early enough to have been known to the Johannine community. Regarding the latter, since there are indications that some of the contributors to the Hermetica were familiar with Christianity, and in some cases they were evidently antagonistic, the closest parallels become problematic. Moreover, in such a large and syncretistic corpus of theosophic materials one should expect to find some parallels with any writing, such as the Fourth Gospel, which addresses

1. Dodd, *Interpretation of the Fourth Gospel*, p. 53.
2. See Dodd, *Interpretation of the Fourth Gospel*, p. 53 n. 1.

similar general themes. For these reasons and others scholars have been reluctant to make much of the Hermetic parallels.[1]

Assessment

Viewing the *Trimorphic Protennoia* as providing the natural context or closest parallel for the Prologue of John is problematic for three basic and very important reasons. First, because of the probability that the *Protennoia* was familiar with Christian ideas and may have made use of the Fourth Gospel itself, it is difficult to say with confidence which significant parallels are truly independent. Secondly, the *Protennoia* sheds very little light on the Prologue. Our understanding of the Prologue or the Fourth Gospel is hardly enhanced. If Robinson and his colleagues are correct, we are left wondering why so little of the myth presupposed by the *Protennoia* is utilized by the Johannine Prologue. Thirdly, other traditions, yet to be considered, shed light on the Johannine Prologue. These traditions antedate the Fourth Gospel and were part of its milieu. In view of these considerations, appeal to the *Trimorphic Protennoia* becomes redundant and possibly misleading.

The *Trimorphic Protennoia* and the *Odes of Solomon* are independent examples of mystical approaches to Wisdom. Whereas there may not be any Gnosticism at all in the latter (as Charlesworth claims), the former has portrayed the figure of Wisdom as a 'Protennoia', a revealing Word (or Voice or Speech), who can claim many attributes. The portrait here is similar to that found in Sirach 24 and in other Wisdom traditions. Even the presence of Gnosticism in the *Trimorphic Protennoia* appears to be secondary. The only distinctive parallels with the Johannine Prologue involve the incarnation, which may very well indicate the dependence of the former on the latter. There is simply no clear evidence that the *Trimorphic Protennoia* is based upon a redeemer myth that lies behind Johannine Christology in general or the Johannine Prologue in particular. At most one can say that

---

1.   As representative, see F.-M. Braun, 'Hermétisme et Johannisme', *RevThom* 55 (1955), pp. 22-42, 259-99; G.D. Kilpatrick, 'The Religious Background of the Fourth Gospel', in F.L. Cross (ed.), *Studies in the Fourth Gospel* (London: Mowbrays, 1957), pp. 36-44; Brown, *Gospel according to John*, I, pp. lviii-lix; and more recently D. Burkett, *The Son of the Man in the Gospel of John* (JSNTSup, 56; Sheffield: JSOT Press, 1991), pp. 28-30.

the typical speculative sapiential tradition of Wisdom revealing herself among humankind is presupposed by the *Trimorphic Protennoia*, the Johannine Prologue and the *Odes of Solomon*. The antecedents of the Johannine Prologue will have to be sought elsewhere.

Chapter 3

BIBLICAL PARALLELS

The Prologue of the Fourth Gospel presupposes several biblical materials, all of them reflecting Wisdom traditions. Even the opening verses, which clearly allude to the creation story of Genesis, should be interpreted in the light of Wisdom traditions. Wisdom herself, it should be remembered, was understood to have been present and in some ways involved with creation. These biblical materials have been assembled in three basic groupings, moving from the more direct to the less direct: (1) Genesis 1–2 and Exodus 33–34; (2) Sirach 24; and (3) other parallels from the LXX and Pseudepigrapha.

A word needs to be said about the relevance and interpretation of 'parallels'. I do not mean to imply that all of the following Old Testament parallels necessarily lie behind the Johannine Prologue. In some cases they obviously do. But in most cases these parallels only point out the biblical flavor of the Prologue. As will be shown they give evidence of a biblical sapiential heritage. The following parallels should also make it clear, moreover, to what extent the themes, language and contents of the Prologue are indebted to the themes, language and contents of Old Testament Scripture. Finally, the parallels also identify those portions of Scripture that have contributed to the exegetical speculations reflected in the traditions that will be considered in Chapter 4.

Genesis 1–2 and Exodus 33–34

Genesis 1–2
Even a casual reader of Scripture cannot help but hear the echo of Genesis 1–2 in the opening verses of the Johannine Prologue. Although there are not many verbal agreements, the conceptual parallels are

obvious and quite significant.[1] The parallels presented here are drawn from the LXX, but this does not imply that other versions could not have been in view.

LXX *Genesis 1–2*	John 1
'In the beginning (ἐν ἀρχῇ)' (v. 1a).	'In the beginning (ἐν ἀρχῇ)' (v. 1a; cf. v. 2).
'God (θεός) created the heaven and the earth' (v. 1b).	'and the Word was God (θεός)...all things came into being (ἐγένετο) through him' (vv. 1c, 3).
	'and the world came into being (ἐγένετο) through him' (v. 10).
'and darkness (σκότος) was upon the abyss...and God said, 'Let there be light (φῶς), and light (φῶς) came into being (ἐγένετο)' (vv. 2-3).	'And the light (φῶς) shines (φαίνειν) in darkness (σκοτία), and the darkness (σκοτία) did not overcome it' (v. 5; cf. vv. 7-8).
'and let [the stars] be lights...to shine (φαίνειν) upon the earth' (v. 15).	
'And God said, "Let the earth bring forth living (ζᾶν) life"' (v. 24).	'In him was life (ζωή)' (v. 4a) 'concerning the Word of life (ζωή)' (1 Jn 1.1).
'And God said, "Let us make a human (ἄνθρωπος) according to our image and likeness"' (v. 26).	'And the life (ζωή) was the light (φῶς) of humans (ἄνθρωποι)' (v. 4b).
'And God made the human (ἄνθρωπος), according to the image of God (κατ' εἰκόνα θεοῦ) he made them' (v. 27).	'He was the true light (φῶς), which enlightens every human (ἄνθρωπος), coming into the world' (v. 9).
'And God formed the human (ἄνθρωπος) from the dust of the earth and breathed into his face the breath of life (ζωή), and the human (ἄνθρωπος) became (ἐγένετο) a living (ζᾶν) soul' (2.7).	

---

1. See P. Borgen, 'The Prologue of John—as Exposition of the Old Testament', in *Philo, John and Paul: New Perspectives on Judaism and Early Christianity* (BJS, 131; Atlanta: Scholars Press, 1987), pp. 75-102.

In terms of language Gen. 1.1-3 provides the closest parallels to the opening words of the Prologue. Creation is certainly alluded to, but it is creation as seen through the lens of wisdom.[1] The following passages below will provide closer thematic parallels.

Exodus 33–34

At first glance the parallels with Exodus 33–34 are less obvious. But careful review of the imagery and context makes it clear that the giving of the law at Sinai, particularly the second giving following the incident of the golden calf (Exod. 32), clearly lies behind the second half of the Prologue (Jn 1.14-18).[2] There are five important points of

1.   As is widely recognized; cf. Beasley-Murray, *John*, p. 10; Brown, *Gospel according to John*, I, pp. 4-5; Carson, *Gospel according to John*, pp. 113-14; Haenchen, *John*, I, p. 109 ('That is no mere coincidence; the agreement is intentional'); Hoskyns, *Fourth Gospel*, I, pp. 135-36; Lindars, *Gospel of John*, p. 82; Schnackenburg, *Gospel according to St John*, I, p. 232. Pace Barrett (*Gospel according to St John*, p. 151), it is not 'probable' that John's 'in the beginning' recalls Mk 1.1 ('The beginning of the Gospel'). Barrett's comment reflects his debatable conclusion that the Fourth Gospel was familiar with the Markan Gospel. P. Lamarch ('Le Prologue de Jean', *RSR* 52 [1964], pp. 497-537) tries to argue that the creation portion of the Prologue (vv. 1-9, as he divides it) is 'Gentile', as opposed to the 'Jewish' half (vv. 14-18). I find no warrant for such a distinction. Both parts are rooted in the Old Testament; both are Jewish.

2.   M.-E. Boismard, *St. John's Prologue* (London: Blackfriars; Westminster: Newman, 1957), pp. 135-45; M.D. Hooker, 'The Johannine Prologue and the Messianic Secret', *NTS* 21 (1975), pp. 40-58; A.T. Hanson, 'Jn 1,14-18 and Exodus 34', *NTS* 23 (1976), pp. 90-101; repr. in *The New Testament Intepretation of Scripture* (London: SPCK, 1980), pp. 97-109; M. Rissi, 'Jn 1,1-18', *Int* 31 (1977), pp. 395-401; C.R. Koester, *The Dwelling of God: The Tabernacle in the Old Testament, Intertestamental Jewish Literature, and the New Testament* (CBQMS, 22; Washington: Catholic Biblical Association, 1989), p. 104. In recent years several commentators have heard echoes of Exodus 33–34 in Jn 1.14-18; cf. Beasley-Murray, *John*, pp. 14-15; Brown, *Gospel according to John*, I, p. 36; Carson, *Gospel according to John*, pp. 129, 134; Hoskyns, *Fourth Gospel*, I, pp. 144, 150; Lindars, *Gospel of John*, pp. 95, 98. Schnackenburg's hesitation (*Gospel according to St John*, I, p. 281) is hard to understand.

On σκηνοῦν Bultmann (*Gospel of John*, p. 67 n. 1) acknowledges that it is 'in the Wisdom myth that we find actual parallels'. He cites *1 En.* 42.2; Sir. 24.4, 8; Bar. 3.28 as the best examples.

J.L. Cumming ('"We Beheld His Glory": Some Aspects of the Old Testament/ Semitic Background of Jn 1.14-18 and Exegetical Implications' [unpublished graduate paper, Fuller Theological Seminary, 1991]) and C. Thoma ('Biblisches

convergence. 1. The general contrast between Moses and Jesus presupposes the giving of the Law at Sinai: 'The Law was given through
Moses; grace and truth came to pass through Jesus Christ' (v. 17).[1]
Taking seriously the contrast implied by this verse we are able to
understand correctly the meaning of the preposition ἀντί in v. 16:
'from his fulness we have all received, even grace in place of (ἀντί)
grace'.[2] For the Johannine community, the grace of the new covenant
established through Jesus supersedes the grace of the covenant established through Moses.[3] 2. Moses' request, 'Show me your glory (כבד)'
(Exod. 33.18; cf. 40.31),[4] is presupposed by the Prologue's declaration: 'and we beheld his glory (δόξαν)' (v. 14). This element receives
clarification from the next point. 3. The Prologue's assertion that 'no
one has ever seen God' (v. 18) echoes God's response to Moses: 'You
cannot see my face; for a human shall not see me and live' (Exod.
33.20, cf. v. 23).[5] 4. The Prologue's assertion that the unique God (or

Erbe im Gottesdienst der Synagoge', in H.H. Henrix [ed.], *Jüdische Liturgie:
Geschichte—Struktur—Wesen* [QD, 86; Freiburg: Herder, 1979], pp. 47-65, esp.
pp. 56-57) have pointed out that Exod. 34.6-7 played an important role in community confessions in the liturgy of the synagogue. The text is alluded to in many later
biblical passages (Neh. 9.17; Ps. 112.4; 116.5; 145.8; Joel 2.13; Jon. 4.2).
E.L. Miller (*Salvation-History in the Prologue of John: The Significance of John
1.3/4* [NovTSup, 60; Leiden: Brill, 1989]) also thinks that the original hymn underlying the Prologue served a liturgical function and may have been sung antiphonally.

1. Koester (*The Dwelling of God*, p. 104) believes that Jn 1.17 recalls Exod.
34.32: 'And afterward all the people of Israel came near, and [Moses] gave them in
commandment all that the Lord had spoken with him in Mount Sinai'.

2. Various renderings such as 'grace upon grace' are not true to the basic sense
of the preposition.

3. So also J.S. King, 'The Prologue to the Fourth Gospel: Some Unsolved
Problems', *ExpTim* 86 (1974), pp. 372-75; Carson, *Gospel according to John*,
pp. 132-34; *idem*, 'John and the Johannine Epistles', in D.A. Carson and
H.G.M. Williamson (eds.), *It is Written: Scripture Citing Scripture* (Cambridge:
Cambridge University Press, 1988), pp. 245-64, esp. p. 256. In saying 'supersede' I
do not mean to imply that the Johannine community viewed the Sinai covenant as
obsolete. It is the *grace* of the revelation in Jesus that has superseded the revelation
given through Moses. The Fourth Evangelist presupposed the validity of the Sinai
covenant, though he did not always agree with the synagogue in matters of
interpretation.

4. The LXX paraphrases, 'Manifest yourself to me'. Here it is clear that seeing
God's 'glory' is to see God himself.

5. The Fourth Evangelist's view coheres with that of the targumic tradition.

Son) existed in the 'bosom of the Father' (v. 18) contrasts with
Moses' fleeting glimpse of God's 'back' (Exod. 33.23). In sharp contrast to Moses, the eternal Word existed 'with [or *facing*: πρός] God'
(v. 1) and 'in the bosom [that is, front][1] of the Father' from eternity.
5. The Prologue's 'full of grace and truth' (v. 14), echoed in v. 17, is
very likely an allusion to Exod. 34.6: 'abounding in steadfast love and
faithfulness', though according to the Hebrew (רב־חסד ואמת), not the
LXX (πολυέλεος καὶ ἀληθινός).[2]

The incarnation of the *logos* cannot be correctly understood, unless
it is seen against this comparison and contrast with Moses and the
Sinai covenant. Prior to the second giving of the covenant, God had
been giving Moses instructions for the building of the tabernacle
(Exod. 26–31). After the calf incident (ch. 32) and the renewal of the
covenant (chs. 33–34), the tabernacle is built (chs. 35–40). When it is
completed and consecrated, 'the cloud covered the tent of meeting, and
the glory (כבוד/δόξα) of the Lord filled the tabernacle (מֹשְׁכַּן/ σκηνή)'
(Exod. 40.34). In essence, then, the second half of the Johannine
Prologue presupposes the second half of the book of Exodus (chs. 20–
40), which tells of Israel's meeting God at Sinai. The balance of the

Although the Hebrew says that Moses spoke with God 'face to face' (cf. Exod.
33.11), the targums usually say that Moses spoke to God 'literally'. We encounter
the same perspective in the reference to Isaiah's vision of God (cf. Jn 12.41), which
is discussed in Chapter 5.

1. The NIV's 'at the Father's side' obscures this point of contrast.

2. So many commentators: cf. Barrett, *Gospel according to St John*, p. 167;
Beasley-Murray, *John*, p. 14; Brown, *Gospel according to John*, I, p. 14; Lindars,
Gospel of John, p. 95; J.N. Sanders and B.A. Mastin, *A Commentary on the Gospel
According to St. John* (BNTC; London: A. & C. Black; HNTC; New York: Harper
& Brothers, 1968), p. 82; B.F. Westcott, *The Gospel according to St John* (London:
Macmillan, 1881), p. 13; and other studies: cf. Boismard, *St. John's Prologue*,
p. 139; Hanson, 'John 1,14-18 and Exodus 34', pp. 90-101; Koester, *The Dwelling
of God*, p. 104. Carson (*Gospel according to John*, pp. 130-31) suggests LXX Exod.
33.16: καὶ πῶς γνωστὸν ἔσται ἀληθῶς, ὅτι εὕρηκα χάριν παρὰ σοί. This is
possible. However, χάρις appears several times in the Sinai passage (cf. 33.12, 13,
17; 34.9). In any case, I do not think that Exod. 34.6 and 33.16 are necessarily com-
peting alternatives. J.A. Montgomery ('Hebrew Hesed and Greek Charis', *HTR* 32
[1939], pp. 97-102) has shown that χάρις is a perfectly legitimate translation of חסד.
Dodd (*Interpretation of the Fourth Gospel*, pp. 175-76, 272) thinks that John's
wording reflects חסד ואמת, but he does not single out Exod. 34.6. Not unexpectedly,
Bultmann (*Gospel of John*, p. 74 n. 2) asserts that 'it is not possible' to find here a
reference to Exod. 34.6.

Fourth Gospel bears this out, as we find several comparisons between Jesus, Moses and various aspects of the wilderness story.[1]

The tabernacle is the place where God spoke to Moses (Exod. 33.9) and it is where God's glory was seen (Exod. 40.34). Koester is correct when he says that 'tabernacle imagery is uniquely able to portray the person of Jesus as the locus of God's Word and glory among mankind'.[2] Not only is the incarnation, the 'tabernacling', of the *logos* patterned after Sinai, but it would also have been viewed as a fulfillment of prophetic promises that someday God would tabernacle among his people (Ezek. 37.27; Joel 3.17; Zech. 2.14[10], where in the LXX κατασκηνοῦν is employed).[3]

Koester reasons that since 'the cognate words σκῆνος and σκήνωμα were often used for the tabernacle of the human body [for example, Wis. 9.15; 2 Cor. 5.4; 2 Pet. 1.13, 14; *Diogn.* 6.8]... tabernacle imagery was uniquely able to capture the idea that people encountered God's Word and glory in the person of Jesus'.[4]

It is clear that there are two principal biblical themes presupposed by the Johannine Prologue. The first is creation, primarily alluded to in the opening five verses. The second is the Sinai covenant, primarily alluded to in the final five verses. In Exodus creation and covenant are linked, primarily with respect to the Sabbath (cf. 20.8-11; 31.12-17; 35.1-3).[5]

---

1. For a study of this theme, see T.F. Glasson, *Moses in the Fourth Gospel* (SBT, 40; London: SCM Press, 1963).

2. Koester, *The Dwelling of God*, p. 102.

3. Koester, *The Dwelling of God*, p. 104. For speculation as to how early 'esoteric' ideas about the Temple could bridge the gap between the Jewish belief that God dwells in the Temple to God dwelling in Jesus, see O. Cullmann, 'The Significance of the Qumran Texts for Research into the Beginnings of Christianity', *JBL* 74 (1955), pp. 213-26; repr. in K. Stendahl (ed.), *The Scrolls and the New Testament* (London: SCM Press; New York: Harper & Brothers, 1958), pp. 18-32; *idem*, 'L'Opposition contre le temple de Jérusalem, motif commun de la théologie johannique et du monde ambiant', *NTS* 5 (1959), pp. 157-73; and more recently *idem*, *The Johannine Circle* (London: SCM Press; Philadelphia: Westminster Press, 1976), pp. 39-56. J.C. Meagher ('Jn 1.14 and the New Temple', *JBL* 88 [1969], pp. 57-68) also thinks that Jn 1.14 originally alluded to the tabernacle or Temple.

4. Koester, *The Dwelling of God*, p. 115. See also W. Michaelis, 'σκηνή, κτλ', *TDNT*, VII, pp. 368-94, esp. pp. 381-84.

5. The interesting observation of O. Hofius ('Struktur und Gedankengang des Logos-Hymnus in Jn 1 1-18', *ZNW* 78 [1987], pp. 1-25, esp. p. 14) should also be considered. He draws our attention to the combination of creation

There are certain emphases in the Johannine Prologue that go beyond the biblical parallels. With regard to creation, there is the emphasis on the *logos* who existed with God and through whom God created the world. There is also the antithesis between light and darkness. These features are not found in Genesis 1–2. With regard to the covenant, the biblical materials say nothing about incarnation. God dwells in a tent; in John the Word dwells in a tent—a tent of flesh and blood. The incarnate Word then reveals the Father, something that parallels but goes beyond the role of Moses.

Sirach 24 and Related Jewish Wisdom Traditions

Sirach 24

Perhaps the closest parallels to Johannine thought, particularly with respect to its Christology, are to be found in the Old Testament Wisdom tradition.[1] 'Word', 'Wisdom' and 'Torah' are the usual

---

(vv. 1-5) and covenant (vv. 14-18) in Psalm 19.

1.   So argue many scholars: Boismard, *St. John's Prologue*; J.D.G. Dunn, *Christology in the Making: A New Testament Inquiry into the Origins of the Doctrine of the Incarnation* (London: SCM Press, 1980), pp. 163-212; E.J. Epp, 'Wisdom, Torah, Word: The Johannine Prologue and the Purpose of the Fourth Gospel', in G.F. Hawthorne (ed.), *Current Issues in Biblical and Patristic Interpretation* (Grand Rapids: Eerdmans, 1975), pp. 128-46; A. Feuillet, *Le Prologue du Quatrième Evangile: Etude de Théologie Johannique* (Paris: Desclée de Brouwer, 1968); E.D. Freed, 'Theological Prelude to the Prologue of John's Gospel', *SJT* 32 (1979), pp. 257-69; H. Gese, 'Der Johannesprolog', in *Zur biblischen Theologie: Alttestamentliche Vorträge* (BEvT, 78; Munich: Chr. Kaiser Verlag, 1977), pp. 152-201; J.R. Harris, *The Origin of the Prologue to St. John's Gospel* (Cambridge: Cambridge University Press, 1917); E.F. Harrison, 'A Study of Jn 1.14', in R.A. Guelich (ed.), *Unity and Diversity in New Testament Theology* (Grand Rapids: Eerdmans, 1978), pp. 23-36; J. Jeremias, *The Central Message of the New Testament* (London: SCM Press; Philadelphia: Fortress Press, 1965), pp. 71-90; *idem*, *Der Prolog des Johannesevangeliums (Johannes 1,1-18)* (CH, 88; Stuttgart: Calwer Verlag, 1967); L.J. Kuyper, 'Grace and Truth: an Old Testament Description of God and its Use in the Johannine Gospel', *Int* 18 (1964), pp. 3-19; B. Lindars, 'Traditions behind the Fourth Gospel', in M. de Jonge (ed.), *L'Evangile de Jean: Sources, rédaction, théologie* (BETL, 44; Leuven: Leuven University Press, 1977), pp. 107-24; T.E. Pollard, *Johannine Christology and the Early Church* (SNTSMS, 13; Cambridge: Cambridge University Press, 1970), pp. 9-15; M. Rissi, 'Die Logoslieder im Prolog des vierten Evangeliums', *TZ* 31 (1975), pp. 321-36; 32 (1976), pp. 1-13; E. Ruckstuhl, 'Kritische Arbeit am Johannesprolog', in W.C. Weinrich (ed.), *The*

designations. The parallels are numerous and significant. The following verses in Sirach 24 offer some of the closest parallels (the parallels from here on are numbered to simplify the exegetical discussion that will follow). Wisdom (σοφία) is speaking 'before the assembly of the Most High... and his host':

	Sirach 24	John 1
1.	'I came forth from the mouth of the Most High...' (v. 3).	'the Word' (v. 1). 'in the bosom of the Father' (v. 18; cf. 3.31: 'he who comes from above is above all').
	'My dwelling-place was (κατασκηνοῦν) in high heaven; My throne was in a pillar of cloud' (v. 4).	
2.	'The Creator of all things (ὁ κτίστης ἀπάντων)' (v. 8).	'all things (πάντα) came into existence through him' (v. 3).
3.	'Then the Creator of the universe laid a command upon me; my Creator decreed where I should dwell (σκηνή). He said, "Make your home (κατασκηνοῦν) in Jacob; find your heritage in Israel"' (v. 8).	'and the Word became flesh and dwelt (σκηνοῦν) among us' (v. 14).
	'In the sacred tent (σκηνή) I ministered in his presence, and so I came to be established in Zion' (v. 10).	
4.	'Before time began (ἀρχή) he created me, and I shall remain forever (αἰών)' (v. 9).	'in the beginning (ἀρχή)' (v. 1; cf. 12.34 [αἰών]).

New Testament Age, II (2 vols.; Macon: Mercer University Press, 1984), pp. 443-54; G. Schimanowski, *Weisheit und Messias: Die jüdischen Voraussetzungen der urchristlichen Präexistenzchristologie* (WUNT, 2.17; Tübingen: Mohr [Paul Siebeck], 1985); C. Spicq, 'Le Siracide et la structure littéraire du Prologue de saint Jean', in *Mémorial Lagrange: Cinquantenaire de l'école biblique et archéologique française de Jérusalem (15 novembre 1890–15 novembre 1940)* (Paris: Gabalda, 1940), pp. 183-95; M. Theobald, *Im Anfang war das Wort: Textlinguistische Studie zum Johannesprolog* (SBS, 106; Stuttgart: Katholisches Bibelwerk, 1983); G. Ziener, 'Weisheitsbuch und Johannesevangelium', *Bib* 38 (1957), pp. 396-418.

5.	'Thus he settled me in the city he loved, and in Jerusalem was my authority (ἐξουσία)' (v. 11).	'he gave authority (ἐξουσία)' (v. 12).
6.	'I took root among the people whom the Lord had honored by choosing them to be his special possession' (v. 12).	'he came to his own things, and his own people' (v. 11).
7	'my branches are branches of glory (δόξα) and grace (χάρις)' (v. 16).	'we beheld his glory (δόξα) . . . full of grace (χάρις) and truth' (v. 14).
8.	'the law (νόμος) which Moses commanded us' (v. 23).	'the law (νόμος) was given through Moses' (v. 17).
9.	'[wisdom] makes them full (ἀναπληροῦν) of understanding' (v. 26);	'full (πλήρης) of grace and truth' (v. 14); 'of his fulness (πλήρωμα) we all received' (v. 16).
	'Her thought is fuller (ἐπληθύνθη) than the sea' (v. 29).	
10.	'The first human did not know (γινώσκειν) wisdom' (v. 28).	'The world did not know (γινώσκειν) him' (v. 10).
11.	'It makes instruction shine forth (ἐκφαίνειν) like light (φῶς)' (v. 27).	'The life was the light (φῶς) of humanity' (v. 4).
	'I will again make instruction shine forth (φωτίζειν) like the dawn' (v. 32a).	'the true light which enlightens (φωτίζειν) every person' (v. 9).
	'and I will make it shine (ἐκφαίνειν) afar' (v. 32b).	'The light shines (φαίνειν) in the darkness' (v. 5).

There are other noteworthy parallels between Sirach 24 and other parts of the Fourth Gospel:

	Sirach 24	*John*
12.	'I shall remain forever (αἰών)' (v. 9).	'The Christ remains forever (αἰών)' (12.34).
13.	'I gave forth the aroma (ὀσμή) of spices, and like choice myrrh (σμύρνα) I spread a pleasant odor. . . like the fragrance of frankincense. . .' (v. 15).	'filled with the aroma (ὀσμή) of the perfume (μύρον)' (12.3).

14.	'Like a terebinth I spread out my branches' (v. 16).	'you are the branches' (15.5).
15.	'Like a vine (ἄμπελος) I caused loveliness to bud, and my blossoms became glorious and abundant fruit (καρπός)' (v. 17).	'I am the true vine (ἄμπελος)' (15.1); 'he bears much fruit (καρπός)' (15.2, 5).
16.	'Come to me, you who desire me, and eat your fill (ἐμπίπλημι) of my produce' (v. 19).	'they were filled (ἐμπίπλημι)' (6.12).
17.	'Those who eat (ἐσθίειν) me will hunger (πεινάζειν) for more, and those who drink (πίνειν) me will thirst (διψᾶν) for more' (v. 21).	'he who comes to me will not hunger (πεινάζειν) and... will not thirst (διψᾶν)... unless you eat (ἐσθίειν) the flesh... and drink (πίνειν) the blood' (6.35, 53).
18.	'I went forth like a canal from a river (ποταμός) and like a water channel into a garden. I said, "I will water my orchard and drench my garden plot"' (v. 30-31).	'rivers (ποταμοί) of living water will flow from his belly' (7.38).

Other Parallels from the LXX and Pseudepigrapha

There are important parallels from elsewhere in the LXX, as well as a few from the Hebrew and from the Pseudepigrapha:

	LXX *(and Pseudepigrapha)*	*John*
19.	'Before eternity (αἰών) he established me in the beginning (ἐν ἀρχῇ)' (Prov. 8.23; cf. Sir. 1.1).	'In the beginning (ἐν ἀρχῇ) was the Word' (1.1).
		'Christ remains forever (αἰών)' (12.34).
20.	'I was with him (ἤμην παρ' αὐτῷ)' (Prov. 8.30). 'Give to me the wisdom that sits by your throne' (Wis. 9.4).	'The Word was with God (ἦν πρὸς τὸν θεόν)' (1.1).
	'When he prepared heaven, I was with him' (Prov. 8.27).	
	'She glorifies her noble birth by living with God' (Wis. 8.3).	

'Forever, O Lord, your word (ὁ
λόγος σου) abides in heaven' (Ps.
118[119].89).

'And the angel of the presence spoke
to Moses by the Word of the Lord,
saying, "Write the whole account of
creation"' (*Jub.* 2.1).

'Before his face the Word will go
(πρὸ προσώπου αὐτοῦ
πορεύσεται λόγος)' (Hab. 3.5).

21. 'Thy all-powerful word leaped from   'and the Word (ὁ λόγος) was with
heaven (ὁ... λόγος ἀπ' οὐρανοῦ),   God' (1.1).
from the royal throne, into the midst
of the land' (Wis. 18.15).

    'and the Word... dwelt among us'
    (1.14; cf. Rev. 19.13: 'The name by
    which he [Jesus] is called is "The
    Word (ὁ λόγος) of God"').

22. 'who made all things (πάντα) by   'all things (πάντα) came into being
your word (ἐν λόγῳ)' (Wis. 9.2; cf.   through him [that is, the Word]'
7.22).   (1.3a).

'God founded the earth by wisdom
(τῇ σοφίᾳ)' (Prov. 3.19; cf. 8.30).

'By the word (ἐν λόγῳ) of the Lord
the heavens were made' (Ps.
33[32].6).

'Wisdom... was present when you
made the world' (Wis 9.9; cf. 8.5-
6).

23. 'and without him nothing is made'   'and without him nothing came into
(1QS 11.11).   being' (1.3b).

24. 'For my ways are the ways of life   'In him was life (ζωή)' (1.4).
(ζωή)' (Prov. 8.35).

'Make me alive according to your
word (λόγος)' (Ps. 118[119].25,
107).

'Because of her I shall have
immortality' (Wis. 8.13).

'[Wisdom] is the book of the
commandments of God, and the
Law that endures for ever. All who
hold her fast will live, and those who
forsake her will die' (Bar. 4.1).

25. 'From you there is a fountain of life   'and the life (ζωή) was the light
     (ζωή), in your light (φῶς) we shall   (φῶς) of humanity' (1.4).
     see light (φῶς)' (Ps 35[36].10).

     'Your word (λόγος) is a lamp to
     my feet and a light to my path'
     (Ps. 118[119].105).

     'Turn, O Jacob, and take [wisdom];
     walk toward the shining of her light
     (φῶς)' (Bar. 4.2).

26. 'Compared with the light (φῶς) she   'and the light (φῶς) shines in the
     [Wisdom] is found to be superior,   darkness, and the darkness did not
     for it is succeeded by the night, but   overcome it' (1.5).
     against wisdom evil does not
     prevail' (Wis. 7.29-30).

     'Darkness and silence were before
     the world was made, and silence
     spoke a word and the darkness
     became light' (Ps.-Philo, *LAB* 60.2).

     'The world lies in darkness and its
     inhabitants are without light' (*4 Ezra*
     14.20).

     'The lamp of the eternal Law which
     exists forever and ever illuminated
     all those who sat in darkness'
     (*2 Bar.* 59.2).

     'I prepared light (φῶς) and I made
     darkness (σκότος), I made peace
     and I created evil' (Isa. 45.7).

27. 'because you want to destroy the   'the true light (τὸ φῶς) which en-
     light of the Law (τὸ φῶς τοῦ   lightens every human (φωτίζει
     νόμου) which was granted to you   πάντα ἄνθρωπον)' (1.9a).
     for the enlightenment of every
     human (εἰς φωτισμὸν παντὸς
     ἀνθρώπου)' (*T. Levi* 14.4).

'to be lighted with the light of life
(לאור באור החיים)' (Job 33.30b).

'the life was the light... the true light
which enlightens' (1.4, 9).

28. 'Send (ἐξαποστέλλειν) her
[Wisdom] forth from the holy
heavens, and from the throne of
your glory send her, that she may be
with me... and that I may know
(γινώσκειν) what is pleasing to you'
(Wis. 9.10).

'coming into the world' (1.9b); 'He
was in the world... and the world
did not know (γινώσκειν) him... to
his own he came' (1.10-11).

'He sends forth (ἀποστέλλειν) his
command (λόγιος) to the earth;
his word (λόγος) runs swiftly'
(Ps. 147.15[14]).

'God did not send (ἀποστέλλειν)
his son into the world to judge the
world' (3.17; cf. 3.34; 6.29, 57
passim).

29. 'You have forsaken the fountain of
wisdom' (Bar. 3.12).

'the world did not know him'
(1.10).

'They did not believe in his word
(λόγος)... they did not obey the
voice of the Lord' (Ps. 105[106].24-
25).

'his own did not receive him' (1.11).

'... for they hated (μισεῖν) wisdom'
(Prov. 1.29).

'Every one who practices evil hates
(μισεῖν) the light (φῶς)' (3.20; cf.
1.5).

'[The world] hates (μισεῖν) me'
(7.7; cf. 15.18, 19, 23, 24, 25).

30. 'She passes into souls of holiness
and makes them friends of God
(φίλους θεοῦ) and prophets'
(Wis. 7.27).

'But as many as received him to
them he gave the authority to
become children of God (τέκνα
θεοῦ)' (1.12).

'Those who get [wisdom] obtain
friendship with God' (Wis. 7.14).

31. 'My name (ὄνομα) shall dwell
(κατασκηνοῦν) in the midst of
the house of Israel forever'
(Ezek. 43.7).

'who believe on his name (ὄνομα)'
(1.12; cf. 2.23; 3.18; 5.43; 10.25).

'While your name dwells
(κατασκηνοῦν τὸ ὄνομα) among
us, we shall receive mercy'
(*Pss. Sol.* 7.6).

32. 'Before the mountains were shaped, before all the hills, he begets me (γεννᾶν)' (Prov. 8.25).

'who were begotten (γεννᾶν) of God' (1.13):

'the only begotten (μονογενής) God' (1.18; cf. 3.16).

33. 'She [Wisdom] dwells with all flesh (μετὰ πάσης σαρκός), and he supplied her to those who love (ἀγαπᾶν) him' (Sir 1.10).

'And the Word became flesh (σάρξ)' (1.14a). 'He who loves (ἀγαπᾶν) me will be loved (ἀγαπᾶν) by my Father' (14.21).

'And let them construct a sanctuary for me, that I may dwell among them (ועשׂו לי מקדשׁ ושׁכנתי בתוכם; LXX reads ὀφθήσομαι ἐν ὑμῖν)' (Exod. 25.8).

'and dwelt among us (ἐσκήνωσεν ἐν ἡμῖν)' (1.14b).

'that I might dwell among them (ושׁכני בתוכם; LXX reads ἐπικληθῆναι αὐτοῖς)' (Exod. 29.46).

'And the cloud covered the tent (σκηνή) of the witness (μαρτύριον), and the tent (σκηνή) was filled with the glory (δόξα) of the Lord' (Exod. 40.34).

'You will know that I am the Lord your God who makes his dwelling (κατασκηνοῦν) in Zion' (Joel 3.17).

'Sing and rejoice, O daughter of Zion, for look, I come and will make my dwelling (κατασκηνοῦν) in your midst' (Zech. 2.10[14]).

'and [Wisdom] appeared upon the earth and lived among people (ἐν τοῖς ἀνθρώποις)' (Bar. 3.37).

34. 'And he [Moses] said, 'Show me your glory (δόξα)' (Exod. 33.18).

'and we beheld his glory (δόξα)' (1.14c).

'and the tent (σκηνή) was filled with the glory (δόξα) of the Lord' (Exod. 40.34).

'Jesus says to her, "... if you believe, you will see the glory (δόξα) of God"' (11.40; cf. 12.41; 17.24).

35. 'For in her there is a spirit that is...
     unique (μονογενές)...for she is the
     breath of the power of God and an
     emanation of the glory of the
     Almighty' (Wis. 7.22, 25).

     'glory as of the only begotten of the
     Father (δόξαν ὡς μονογενοῦς
     παρὰ πατρός)' (1.14d).

36. 'And he said, "The Lord, the Lord
     God...abounding in loving
     kindness and truth (רב־חסד ואמת)"'
     (MT Exod. 34.6).

     'full of grace and truth (πλήρης
     χάριτος καὶ ἀληθείας)' (1.14e; cf.
     v. 17b).

37. 'And the cloud covered the tent
     (σκηνή) of the witness
     (μαρτύριον), and the tent (σκηνή)
     was filled with the glory (δόξα) of
     the Lord' (Exod. 40.34).

     'He came for a witness (μαρτυρία)
     that he might witness (μαρτυρεῖν)
     concerning the light (φῶς)' (1.7, 8).

     'John bears witness (μαρτυρεῖν)
     concerning him' (1.15).

38. 'Who has seen (ἑώρακεν) him
     [God] and can describe
     (ἐκδιηγεῖσθαι) him?' (Sir. 43.31).
     'And [God] said,'You cannot see
     (εἶδον) my face, for no one can see
     (εἶδον) my face and live' (Exod.
     33.20).

     'no one has ever seen (ἑώρακεν)
     God...that one has interpreted
     (ἐξηγεῖσθαι) him' (1.18a, c).

     'I was with him united [or betrothed;
     MT var.: 'in his bosom']...Every
     day I rejoiced in his presence at all
     times' (Prov. 8.30).

     'who was in the bosom of the
     father' (1.18b).

39. 'Who ascended into heaven and
     descended (τίς ἀνέβη εἰς τὸν
     οὐρανὸν καὶ κατέβη)?' (Prov.
     30.4).

     'no one has ascended into heaven
     (ἀναβέβηκεν εἰς τὸν οὐρανόν)
     except the one who descended
     (καταβάς) from heaven' (3.13; cf.
     Rom. 10.6-7; Eph. 4.9-10).

     'Who has gone up into heaven (τίς
     ἀνέβη εἰς τὸν οὐρανόν), and
     taken her, and brought her down
     from the clouds?' (Bar. 3.29).

40.	'Afterward she [Wisdom] appeared upon earth (γῆ) and lived among humans (ἄνθρωποι)' (Bar. 3.37 [38]).[1]	'if I be lifted up from the earth (γῆ) (12.32; cf. 3.31; 1.9: 'enlightens every human [ἄνθρωπος], coming into the world').
41.	'people were taught what pleases you, and were saved (σώζειν) by wisdom' (Wis. 9.18).	'I did not come to judge the world, but to save (σώζειν) the world' (12.47).
42.	'Wisdom found no place where she might dwell; then a dwelling-place was assigned her in the heavens. Wisdom went forth to make her dwelling among the children of men, and found no dwelling-place; Wisdom returned to her place, and took her seat among the angels.	'and the Word was with God' (1.1). 'and the Word...dwelt among us' (1.14). 'I leave the world and go to the Father' (16.28; cf. 8.14; 13.3). 'You will see angels ascending and descending upon the Son of Man' (1.51).
	And righteousness went forth from her chambers: whom she sought not she found, and dwelt with them, as rain in a desert and dew on a thirsty land' (*1 En.* 42.1-3).	'and the Word...dwelt among us' (1.14). 'Whoever drinks of the water that I shall give him will never thirst, but the water that I shall give him will become in him a well springing up into eternal life' (4.14; cf. 7.37-38).

The interpretation of these parallels is deferred to Chapters 4 and 5. For now it is only necessary to say that their importance for interpreting the Johannine Prologue can hardly be overestimated. All of the elements of the Prologue are paralleled. Even when the Prologue is divided into two parts, reflecting the λόγος ἄσαρκος (vv. 1-5), the 'creation' half, and the λόγος ἔνσαρκος (vv. 6-18),[2] the 'covenant'

1.   R. Bultmann ('The History of Religions Background of the Prologue to the Gospel of John', in J. Ashton [ed.], *The Interpretation of John* [London: SPCK; Philadelphia: Fortress Press, 1986], p. 29) rightly argues that Bar. 3.37 should not be regarded as a Christian interpolation, but as 'a remnant of ancient wisdom-speculation'.

2.   On the distinction between the λόγος ἄσαρκος and the λόγος ἔνσαρκος, see Schnackenburg, *Gospel according to St John*, I, pp. 228-30.

half, we find that the biblical Wisdom materials parallel all of the principal components. With respect to the former we hear echoes of the attributes and activities of Sophia (and, in many instances, of God's *logos* as well):

1. Sophia was 'in the beginning' (Jn 1.1a; see §4 [Sir. 24.9], §19 [Prov. 8.23]).
2. Sophia 'was with' God (Jn 1.1b; see §1 [Sir. 24.4], §20 [Prov. 8.27, 30], §42 [*1 En.* 42.1-3]). Similarly, God's *logos* abides in heaven (see §20 [Ps. 118(119).89], §21 [Wis. 18.15]).
3. The world was created 'by Sophia' (Jn 1.3; see §22 [Prov. 8.30; Wis. 9.9]). Similarly, the world was created by God's *logos* (see §22 [Wis. 7.22; 9.2]).
4. In Sophia was 'life' (Jn 1.4a; see §24 [Prov. 8.35; Wis. 8.13], §25 [Ps 35(36).10]. Likewise, God's *logos* makes alive (see §24 [Ps 118(119).25, 107]).
5. Sophia gave 'light' to the world (Jn 1.4b-5a; see §25 [Bar. 4.2]). Similarly, God's *logos* is light (see §25 [Ps. 118(119).105]), and his Torah enlightens humankind (see §27 [*T. Levi* 14.4; Job 33.30b]).
6. Sophia prevailed against darkness and evil (Jn 1.5b; see §26 [Wis. 7.29-30]). Similarly, God's spoken word at the time of creation brought light into being (see Gen. 1.2-3).

We find that many of the assertions regarding the λόγος ἔνσαρκος in the Prologue's final five verses, with the exception of the incarnation itself, are true of Sophia:

1. Sophia 'tabernacled' among humankind (Jn 1.14a; see §3 [Sir. 24.8, 10], §40 [Bar. 3.37 [38]]).
2. Sophia 'dwelt with flesh' (Jn 1.14a; see §33 [Sir. 1.10]).
3. Sophia's 'branches are branches of glory' (Jn 1.14b; see §7 [Sir. 24.16]).
4. Sophia's 'understanding' is 'full' (Jn 1.14c, 16, 17; see §9 [Sir. 24.26, 29]).
5. Sophia is God's 'unique' (or 'only begotten') creation, reflecting his 'glory' (Jn 1.14d; see §35 [Wis. 7.22]).
6. Although no one 'has seen' God, Sophia has and she can 'interpret him' (Jn 1.18; see §38 [Sir. 43.31]).

It is evident that we have here the raw materials from which the

Prologue may have taken shape.[1] That there is a gap between the biblical materials and what we find in the Johannine Prologue is undeniable. Some, such as Rudolf Bultmann and James Robinson, have argued that this gap can only be bridged by an appeal to Gnosticism. The problems with this solution were reviewed in Chapters 1 and 2. Others contend that the gap can be bridged by appealing to exegetical and speculative traditions that are known to have predated the Fourth Gospel. To these traditions we shall turn in Chapter 4.

Further Comments on Johannine Christology and the Old Testament

Before leaving this chapter it would be useful to consider briefly one recent study that has concluded that the Old Testament supplies all of the necessary ingredients for understanding important aspects of Johannine Christology. Although this work is not limited to the Prologue, it is worth reviewing because it offers additional evidence of the foundational role played by the Scriptures of Israel in the formation of Johannine theology, including the theology of the Prologue.

Delbert Burkett has recently observed that all of the Johannine passages that speak of descent or ascent are based upon various Old Testament passages:[2] (1) Jn 1.51, which alludes to the ascending and descending angels of Gen. 28.12; (2) Jn 3.13, which apparently answers the question posed in Prov. 30.4: 'Who has ascended to heaven and descended?'; (3) Jn 3.14 and 12.32-34, passages which speak of the need for the Son of (the) Man to be lifted up, allude to Num. 21.9 and Isa. 52.13, respectively; and (4) John 6, which quotes Ps. 78.24 and speaks of the 'bread from heaven', but probably also presupposes Isa. 55.10-11. The allusions in the first and second passages are routinely noted by interpreters.[3] The allusion to Isa. 55.10-11

1. See G. Rochais, 'La formation du Prologue (Jn 1,1-18)', *ScEs* 37 (1985), pp. 161-87, esp. pp. 174-82.

2. Burkett, *Son of the Man*.

3. On Jn 1.51, see Barrett, *Gospel according to St John*, pp. 186-87; Beasley-Murray, *John*, p. 28; Brown, *Gospel according to John*, I, p. 90; Bultmann, *Gospel of John*, p. 105 n. 3 (though with a Gnostic twist); Carson, *Gospel according to John*, pp. 163-64; Dodd, *Interpretation of the Fourth Gospel*, pp. 245-46; Haenchen, *John*, I, p. 166; Hoskyns, *Fourth Gospel*, I, p. 189; Lindars, *Gospel of John*, p. 121; Schnackenburg, *Gospel according to St John*, I, pp. 320-22. On Jn 3.13, see Bultmann, *Gospel of John*, p. 150 n. 2 (though again with a Gnostic twist); Carson, *Gospel according to John*, p. 201; Lindars, *Gospel of John*, p. 156; Schnackenburg,

is less obvious, although scholars before Burkett have suggested that
this prophetic passage has contributed to Johannine Christology.[1]
Burkett himself has provided a very helpful listing of the parallels
between Isa. 55.1-3, 10-11 and Jn 6.27-71.[2] The allusion to Num. 21.9
is obvious,[3] while the allusion to Isa. 52.13 seems apparent enough
(see the discussion in Chapter 5).[4]

An important feature that is common to all of these Johannine passages is the reference to 'the Son of (the) Man' (see 1.51; 3.13; 3.14;
6.27, 53; 12.23, 34). Burkett concludes that not only does Prov. 30.4
lie behind Jn 3.13, but that the Johannine 'Son of (the) Man' comes
from this passage (as opposed to Daniel 7, the passage which apparently lies behind the synoptic Son of Man sayings). He reaches this
conclusion by observing first that the clearest biblical language for the
ascent/descent language (as expressed in Jn 3.13) comes from
Prov. 30.4. Burkett correctly wonders if the passage may have contributed more to the evangelist's Christology than only this single
element. He next observes in John 3 allusions to several elements

Gospel according to St John, I, p. 374; E.M. Sidebottom, 'The Ascent and Descent
of the Son of Man in the Gospel of St. John', *ATR* 39 (1957), pp. 115-22, esp.
p. 120; B.F. Westcott, *The Gospel according to St John* (London: Macmillan, 1881),
p. 53.

1. F.W. Young, 'A Study of the Relation of Isaiah to the Fourth Gospel', *ZNW*
46 (1955), pp. 215-33, esp. pp. 227-30; H. Lausberg, *Minuscula philologia (V):
Jesaja 55,10–11 im Evangelium nach Johannes* (Nachrichten der Akademie der
Wissenschaften in Göttingen, Philologisch-historische Klasse, 7; Göttingen:
Vandenhoeck & Ruprecht, 1979), p. 6. Lausberg believes that Isa. 55.10-11 has
supplied the framework against which much of Johannine Christology should be
understood. Among commentators, see Carson (*Gospel according to John*, p. 115)
and Schnackenburg (*Gospel according to St John*, I, p. 483) who relates Isa. 55.10-
11, among other passages, to the general background of the Johannine *logos*. See
Burkett's discussion (*Son of the Man*, pp. 46-47).

2. Burkett, *Son of the Man*, pp. 130-34.

3. The Nestle–Aland and Metzger (*et al.*) editions of the Greek New Testament
cite Num. 21.9 in the margin or footnotes.

4. Barrett, *Gospel according to St John*, p. 427; Brown, *Gospel according to
John*, I, pp. 146, 478; Carson, *Gospel according to John*, p. 444; Dodd, *Interpretation
of the Fourth Gospel*, p. 247; G. Reim, *Studien zum alttestamentlichen Hintergrund
des Johannesevangeliums* (SNTSMS, 22; Cambridge: Cambridge University Press,
1974), pp. 174-76; Schnackenburg, *Gospel according to St John*, I, p. 397; II,
pp. 405, 407. See Burkett's discussion (*Son of the Man*, pp. 126-27).

expressed in Prov. 30.1-4.[1] 1. In the first line of Prov. 30.1 the 'son' is addressed. In the second line the addressee is identified as 'the Man' (הגבר). The Johannine title, the 'Son of (the) Man', comes from this opening verse. Burkett also believes that 'the Man' is God. Hence, the Johannine title 'Son of (the) Man' is equivalent to 'Son of God'. 2. In the third line of Prov. 30.1 the 'son' is called 'Ithiel' (איתיאל='God is with me'), which apparently is a proper name (cf. Neh. 11.7). Burkett sees the name 'God is with me' unwittingly alluded to in the opening statement of Nicodemus: 'unless God be with him' (Jn 3.2). Elsewhere Jesus says that his Father is 'with me' (cf. 8.29; 16.32). Thus, the Johannine Jesus has identified himself as Ithiel. 3. The fourth and final line of Prov. 30.1, in synonymous parallelism, reads: 'to "God is with me so that I am able"'. This too is alluded to by Nicodemus when he says to Jesus: 'No is able to do the signs which you do...' (Jn 3.2). In other words, only Ithiel ('God is with me'), who is 'able', can do what Jesus does. 4. Prov. 30.2-3 ('I burn more brightly than a man, and mine is not human understanding; I have not learned wisdom, yet I have knowledge of the holy ones') means that Ithiel, unlike a mere mortal, did not have to learn wisdom; he already knew it. In contrast to Jesus/Ithiel stands Nicodemus, a 'teacher of Israel' who does not understand earthly and spiritual things (Jn 3.9-12). Jesus, like Ithiel who 'burns' with illumination, is the 'light' that illumines the darkness of the world (Jn 3.19-21). 5. Prov. 30.4 poses a question: 'Who has ascended to heaven and descended? Who has gathered wind in his garments? Who has wrapped water in a mantle? Who has established all the ends of the earth? What is his name and what is his son's name? For you know'. Jesus answers the question in Jn 3.13: 'No one has ascended into heaven but he who descended from heaven, the Son of (the) Man'. That is to say, Jesus is Ithiel ('God is with me so that [he] is able'), who is the one who has ascended to heaven and descended to earth, who as God's Wisdom has created all things, and who is the 'son' addressed in Prov. 30.1 and 4.

Burkett's analysis has much to commend it. Given the relevance of Jewish Wisdom tradition for Johannine Christology, defining the Johannine 'Son of (the) Man' in terms of the 'son' called Ithiel ('God with me') of Proverbs 30 makes good sense. Furthermore, the discussion with Nicodemus in John 3 coheres with the substance of

1. Burkett (*Son of the Man*, pp. 51-59) does not follow the pointing of the MT; he repoints a few words usually based on the reading in the LXX.

Prov. 30.1-4. The one detail in Burkett's analysis that is sure to be challenged, however, is his conclusion that הגבר ('the Man') refers to 'God'.[1] But even if this point is questioned, the rest of his analysis appears to be well founded and coheres with emphases found in the Prologue: the *logos* is 'with God' (Jn 1.1); 'All things were created through him' (Jn 1.3); the '*logos* became flesh and dwelt among' human beings, which implies descent. His analysis also makes good sense of many other important themes that express Johannine Christology.[2] There is a fourth point of coherence, with which Burkett is in disagreement. The assertion that 'no one has ascended into heaven except the one who descended from heaven' (Jn 3.13) not only answers the rhetorical question of Prov. 30.4, but may also be intended as a point of contrast between Jesus and Moses. Peder Borgen has argued that the Fourth Evangelist has polemicized against Jewish traditions of Moses' ascent to heaven, a line of interpretation that I think Burkett dismisses too hastily.[3] Sinai traditions probably do not explain the Johannine Son of Man, and I think here Burkett's criticism is on target, but the exclusivistic claim that 'no one has ascended except...the Son of Man' probably would have been interpreted in the synagogue as a challenge to popular speculations about Moses.[4] This

1.   הגבר can be pointed הַגֶּבֶר ('the man') or הַגִּבֹּר ('the Mighty one'). Burkett notes (*Son of the Man*, p. 64) that the word pointed the latter way is used in reference to God (cf. Deut. 10.17; Isa. 42.13; Jer. 20.11; 32.18; cf. *2 Bar.* 21.3). If pointed the former way, the word then becomes a 'veiled or concealed' reference to God. Perhaps.

2.   Burkett, *Son of the Man*, pp. 142-68.

3.   P. Borgen, 'Some Jewish Exegetical Traditions as Background for Son of Man Sayings in John's Gospel (Jn 3, 13-14 and Context)', in de Jonge (ed.), *L'Evangile de Jean*, pp. 243-59; repr. in P. Borgen, *Philo, John and Paul: New Perspectives on Judaism and Early Christianity* (BJS, 131; Atlanta: Scholars Press, 1987), pp. 103-20.

4.   Borgen ('Some Jewish Exegetical Traditions', pp. 243-44) cites Philo, *Vit. Mos.* 1.28 §158; Josephus, *Ant.* 3.5.7 §96; Pseudo-Philo, *LAB* 12.1; *Num. R.* 12.11 (on Num. 7.1); *Midr. Ps.* 24.5 (on Ps. 24.1); 106.2 (on Ps. 106.2). The midrash preserved in *Numbers Rabbah* is based on Prov. 30.4. Some of the interpretations refer to Sinai. One specifically refers to Moses: '"Who has ascended into heaven [Prov. 30.4]?" That was Moses of whom it is written, "And Moses went up unto God" [Exod. 19.3]. "And descended," as it says: "And Moses went down from the Mount unto the people" [Exod 19.14]'. The midrash goes on to explain that in erecting the Tabernacle Moses accomplished the statements about creation that are found in Prov. 30.4. Borgen also cites *Mek.* on Exod. 19.20 (*Bahodeš* §4) which

does not mean that Jn 3.13 or any other passage in John denigrates Moses; it means that at yet one more point Jesus' authority and being surpass those of the Lawgiver. If this interpretation is correct, then

also polemicizes against speculations that Moses went up to heaven: 'Neither Moses nor Elijah ever ascended to heaven, nor did the Glory ever come down to earth'. These exegeses strongly suggest that the Johannine interpretation of Prov. 30.4 was intended as polemic against the view that Moses had ascended into heaven.

Traditions about Moses' ascension begin with the mystery surrounding his death and burial: 'So Moses the servant of the Lord died there...but no man knows the place of his burial to this day' (Deut. 34.5-6). The idea of Moses' ascension may lie behind the *Testament of Moses*, especially 10.12: 'Keep these words and this book, Joshua of Nun, for from my death and burial [*or* ascension] until his coming there shall be 250 times'. According to Pseudo-Philo, when Moses 'was dying God established for him a platform and showed him then what we now have as witnesses, saying, "Let there be as a witness between me and you and my people the heaven that you are to enter and the earth on which you walk until now"' (*LAB* 32.9); trans. from D.J. Harrington, 'Pseudo-Philo', in J.H. Charlesworth (ed.), *The Old Testament Pseudepigrapha*, II (Garden City, NY: Doubleday, 1985), p. 346. Josephus is apparently aware of beliefs that at death Moses had been taken up to heaven, though he himself rejects the notion. Nevertheless, his own description only contributes to the mysteriousness of Moses' death: 'While [Moses] bade farewell to Eleazar and Joshua and was yet communicating with them, a cloud of a sudden descended upon him and he disappeared [ἀφανίζεσθαι]' (*Ant.* 4.8.48 §326); trans. from H. St. J. Thackeray, *Josephus* (LCL, 4; Cambridge, MA: Harvard University Press, 1961) 633. Note that Josephus also uses ἀφανίζεσθαι in his description of the disappearance of Elijah (*Ant.* 9.2.2 §28). Thackeray (*Josephus*, pp. 632-33 n. b) notes that Josephus's description of Moses' disappearance is reminiscent of legends of the assumptions of Aeneas and Romulus (see Dionysius of Halicarnassus, *Ant. Rom.* 1.64.4; 2.56.2). Josephus's description is somewhat similar to Luke's in Acts 1.9 where 'a cloud took [Jesus] out of sight'. According to Philo (*Vit. Mos.* 2.51 §288, 291), the death of Moses was a journey to heaven in spirit. These speculations make it clear that at least some Jews in the first century believed that Moses had been caught up into heaven, either at death or at Sinai. In fact, Moses' reception of the Law at Sinai is often portrayed as a heavenly ascent. In addition to the passage cited by Borgen above, see *Fragmentary Targum* and *Neof. Deut.* 30.12; *Pes. R.* 20.4.

In later writings the ascension of Moses is clearly accepted. According to Clement of Alexandria (*Strom.* 6.15.132), Joshua saw Moses ascend with the angels. In what may be a reference to a portion of the *Assumption of Moses* that is no longer extant, Origen (*Hom. Josh.* 2.1) says that Moses was alive in the spirit, but dead in the body. According to Jerome (*Hom. Amos* 9.6), 'The Lord ascended in a cloud with Enoch, ascended with Elijah, ascended with Moses'. *Acts Pil.* 16.7 compares Moses

we have coherence with the Prologue's comparisons between Jesus and Moses: 'the Law was given through Moses; grace and truth were realized through Jesus Christ' (1.17); 'no one has ever seen God [including Moses]; the only begotten God who exists in the bosom of the Father has interpreted him' (1.18).

The point to all of this is that we have here another compelling indication that Johannine Christology is founded squarely on Old Testament language, imagery and concepts.[1] Turning to non-Jewish, non-Old Testament sources becomes less and less necessary or justified. The relevance of Burkett's work for the present study is clear: if the Fourth Evangelist's ascent and descent Christology can be adequately explained on the basis of the Old Testament, then appeal to Gnostic mythologies of a descending/ascending redeemer becomes superfluous.[2]

with Enoch (who was widely thought of as assumed): 'No one saw the death of Enoch or the death of Moses'. Finally, according to *Sifre Deut.* §357 (on 34.5), some say that 'Moses never died, and he stands and serves on high'; trans. from R. Hammer, *Sifre: A Tannaitic Commentary on the Book of Deuteronomy* (Yale Judaica, 24; New Haven: Yale University Press, 1986) 381; and *Midrash haGadol* on Deuteronomy: 'Three went up alive into heaven: Enoch, Moses, and Elijah'; trans. from J. Jeremias, 'Μωυσῆς', *TDNT*, IV, p. 855. The evidence seems to indicate that there was the belief that although Moses physically died and was buried, his soul was taken up into heaven. This idea in reference to other Old Testament worthies is found in other writings (*T. Abr.* 14.6-7; *T. Job* 52.8-12; *T. Isaac* 7.1).

1. Burkett (*Son of the Man*, p. 66 n. 1) reminds us that in the Old Testament the ascent and descent of God is common. For passages which speak of God's ascent, see Gen. 17.22; 35.13; Pss. 47.5; 68.18; for passages that speak of God's descent, see Gen. 11.5, 7; Exod. 3.8; 19.11, 18, 20; Neh. 9.13; 2 Sam. 22.10 = Ps. 144.5; Isa. 31.4; 64.1, 3; Mic. 1.3.

2. Burkett (*Son of the Man*, pp. 21-24, 26-27) criticizes the theory of the Gnostic redeemer myth. He says that the results of his study 'suggest that perhaps the only Gnostic myth associated with John is the myth that its Christology is Gnostic...In this respect, therefore, the findings of the present study are in accord with recent Johannine scholarship, which has moved increasingly toward understanding the [Fourth] Gospel against a Jewish and Old Testament background' (p. 177).

Chapter 4

JEWISH INTERPRETIVE PARALLELS

Genesis 1–2 clearly underlies the first half of the Prologue, especially vv. 1-5. But the Johannine Prologue contains ideas not even hinted at in the creation story. Most of these ideas are found in the Wisdom traditions, as the parallels outlined in Chapter 3 demonstrate. But have all the essential elements been taken into account? Most interpreters do not think so. With respect to the second half of the Prologue (esp. vv. 14-18), which clearly echoes the giving of the law at Sinai, especially Exodus 33–34, we may raise the same question. Can the biblical parallels alone provide a backdrop that is adequate for explaining the Prologue? Most interpreters have rightly recognized that the biblical parallels do not in themselves fully explain the ideas presupposed by the Johannine Prologue.

As discussed above in Chapters 1 and 2, some scholars think that a Gnostic myth underlies the Prologue and so acts as the bridge between Jewish or biblical ideas and the Prologue. Others think that the bridge is to be found in Jewish interpretations of the biblical materials surveyed in Chapter 3. To these interpretive traditions I shall now turn. Philo will be considered first, then the interpretive traditions preserved in the targums and in rabbinic writings.

Philo's Exegesis

Scholars have always pointed to important parallels between Philo's use of the *logos* and that found in the Johannine Prologue.[1]

---

1. Dodd, *Interpretation of the Fourth Gospel*, pp. 54-73, esp. pp. 71-72; A.F. Segal, *Two Powers in Heaven: Early Rabbinic Reports about Christianity and Gnosticism* (SJLA, 25; Leiden: Brill, 1977), pp. 159-81; L. Hurtado, *One God, One Lord: Early Christian Devotion and Ancient Jewish Monotheism* (Philadelphia: Fortress Press, 1988), pp. 44-50. For a sketch of the Hellenistic antecedents to

The most impressive include the following:

Philo	John
43. God's 'First-born' and 'Son' is 'the Word (τὸν...λόγον)' who is called 'the beginning (ἀρχή)' (*Conf. Ling.* 28 §146)	'in the beginning (ἀρχῇ) was the Word (ὁ λόγος)' (1.1a, 2)
44. 'The Divine Word (ὁ...λόγος θεῖος)...is placed nearest, with no intervening distance, to the only truly existent One' (*Fug.* 19 §101)	'and the Word (ὁ λόγος) was with God' (1.1b)
45. 'the title "God (θεόν)" is given to his principal Word (λόγον)' (*Somn.* 1.39 §230)	'and the Word (ὁ λόγος) was God (θεός)' (1.1c)
The greatest power is 'the Divine Word (λόγον θεῖον)'; to the next 'Moses gives the name "God (θεόν)"' (*Fug.* 18 §97)	
'And from the Divine Logos (θείου λόγου), as from a spring, there divide and break forth two powers. One is the creative [power], through whom the Architect placed and ordered all things; this is named "God (θεός)". And (the other)...is called "Lord (κύριος)"' (*Quaest. in Exod.* 2.68 [on Exod. 25.22]).	
46. the instrument of creation is 'the Word of God (λόγον θεοῦ) through whom (δι' οὗ) it was framed' (*Cher.* 35 §127; cf. *Fug.* 18 §95)	'all things came into being through him (δι' αὐτοῦ)' (1.3a)
Author of creation is 'the divine Word (τὸν θεῖον λόγον)' (*Op. Mund.* 5 §20)	'apart from him nothing came into existence' (1.3b)
47. the 'light (φῶς)' is a source of 'life (ζωῆς)' (*Op. Mund.* 8 §30)	'and the life (ζωή) was the light (φῶς) of humanity' (1.4)

Philo's *logos*, see H. Kleinknecht, 'λέγω, λόγος, κτλ', *TDNT*, IV, pp. 77-91; R.L. Duncan, 'The Logos: From Sophocles to the Gospel of John', *Christian Scholar's Review* 9 (1979), pp. 121-30.

48.	'darkness (σκότος), the adversary [of φῶς], withdrew' (*Op. Mund.* 9 §33)	'and the light (φῶς) shines in the darkness (σκότος), and the darkness did not overcome it' (1.5)
49.	'the Word of God (θεοῦ λόγον) already making the world (κοσμοποιοῦντες)' (*Op. Mund.* 6 §24)	'the world (κόσμος) came into existence through him' (1.10)
50.	God's 'Word (λόγος)' is 'the human being (ἄνθρωπος) after his image' (*Conf. Ling.* 28 §146)	'and the Word (ὁ λόγος) became flesh' (1.14a)
51.	'For nothing mortal can be made in the likeness of the most high One and Father of the universe but [only] in that of the second God, who is his Logos (τὸν δεύτερον θεόν, ὅς ἐστιν ἐκείνου λόγος)' (*Quaest. in Gen.* 2.62 [on Gen. 9.6])	'and the Word (ὁ λόγος) became flesh and we beheld his glory' (1.14ab)
52.	'Not even to Moses' did God reveal himself (*Poster. C.* 48 §169, in reference to Exod. 33.23; cf. *Fug.* 29 §164-65; *Mut. Nom.* 2 §7-10; *Spec. Leg.* 1.8 §41-50)	'No one has ever seen God' (1.18a; cf. Exod. 33.20, 23)
53.	'The Divine Word (ὁ...λόγος θεῖος)...is placed nearest, with no intervening distance, to the only truly existent One' (*Fug.* 19 §101)	'who was in the bosom of the Father...' (1.18b); 'and the Word (ὁ λόγος) was with God' (1.1b, cf. v. 2)
54.	Abraham had 'the Divine Word (λόγῳ θείῳ) as his leader (ἡγεμόνι)' (*Migr. Abr.* 31 §174)	'the only begotten God (θεός)... has explained (ἐξηγήσατο) him' (1.18b)
	'The Divine Word (ὁ λόγος θεῖος)...is the image of God' (*Fug.* 19 §101)	

Philo's speculative interpretations coincide with the attributes and function of the *logos* of the Johannine Prologue in several important areas:

1. Just as the *logos* of the Johannine Prologue was 'in the beginning' (1.1a), so Philo's *logos* is called 'the beginning' (see §43 [*Conf. Ling.* 28 §146]), which probably implies that

the *logos*, like Wisdom and like God himself, antedated the created universe.

2. Philo's *logos*, moreover, exists very close to God, 'with no intervening distance' (see §44 and §53 [*Fug.* 19 §101]), something that the Johannine Prologue says about the *logos*: 'the Word was with God' (1.1b), even 'in the bosom of the Father' (1.18).

3. As in the Johannine Prologue (1.1c), Philo calls the *logos* 'God' (see §45 [*Somn.* 1.39 §230; *Fug.* 18 §97; *Quaest. in Exod.* 2.68]).

4. As in the Johannine Prologue (1.3, 10), Philo says that the world was created 'through' the agency of the *logos* (see §46 [*Cher.* 35 §127; *Op. Mund.* 5 §20]; §49 [*Op. Mund.* 6 §24]).

5. As in the Johannine Prologue (1.4-5), Philo says the *logos* brings 'light' and 'life' and that 'darkness' withdrew when confronted by the light (see §47 and §48 [*Op. Mund.* 8 §30, §33]).

6. As in the Johannine Prologue (1.18a), Philo emphasizes that no one, not even the great Moses, has seen God (see §52 [*Poster. C.* 48 §169]).

Philo's speculations about the *logos* entertain characteristics and functions that in important ways go beyond the characteristics and functions of Wisdom. In a recent study Thomas Tobin has argued that some of these elements in Philo's *logos* parallel the Johannine *logos* in precisely those areas where the latter also seems to go beyond speculations about Wisdom, especially with respect to interpretations of the Genesis creation account.[1] According to Philo the *logos* was the true image of God (*Fug.* 19 §101), God's first-born son (*Conf. Ling.* 14 §62-63; 28 §146-47), who indeed could even be called θεός (*Somn.* 1.39 §228-30). All of these attributes assigned to the *logos* find close parallels in the Fourth Gospel. Moreover, unlike the wisdom literature, which speaks of God creating *by* Wisdom (σοφία) or *by* the Word (λόγῳ), which expresses instrumentality (cf. Wis. 9.2; Ps. 32[33].6), Philo speaks of creation *through* the Word (δι' οὗ), which expresses agency (cf. *Cher.* 35 §127). In this Philo closely parallels the Johannine Prologue, which also speaks of all things having

1. T.H. Tobin, 'The Prologue of John and Hellenistic Jewish Speculation', *CBQ* 52 (1990), pp. 252-69.

been created through the Word (δι' αὐτοῦ).

Tobin also observes that Jn 1.4-5 implies an antithesis between light and darkness,[1] something that seems to go beyond the plain statements of Gen. 1.2-4. Whereas Genesis only speaks of God *separating* the light from the darkness, the Johannine Prologue evidently presupposes conflict and hostility. Furthermore, Jn 1.4 states that 'life' was in the Word,[2] another idea that is not expressed in Genesis 1. Both of these ideas are clarified by Philo's exegesis, which describes darkness as an 'adversary' of the light, making it necessary for God to separate them (*Op. Mund.* 9 §33-34), and which interprets the hovering Spirit of Gen. 1.2, all part of the Word's creative activity (*Op. Mund.* 6 §24), as 'life-giving' (*Op. Mund.* 8 §30).[3]

There is, however, one important element that lacks a clear parallel: the idea of the *logos* becoming a human being. In a few places Philo seems to say that God can appear as a human. He says that the first human (ἄνθρωπος) was made in the likeness of the Word (*Op. Mund.* 48 §139). With reference to Moses Philo says: 'For he was named god and king of the whole nation, and entered...into the darkness where God was, that is, into the unseen, invisible, incorporeal and archetypal essence of existing things' (*Vit. Mos.* 1.28 §155-58). Elsewhere Philo says that God 'makes the worthy man [here Moses] sharer of his nature' (*Poster. C.* 9 §28). One more important passage should be noted: 'But he who is resolved into the nature of unity, is said to come near God in a kind of family relation, for having given up and left behind all mortal kinds, he is changed into the divine, so that such men become kin to God and truly divine' (*Quaest. in Exod.* 2.29 [on Exod. 24.2]). But did Philo actually understand Moses as deity?[4]

1. Jn 1.5b should be rendered, 'the darkness did not overcome it', as opposed to 'did not comprehend it'. See the use of καταλαμβάνειν in Jn 12.35. See W. Nagel, '"Die Finsternis hat's nicht begriffen" (Joh i 5)', *ZNW* 50 (1959), pp. 132-37. Carson (*Gospel according to John*, pp. 119-20) points out that the meaning of καταλαμβάνειν in 1.5 could be ambiguous, and deliberately so, meaning both overcoming and comprehending.

2. See B. Vawter, 'What Came to Be in Him Was Life (Jn 1, 3ᵇ-4ᵃ)', *CBQ* 25 (1963), pp. 401-406. Vawter's arrangement underscores the importance of life and fits Johannine theology better; cf. Jn 5.26; 6.57.

3. The idea of the Word as the source of life is expressed in Scripture: 'For this is no vain word (λόγος) for you; for it is your life (ζωή), and because of this word you will live long upon the land' (LXX Deut. 32.47).

4. On the basis of these passages and others like them E.R. Goodenough (*By*

Probably not.[1] Philo's position in this matter becomes quite clear in his discussion of Exod. 7.1: 'And the Lord said to Moses, "See, I make you as God to Pharaoh"'. Philo explains: 'When Moses is appointed "a god to Pharaoh", he did not become such in reality, but only by a convention is supposed to be such...the wise man is said to be a god to the foolish man, but in reality he is not God' (*Det. Pot. Ins.* 44 §161-62). Philo's statements make it clear that he did not hold to such an idea.[2]

With regard to 'the Divine Word (ὁ...λόγος θεῖος)', Philo asserts that although 'he is himself the image (εἰκών) of God', 'he has not been visibly portrayed' (*Fug.* 19 §101). This 'image' can be perceived (with the mind or with the soul), but it cannot literally be seen. Elsewhere Philo explains that 'the invisible Logos in heaven' (*Quaest. in Exod.* 2.81 [on Exod. 25.39]) is 'immaterial' (*Quaest. in Exod.* 2.122 [on Exod. 28.32]).

But Philo's speculations could still explain in part the application of the *logos* to Johannine Christology. Tobin speaks to this problem as well. He points out that the Johannine Prologue's explicit identification of the Word with an individual human, Jesus of Nazareth, goes well beyond anything in the wisdom tradition. Philo's exegesis, Tobin believes, seems to form a bridge, as seen in his description of the *logos* as the 'man after [God's] image' (*Conf. Ling.* 28 §146). This is the ἄνθρωπος created in Gen. 1.27, not the ἄνθρωπος created from dust in Gen. 2.7 (*Conf. Ling.* 14 §62; see also *Quaest. in Gen.* 1.4 [on Gen. 2.7]). Philo identifies the *logos* with the 'heavenly man' of Gen. 1.27. Tobin comments that this interpretation of the *logos* as 'the figure of the heavenly man may have served as an important step in the kind of reflection that led to the identification of the *logos* with a particular human being, Jesus of Nazareth, in the hymn in the Prologue

Light, Light: The Mystic Gospel of Hellenistic Judaism [New Haven and London: Yale University Press, 1935], pp. 227-29) concluded that Philo actually did think of Moses as divinized, a sort of θεῖος ἄνθρωπος bridging the gulf between God and humanity.

1. See Hurtado, *One God, One Lord*, pp. 59-63.

2. Philo affirms that 'God is neither in human form, nor is the human body God-like' (*Op. Mund.* 23 §69). Moreover, Scripture, he acknowledges, sometimes 'likens God to man', but not 'to any particular man' (*Somn.* 1.39 §234). For other passages where Philo grapples with Exod. 7.1, see *Leg. All.* 1.13 §40; *Sacr.* 3 §9; *Det. Pot. Ins.* 12 §39-40; *Migr. Abr.* 15 §84; 31 §169; *Mut. Nom.* 3 §19-20; 22 §§125, 128-29; *Omn. Prob. Lib.* 7 §43-44.

of John'.[1] Indeed, Philo's understanding of Gen. 1.27 probably represents the kind of speculation that lies behind some of the other New Testament christological hymns (for example, Col. 1.15-17; Heb. 1.2-4).

There are two other characteristics of Philo's description of the *logos* that may contribute to a bridge between the biblical materials and the Johannine declaration that the 'Word became flesh'.[2] The first has to do with the role of the intermediary. An important feature of early Christology is the belief that the risen Christ is an intermediary and reconciler between God and humanity (cf. Rom. 8.34; 2 Cor. 5.18-19; Col. 1.20-22). This is the principal function of Philo's *logos*. We often find this idea expressed with respect to the cosmos: 'The incorporeal world is set off and separated from the visible one by the mediating Logos (ὑπὸ τοῦ μεθορίου λόγου) as by a veil' (*Quaest. in Exod.* 2.94 [on Exod. 26.33]). 'The Divine Logos, inasmuch as it is appropriately in the middle (μέσος), leaves nothing in nature empty, but fills all things and becomes a mediator (μεσιτεύει[3]) and arbitrator for the two sides which seem to be divided from each other, bringing about friendship and concord, for it is always the cause of community (κοινωνίας[4]) and the artisan of peace (εἰρήνης[5])' (*Quaest. in Exod.* 2.68 [on Exod. 25.21]). The 'Divine Logos (τοῦ θείου λόγου)' is a 'mediator (μεσίτου)',[6] Philo explains elsewhere, and 'the strongest and most stable bond of all things', binding and

---

1.   Tobin, 'The Prologue of John', p. 267. See also D.A. Hagner ('The Vision of God in Philo and John', *JETS* 14 [1971], pp. 81-93) who points out that John's concept of God is not as transcendent (that is, Platonic) as Philo's. Hence, the Fourth Evangelist is more open to identifying God with a human being.

2.   Pace J.C. O'Neill, 'The Word Did Not "Become Flesh"', *ZNW* 82 (1991), pp. 125-27. It is not likely that v. 14 means 'and the Word was born flesh'. When O'Neill says ἐγένετο in this context 'cannot mean that Christ changed into man' (p. 127), he has confused Christ with the *logos*. The Prologue does not say that 'Christ' became flesh. It only says that 'the Word' became flesh. These statements are not identical.

3.   For an example of μεσιτεύειν in early Christian literature, see Heb. 6.17.

4.   For examples of κοινωνίας in early Christian literature, see 1 Cor. 1.9; 1 Jn 1.3, 6, 7.

5.   For an example of 'making peace' (εἰρηνοποιεῖν) in early Christian literature, see Col. 1.20.

6.   For examples of μεσίτης in early Christian literature, see 1 Tim. 2.5; Heb. 8.6; 9.15; 12.24; cf. Gal. 3.19-20.

weaving 'together the parts of the universe and their contraries, and by the use of force bring[ing] into unity and communion and loving embrace those things which have many irreconcilable differences' (*Quaest. in Exod.* 2.118 [on Exod. 28.28]). We also find this idea expressed with respect to humanity's relationship with heaven: The 'Logos was appointed as judge and mediator (μεσίτης)' (*Quaest. in Exod.* 2.13 [on Exod. 23.20-21]). In the Fourth Gospel Jesus is judge (5.22, 30; 8.15-16) and mediator in the sense of providing access to the Father (14.6).

A second characteristic of Philo's *logos* that could clarify the Johannine *logos* is the identification of the *logos* with the 'angel of the Lord'. Philo frequently says that the *logos* is this angel: the 'Logos... is called "angel"' (*Quaest. in Exod.* 2.13 [on Exod. 23.20-21]). In the discussion of the passage where Hagar met the 'angel of the Lord' it is assumed that this angel is the *logos* (*Quaest. in Gen.* 3.27-32 [on Gen. 16.7-11]). God appeared to Sarah (a symbol of 'wisdom'), while the *logos* appeared to Hagar (wisdom's 'attendant') (*Quaest. in Gen.* 3.34 [on Gen. 16.13]). The 'angel of God' that spoke to Jacob (Gen. 31.11) is the 'Divine Word (ὁ θεῖος λόγος)'. The *logos* is called the 'angel of the Lord' in several other passages (cf. *Agr.* 12 §51; *Quaest. in Gen.* 4.90 [on Gen. 24.7]; 4.91 [on Gen. 24.8]; *Quaest. in Exod.* 2.13 [on Exod. 23.20-21]); 2.16 [on Exod. 23.22]).[1] This common identification of the *logos* with the 'angel of the Lord' could make an important contribution to the bridge between Wisdom and *logos* speculations and the Johannine confession that the 'Word became flesh'. If the *logos* could be identified as the angel that walked the earth and was seen by the patriarchs, then it would not be too difficult to equate the *logos* with Jesus who walked the earth and taught his disciples.[2]

In addition to these two important elements, Philo's *logos* possesses other functions and attributes that cohere with Johannine Christology. Of major importance is the *logos*'s function as 'advocate' (παράκλητος): 'He thought it best to be called, not a servant of God, but an attendant of the intercessor [probably the *logos*]. And the inter-

---

1.   The angels of Gen. 28.12 are the 'words' of God, which facilitate communication between God and humankind (*Somn.* 1.22 §142).

2.   J.-A. Bühner, *Der Gesandte und sein Weg im 4. Evangelium: Die kultur- und religionsgeschichtlichen Grundlagen der johanneischen Sendungschristologie sowie ihre traditionsgeschichtliche Entwicklung* (WUNT, 2.2; Tübingen: Mohr [Paul Siebeck], 1977), pp. 316-73.

cessor is a servant of the Creator of all and Father' (*Quaest. in Gen.*
4.114 [on Gen. 24.27]). In reference to the High Priest, Philo says:
'For it was necessary for the one consecrated to the Father (πατήρ) of
the world to act as an advocate (παρακλήτῳ), that sins (ἁμαρτήματα)
will no more be remembered' (*Vit. Mos.* 2.26 §134). Philo's use of
παράκλητος is similar to aspects of its use in the Johannine writings
(cf. Jn 14.16, 26; 15.26; 16.7), especially as seen in 1 Jn 2.1: 'If anyone should sin (ἁμαρτάνειν), we have an advocate (παράκλητον)
with the Father (πατήρ): Jesus Christ the righteous'.[1]

The 'Divine *logos* (ὁ θεῖος λόγος)' also pursues those in need of
reform and acts as a 'disciplinarian' (*Quaest. in Gen.* 3.27 [on Gen.
16.7]). The *logos* is further described as a 'healer of the weakness of
the soul' (*Quaest. in Gen.* 3.28 [on Gen. 16.8]). Philo elaborates: 'the
Divine Word (τὸν θεῖον λόγον) is appointed over the body also, to

---

1. 'Paraclete' in the passages in the Fourth Gospel refers to the Holy Spirit. But
the expression 'another paraclete' (14.16: ἄλλον παράκλητον δώσει ὑμῖν)
implies that Jesus is himself a paraclete. The paraclete of 1 Jn 2.1 is, of course,
'Jesus Christ the righteous'. Whereas παράκλητος in Philo is usually employed in
a legal sense (for example, *Jos.* 40 §239, where Joseph says to his brothers: 'ask for
no other advocate'), there are several examples in the targums and rabbinic writings
where the word is used in reference to mediation between humans and God: 'If a
man has merits, an angel intervenes as an advocate (פרקליטא)' (*Targ. Job* 33.23);
'All the benevolences and good works which the Israelites do in this world...are
great advocates (פרקליטין) between the Israelites and their Father in heaven' (*b. B.
Bat.* 10a; cf. *Ab.* 4.11; *t. Pe'ah* 4.21; *b. Šab.* 32a; *Zeb.* 7b; *Sifre Deut.* §277 [on
14.19-20]; *Exod. R.* 18.3 [on Exod. 12.29]). παράκλητος appears in Hebrew and
Aramaic as a loanword.

Not surprisingly, Bultmann (*Gospel of John*, pp. 570-72) finds the closest parallels
to the Johannine paraclete in the *Odes of Solomon* and the Mandaean literature. In all
likelihood these writings have been influenced by the Fourth Gospel. Many scholars
have disagreed with Bultmann; cf. J. Behm, 'παράκλητος', *TDNT*, V, pp. 800-14,
esp. p. 809; G. Bornkamm, 'Der Paraklet im Johannes-Evangelium', in E. Wolf
(ed.), *Festschrift Rudolf Bultmann zum 65. Geburtstag überreicht* (Stuttgart:
Kohlhammer, 1949), pp. 12-35; revised and repr. in G. Bornkamm, *Geschichte und
Glaube*, III (GA; 3 vols.; Munich: Chr. Kaiser Verlag, 1968), pp. 68-89; O. Betz,
Der Paraklet (AGJU, 2; Leiden: Brill, 1963), pp. 28-30; and G.M. Burge, *The
Anointed Community: The Holy Spirit in the Johannine Tradition* (Grand Rapids:
Eerdmans, 1987), pp. 10-12. The principal problem is that the 'paraclete' of the
Mandaean literature in reality is a 'helper' (βοηθός), not an 'advocate'
(παράκλητος). For a recent and helpful assessment of the antecedents of the para-
clete tradition in the Fourth Gospel, see Burge, *Anointed Community*, 13-31. Burge
concludes that the Johannine paraclete derives from 'a well-formulated Jewish idea'.

be, as it were, its physician' (*Quaest. in Gen.* 3.51 [on Gen. 17.13]; cf.
2.29 [on Gen. 8.2]); 'the angel, who is the Word (λόγος), [is] a healer
of ills' (*Leg. All.* 3.62 §177).¹ Commenting on Ps. 23.1 ('The Lord is
my Shepherd and I shall lack nothing') Philo says that the world and
all the creatures in it 'are like some flock under the hand of God its
King and Shepherd. This hallowed flock He leads in accordance with
justice and law, setting over it His true Word (τὸν... λόγον) and
Firstborn Son (πρωτόγονον) who shall take upon him its government
like some viceroy of a great king; for it is said in a certain place:
"Behold I am, I send my angel before your face to guard you in the
way"' (*Agr.* 12 §51, quoting Exod. 23.20; cf. Jn 10.7-18). Finally, the
'Divine Word (λόγον θεῖον) [is] the fountain of wisdom (σοφίας)'
(*Fug.* 18 §97). The diverse qualities of Philo's *logos*—advocate, disciplinarian, physician, shepherd, and fountain of wisdom—parallel
some of the elements explicitly asserted or implicitly assumed in the
Christology of the Fourth Gospel.

Tobin's observations, in combination with the biblical materials
surveyed above, make it very clear that the Prologue of the Fourth
Gospel must be viewed against the interpretive and theological background of Jewish biblical interpretation, especially as illustrated by
Philo. But there are also elements within the wisdom tradition itself
that contribute to the three areas that Tobin has isolated.

First, with regard to the reality and functions of the *logos*, in at
least one instance there is an explicit movement from *sophia* to *logos*
in the Wisdom tradition. Whereas the Wisdom of Solomon begins
with σοφία (Wis. 1.4; 9.4), it concludes with ὁ λόγος which leaped
out of heaven to punish the Egyptians (Wis. 18.15; see §21 above). As
to the filial dimension of *logos* in Philo, there is something of filiality
in the wisdom tradition where Sophia is portrayed as having been
raised and nurtured by God (Prov. 8.30-31; see §38 above).

Tobin's point about the intermediacy of the *logos* in Philo seems, at
first blush, to be very important. So far as I have been able to determine, this aspect does not appear in reference to creation in the
Wisdom literature or in the targums and rabbinic writings (where in
the latter it would be in reference to Wisdom or Torah and not to
memra). In some ways, however, this is an argument from silence,

---

1.   The λόγος as healer is depicted in Scripture itself: 'He sent forth his word
(ἀπέστειλε τὸν λόγον αὐτοῦ), and healed them, and delivered them from their
destructions' (LXX Ps. 106.20).

for there is no word in Hebrew that means 'through' in quite the same sense as διά. The word that comes closest is ביד, which literally means 'by the hand of'.[1] In the LXX it is usually translated with the instrumental dative, with or without a preposition (for example, Exod. 9.35: τῷ Μωυσῇ; Judg. 3.15: ἐν χειρὶ αὐτοῦ), other times with διά and the genitive (for example, 1 Chron. 11.3: διά χειρός). In the examples cited above in §22 (Prov. 3.19; Ps. 33[32].6), where in the LXX the instrumental is employed, and below in §58 (*Frag. Targ.* Gen. 1.27; *Targ. Isa.* 44.24; 45.12; 48.13) the prefix ב is used meaning 'by' or 'with'.[2] In Greek the dative is almost always used to translate this preposition. Consequently, the regular usage of the instrumental dative in the Greek Scriptures and the absence of any clear examples of intermediacy in the Hebrew and Aramaic materials may not be particularly significant.[3] Of course, Philo's use of διά, at least as he explains it in *Cher.* 35 §127, certainly constitutes the closest Greek parallel to the Johannine Prologue.

Secondly, with regard to the observation of the antithesis between light and darkness in the Prologue, I think that Tobin once again has made a helpful observation. The antithesis, indeed the conflict, between light and darkness in Philo's exegesis is explicit and certainly aids in our interpretation of John. If there is any antithesis in Genesis 1, it is only inferential at best. There God pronounces the light 'good', possibly implying that the darkness was not good. This seems to be the understanding of Second Isaiah (Isa. 45.7), whose synonymous parallelism links light with peace and darkness with evil (see §26).

It is possible that the first-century eschatological, and possibly cosmological, antithesis expressed at Qumran, where, according to the

---

1.   ביד is used in the Peshitta version of the Prologue to translate διά.

2.   In one case it appears that ב should be understood in the sense of intermediacy: 'I let myself be entreated through my Word (במימרי)' (*Targ. Isa.* 65.1; so translated by J.F. Stenning, *The Targum of Isaiah* [Oxford: Clarendon Press, 1949], p. 214, and Chilton, *The Glory of Israel*, p. 64). But the passage has nothing to do with creation. In two texts having to do with creation M.L. Klein (*The Fragment-Targums of the Pentateuch*, II [AnBib, 76; 2 vols.; Rome: Pontifical Biblical Institute, 1980], pp. 3, 47) translates ב in the intermediate sense, rather than the instrumental: 'And there was light through his Memra (במימריה)' (*Frag. Targ.* Gen. 1.3); and 'through his Memra (במימריה) there was light and illumination' (*Frag. Targ.* Exod. 15.18).

3.   Note, however, that twice בי is translated δι' ἐμοῦ in Prov. 8.15-16, where Wisdom boasts, 'through me kings reign...through me princes rule'.

War Scroll, one of the objectives of the 'day of great battle against darkness' was 'to strike down darkness and to raise up light' (1QM 13.15; see also the description of the struggle between the 'Prince of light' and the 'Angel of darkness' in 1QS 3.18-25) represents a first-century link in a chain that comes to a fuller and more varied expression in the later interpretations of the rabbis. The antithesis articulated in the Fourth Gospel may have been part of this chain. Paul himself may witness this link. In 2 Cor. 4.6 Paul says, 'God who said, "From darkness light will shine" [cf. Gen 1.2-3], has shone in our hearts to the light of the knowledge of the glory of God in the face of Christ'. Not only does this light stand in an antithetical relationship to the blindness and unbelief described in 2 Cor. 4.3-4, but it stands in contrast to the Mosaic covenant described in Exodus 34, a passage that plays an important background role in the Johannine Prologue.[1]

Tobin's point about the life as the source of light is another good observation. John and Philo understood this life in terms of eternal life, not simply as biological life, as it is in Genesis 1–2. But the Wisdom tradition also hints of eternal life. Proverbs (8.35) speaks of Sophia's ways as the 'ways of life', while Wisdom of Solomon (8.13) promises 'immortality' (ἀθανασία). Does this not approximate the promise of the Johannine Jesus that those who believe in him will not die (11.26: οὐ μὴ ἀποθάνῃ)?

Thirdly, with regard to the Word being identified with a specific human being, Tobin's assessment of Philo's exegesis of Gen. 1.27 is quite helpful. The early church compared Jesus with Adam (Rom. 5.12-21; 1 Cor. 15.21-22, 45-49; Lk. 3.38–4.13) and interpretation such as that found in Philo would have facilitated such comparison. But there are two passages in the Wisdom literature that appear to be precursors to the Johannine doctrine of incarnation. Joshua ben Sira spoke of Wisdom 'dwelling with all flesh (μετὰ πάσης σαρκός)' (Sir. 1.10). The other passage, 'Wisdom will not enter a deceitful soul, nor dwell (κατοικήσει) in a body (ἐν σώματι) enslaved to sin' (Wis. 1.4), implies that Wisdom can dwell in a righteous body. Obviously these passages are speaking in general terms; they do not have a particular person in view, such as an agent of redemption. It is intriguing to observe, however, that the last line of Sir. 1.10 ('for those who love him') is cited by Paul in 1 Cor. 2.9 as part of a

---

1. The very way in which Paul paraphrases Gen. 1.3 (that is, by bringing the darkness of Gen. 1.2 into the quotation) seems to imply an antithesis.

conflated quotation that explains why the 'rulers of this age' failed to perceive who Jesus really was and therefore 'crucified the Lord of glory' (1 Cor. 2.8). Since the wider context of 1 Corinthians speaks of God's wisdom (see chs. 1–3), it is possible that Paul is here thinking of Wisdom in (or as) Christ (cf. 1.24: 'Christ the power of God and the wisdom of God'; 1.30: 'Christ Jesus, whom God made our wisdom'). According to Paul, this wisdom had been decreed by God 'before the ages' (2.7). This idea coheres with statements about Wisdom existing with God before the creation of the world (see §4, §19, §22; cf. §55 and §65 below). Of course, even if Paul does have in mind ideas about Jesus as the incarnation of Wisdom, Philo's exegesis, in which the *logos* is identified with the 'man' of Gen. 1.27, may very well be the most important link between Genesis and the wisdom literature and the incarnational theologies found in John and Paul.[1]

To sum up, it appears that the biblical materials themselves, particularly the Wisdom tradition, provide all of the essential background necessary to understand the Johannine Prologue. In my judgment, Philo's biblical exegesis makes explicit certain Wisdom features that constitute the important components in the bridge between Genesis 1–2 and Jn 1.1-18. The significance of all of this is that the biblical materials and Philo's exegesis predate the Johannine Prologue.

---

1.   J. Ashton ('The Transformation of Wisdom: A Study of the Prologue of John's Gospel', *NTS* 32 [1986], pp. 161-86, esp. p. 179) has concluded that the Fourth Evangelist has portrayed Jesus Christ as the incarnation of Wisdom. He also speaks of the 'Jewish ancestry of the Prologue' and of the Johannine community in relation to the 'Jewish community' (p. 182). J. Painter ('Christology and the Fourth Gospel: A Study of the Prologue', *AusBR* 31 [1983], pp. 45-62; 'Christology and the History of the Johannine Community in the Prologue of the Fourth Gospel', *NTS* 30 [1984], pp. 460-74) believes that the source originally underlying the Prologue was a hymn in honor of Wisdom/Torah, now transformed into a hymn in honor of the incarnation of the *logos*. For additional studies which understand the Johannine Prologue in terms of divine wisdom, see Dodd, *Interpretation of the Fourth Gospel*, pp. 274-77; B. de Pinto, 'Word and Wisdom in St. John', *Scr* 19 (1967), pp. 19-27; D.K. Clark, 'Signs and Wisdom in John', *CBQ* 45 (1983), pp. 201-209; W. Grundmann, *Der Zeuge der Weisheit: Grundzüge der Christologie des Johannesevangeliums* (ed. W. Wiefel; Berlin: Evangelische Verlagsanstalt, 1985), pp. 16-29; P. Schoonenberg, 'A Sapiential Reading of John's Prologue: Some Reflections on Views of Reginald Fuller and James Dunn', *TD* 33 (1986), pp. 403-21; M. Scott, *Sophia and the Johannine Jesus* (JSNTSup, 71; Sheffield: JSOT Press, 1992).

Moreover, they are part of the cultural and religious context, at least broadly speaking, against which the Fourth Gospel should be understood. Nothing of the sort can be said for the Gnostic parallels that have been surveyed. There is no evidence that their ideas (never mind the earliest copies of the texts themselves) predate the Fourth Gospel, nor is there any evidence that these documents derive from the same cultural and religious context.

The biblical materials were studied and discussed in the context of the synagogue, as well as the academies. The Fourth Gospel three times makes explicit reference to the synagogue (9.22; 12.42; 16.2). It refers to 'searching the scriptures' (7.39), which was the word that rabbis used for biblical interpretation (that is, 'midrash'). The Fourth Gospel contains involved exegeses which some scholars have identified as instances of rabbinic-like midrash. Moreover, at several points Johannine biblical interpretation coheres with the exegesis preserved in the midrashim and the targumim. Although these materials were committed to writing at some time during the five hundred years after the Fourth Gospel, there are scholars who think that they contain interpretive traditions that shed light on this writing, including its Prologue. This is possible for two reasons at least: (1) some Tannaic traditions, perhaps even some traditions now extant in early Amoraic traditions, originated in the first century; and (2) the synagogue, particularly with reference to the targumim, provided a context in which such traditions could be preserved and handed on. Since the Johannine Gospel apparently emerged from a context with reasonably close contact with the late first-century synagogue (see Chapter 5), it is plausible to suspect that some of its interpretive elements parallel traditions now extant in the later rabbinic materials.[1] Should this be so in the case of the Prologue, especially at points that bridge the gap between Genesis 1–2 and the thought of the Prologue, not only will this support the contention of some that the targums and rabbinic materials have a measure of relevance to the interpretation of the Fourth Gospel, but it will add further confirmation to the conclusion

---

1. Several studies in recent years have concluded that the targums preserve traditions that originated in the first century CE (or earlier). See McNamara, *The New Testament and the Palestinian Targum to the Pentateuch*; G. Vermes, *Scripture and Tradition in Judaism* (SPB, 4; Leiden: Brill, 2nd edn, 1973); Chilton, *The Glory of Israel*. For additional bibliography, see J.T. Forestell, *Targumic Traditions and the New Testament* (SBL Aramaic Studies, 4; Chico, CA: Scholars Press, 1979).

already reached, to the effect that the Gnostic sources and parallels are not helpful and perhaps even misleading.

Targumic and Midrashic Exegesis

Appeal to targumic and midrashic traditions faces the same challenges faced by appeal to the Coptic and Mandaic materials. Let us consider the four criteria outlined above in Chapter 1. 1. There is external evidence that some of the interpretive traditions preserved in the targums and midrashim date from the first century. Comparatively speaking, little of this tradition can with confidence be assigned such an early date. 2. There is little evidence that the early interpretive traditions preserved in the targums and midrashim have been contaminated by Christian ideas. Parallels should normally be viewed as independent and not in terms of later documents (such as targums or rabbinic writings) borrowing ideas from earlier documents (such as the New Testament). 3. The milieu of the targums especially (and less so the rabbinic writings) is essentially the milieu in which many New Testament ideas took shape. 4. Many of the interpretive traditions preserved in the targums and midrashim cohere with those found in the New Testament. These bodies of writings are mutually illuminating at many points.

The table below exhibits numerous parallels.[1] Some of these may be truly 'parallel' in that the targumic/midrashic and Johannine expressions reflect the same ideas and even originate from a common milieu. Other parallels reflect similar language and similar modes of expression. Some of the parallels may be purely formal. Note especially the parallels between the targumic *memra* and the Johannine *logos*:

Targumic and Midrashic Parallels	*John*
55. 'From the beginning with wisdom the Memra (מימרא) of the Lord created and perfected the heavens and the earth' (*Targ. Neof.* Gen. 1.1).	'In the beginning was the Word' (1.1a).

1. For a recent study that probes many of these parallels and others, see G. Rochais, 'La Formation du Prologue (Jn 1, 1-18)', *ScEs* 37 (1985), pp. 5-44, 161-87, esp. pp. 175-80; also O. Hofius, 'Struktur und Gedankengang des Logos-Hymnus in John 1 1-18', *ZNW* 78 (1987), pp. 1-25, esp. pp. 17-25.

'In wisdom, the Lord created and
perfected the heaven and the earth'
(*Frag. Targ.* Gen. 1.1).

'Before God created the world, he
created Torah' (*Targ. Ps.-J.* Gen.
3.24; cf. *Targ. Neof.* Gen. 3.24).

'Torah declares, "I was the working
tool of the Holy One, blessed be
he..." Thus God consulted Torah
and created the world, while Torah
declares, "In the beginning God
created", "beginning" referring to
Torah, as in the verse, "The Lord
made me [Wisdom/Torah] as the
beginning of his way" [Prov. 8.22]'
(*Gen. R.* 1.1 [on 1.1]).

'Seven things were created before the
world was created: the Torah... and
the name of the Messiah' (*b. Pes.*
54a, with citation of Prov. 8.22).

56.   'From the beginning with wisdom   'and the Word was with God' (1.1b).
       the Word (מימרא) of the Lord
       perfected the heavens and the earth'
       (*Targ. Neof.* Gen 1.1).

       'The Word (מימרא) from before (מן
       קדם)[1] the Lord' (*Targ. Onq.* Gen.
       20.3).

1.   'From before' has a range of possible meanings. In this context it probably
means 'in the presence of' or even 'with'. See M.L. Klein, 'The Preposition קדם
("Before"): A Pseudo-Anti-Anthropomorphism in the Targums', *JTS* 20 (1979),
pp. 502-507. Klein notes (p. 505) that קדם (מן) typically translates the Hebrew
prepositions לפני, בפני, and מפני, among others (cf. BDB, pp. 818, 1110). According
to F. Rosenthal (*A Grammar of Biblical Aramaic* [Wiesbaden: Otto Harrassowitz,
1974], p. 37) this Aramaic idiom constitutes 'a respectful indication of location'.
These prepositions are frequently translated in Greek writings with ἐναντίος and
other words. There are a few examples in the New Testament where the meaning of
πρός is essentially that of Jn 1.1 (cf. Mt. 13.56; Mk 9.19; Gal. 2.5).

57. 'When the Word (מימרא) of the Lord   'and the Word was God' (1.1c).
     will be revealed to redeem his people
     he will say to all the nations: "See
     now that I AM HE WHO IS (אנא   'Before Abraham came into being, I
     הוא דהוי)"' (*Targ. Ps.-J.* Deut 32.39).   AM (ἐγὼ εἰμί)' (8.58).

58. 'And the Word (מימרא) of the Lord   'All things through him [the Word]
     said to Moses: "The One who said to   came into being (ἐγένετο)' (1.3).
     the world in the beginning: 'Come
     into being (הוי)!' and it came into
     being (והוי)"' (*Frag. Targ.* Exod.
     3.14).

     'And the Lord said: "Let us create
     man…" and the Word (מימרא) of the
     Lord created man in his own image'
     (*Targ. Neof.* Gen. 1.26-27).

     'I am the Lord, who made all things;
     I stretched out the heavens by my
     Word (מימר), I founded the earth by
     my might' (*Targ. Isa.* 44.24).

     'By my Word (מימר) I made the
     earth, and created man upon it'
     (*Targ. Isa.* 45.12).

     'Indeed, by my Word (מימר) I
     founded the earth, by my might I
     stretched out the heavens' (*Targ. Isa.*
     48.13).

     'to them was given the precious
     instrument [Torah] by which the
     world was created (ברא)' (*Ab.* 3.18).

59. 'Better is Torah for the one who   'In him [the Word] was life' (1.4a).
     attends to it than the fruits of the tree
     of life: Torah which the Word
     (מימרא) of the Lord has prepared in
     order that it may be kept, so that man   'I am the way, the truth, the life; no
     may live and walk by the paths of the   one comes to the Father except
     way of the life of the world to come'   through me' (14.6).
     (*Targ. Ps.-J.* Gen. 3.24; cf. *Targ.
     Neof.* Gen 3.24; *Ab.* 7.6; *Sifre Deut.*
     §48 [on 2.22]; *Mek.* on Exod 13.3
     [*Pisḥa* §16]).

'Torah is a tree of life' (*Targ. Neof.*
Gen. 3.24).

60. 'And the Word (מימר) of the Lord   'and the light shines in darkness'
said, "Let there be light." And there   (1.5; cf. 1.9)
was light in his Word (מימר)' (*Frag.
Targ.* Gen. 1.3; cf. *Targ. Neof.* Gen.
1.3).

'God is light and in him there is no
'The first night when the Lord was   darkness' (1 Jn 1.5).
revealed above the earth to create it:
The earth was void and empty and
darkness was spread over the face of
the abyss [cf. Gen. 1.1-2]. And the
Word (מימר) of the Lord was the light
and it shone; and he called it the first
night' (*Targ. Neof.* Exod. 12.42).[1]

'And God said, "Let there be light to   'which enlightens every person,
lighten the world"' (*Targ. Ps.-J.*   coming into the world' (1.9).
Gen. 1.3).

Baba ben Buta said to Herod the   'the life was the light of humanity,
Great, who had put to death many   and the light shines in darkness' (1.4-
rabbis: 'You have quenched the light   5)
of the world' (*b. B. Bat.* 4a).

'I am the light of the world' (8.12;
9.5; cf. 1 Jn 1.5: 'God is light').

'As oil is life for the world, so also
are the words of Torah life for the
world. As oil is light for the world,
so also are the words of Torah light
for the world' (*Deut. R.* 7.3 [on
28.1]).

'"The Lord make his face shine upon
you", that is, the light of the Torah'
(*Sifre Num.* §41 [on 6.25]).

---

1. On the proper reading of *Neofiti*, see M. McNamara, *Targum and Testament*
(Shannon: Irish University Press; Grand Rapids: Eerdmans, 1972), p. 103.

'Those who study the Torah give
forth light wherever they may be...
as it says, "Thy word is a lamp unto
my feet, and a light unto my path"
[Ps. 119.105]... What is the lamp of
God? The Torah...' (*Exod. R.* 36.3
[on 27.20]).

61.   'They believed in the name of the
        Word (מימר) of the Lord' (*Frag.
        Targ.* Exod. 14.31).

        'Blessed shall be the man who trusts
        in the name of Word (מימר) of the
        Lord' (*Frag. Targ.* Gen. 40.23).

        'And Abraham worshipped and
        prayed there in the name of the Word
        (מימר) of the Lord' (*Frag. Targ.*,
        Targ. Neof. Gen 22.14).

62.   'Where is he who made the Word
        (מימר) of his holy prophets dwell
        among them?' (*Targ. Isa.* 63.11).

        'And the Lord revealed himself in the
        cloud of the Glory (יקר) of his
        Shekinah (שכינה), and Moses stood
        with him there; and Moses called on
        the name of the Word (מימר) of the
        Lord.

        And the Lord made his Shekinah
        (שכינה) pass by before his face, and
        he proclaimed, "The Lord... full of
        kindness and truth"' (*Targ. Ps.-J.*
        Exod. 34.5-6; cf. *Targ. Neof.* Exod.
        25.22; 29.43; 30.6, 36; where *memra*
        is associated with the tabernacle).

'He gave to them the authority to become the children of God, to those
who believe in his [the Word's]
name' (1.12; cf. 12.28: 'Glorify your
name'; 17.5: 'Now glorify me,
Father'; 10.30: 'I and my Father are
one'[1]).

'In that day you shall ask in my name
... you have believed that I have
come from God' (16.26-27; cf. Rev.
19.13: 'his name is "The Word of
God"').

'And the Word became flesh and
dwelt among us, and we beheld his
glory, glory as of the only begotten of
the Father, full of grace and truth'
(1.14).

'Isaiah said this when he saw his
glory' (Jn 12.41; cf. *Targ.* Isa. 6.1,
5).

[Jesus refers to himself as a temple
(2.19).]

1.   Jesus' petitions in Jn 12.28 and 17.5 could imply that he is in some sense
God's name.

'And my Word (מימר) will be to her,
says the Lord, like a wall of fire
encircling her round about, and I will
make my Shekinah (שכינה) dwell in
her midst in honor' (*Targ. Zech.*
2.5[9]).

'in every place where you remember
my name in prayer, I will be revealed
in my Word [מימר] upon you, and I
will bless you' (*Targ. Neof.* Exod.
20.24)

'at the door of the tent of ordinance,
where I shall appoint my Word
(מימר) to meet you [and] to speak
with you. And there I shall appoint
my Word (מימר) [to meet] with the
sons of Israel...for my Glory (יקר)
...and my Shekinah (שכינה) shall
dwell in the midst of the sons of
Israel, and I shall be their God'
(*Targ. Ps.-J.* Exod. 29.42b-45).

'I will make my Shekinah (שכינה)
dwell there, in the midst of the
children of Israel forever; and the
children of Israel shall no longer
defile my Holy Name... by placing
their threshold beside the threshold of
my Holy Temple... with only a wall
of my Holy Temple between my
Word (מימר) and them' (*Targ. Ezek.*
43.7b-8).

63. 'May the Word (מימר) of the Lord be
among us as a true and faithful
witness' (*Targ. Jer.* 42.5).

'the witness to which he witnesses
concerning me is true' (5.32).

'Does not his Word (מימרא) endure
in truth and virtue?' (*Targ. Isa.* 48.1).

'My witness is true' (8.14, 16).

'full of grace and truth' (1.14).

'Attend to my Word (מימר), you who
pursue the truth' (*Targ. Isa.* 51.1).

64.   'Then he said, "You will not be able   'No one has ever seen God; the only
       to see the face of my Shekinah   begotten God [or Son], who was in
       (שכינה); for no man may see me and   the bosom of the Father, has inter-
       live". And the Lord said, "Here is a   preted him' (1.18).
       place prepared before me...when
       my Glory (יקר) passes by, I will...
       shield you with my Word (מימר) until
       I have passed by. Then I will remove
       the word (דבר) of my Glory (יקר),
       and you will perceive that which is
       behind me, but what is in front of me
       will not be seen"' (*Targ. Onq.* Exod
       33.20-23).[1]

65.   'Rabbi Eliezer ben Jose the Galilean   'in the bosom (κόλπος) of the
       [c. 150 CE] said: "...before the   Father' (1.18).
       world was made, the Torah was
       written and lay in the bosom (חיק)[2] of
       the Holy One, blessed be he, and
       with the ministering angels it uttered
       a song: 'Then I was by him, as one
       brought up with him; and I was daily
       his delight, rejoicing always before
       him' [Prov. 8.30-31]"' (*ARN* A §31;
       cf. *Gen. R.* 8.2 [on 1.26]).

       Torah speaks to God and God
       addresses Torah as 'My daughter'
       (*b. Sanh.* 101a), probably implying
       the equation of Torah with Wisdom.[3]

In sum, virtually every element of the Johannine Prologue is paralleled in targumic and midrashic materials. Moreover, there are many
significant parallels between the targumic *memra* and the Johannine
logos. It appears that every assertion regarding the *asarkos logos* in
the Prologue's opening five verses is true of the targumic *memra*:

     1.   The *memra* was in the beginning (Jn 1.1a; see §56 [*Targ.
            Neof.* Gen. 1.1]).

---

1.   Translation based on B. Grossfeld, *The Targum Onqelos to Exodus* (ArBib,
7; Wilmington, DE: Michael Glazier, 1988), p. 94.
   2.   The LXX almost always translates חיק with κόλπος.
   3.   U. Wilckens, 'σοφία, κτλ', *TDNT*, VII, pp. 507.

2. The *memra* was with God (Jn 1.1b; see §56 [*Targ. Onq.* Gen. 20.3]).
3. The *memra* was God (Jn 1.1c; see §57 [*Targ. Ps.-J.* Deut. 32.39] and §58 [*Targ. Neof.* Gen. 1.26-27; *Targ.* Isa. 44.24]).
4. Everything came into being through the *memra* (Jn 1.3; see §58 [*Frag. Targ.* Exod. 3.14]).
5. In the *memra* was life (Jn 1.4; see §59 [*Targ. Ps.-J.* Gen. 3.24]).
6. The *memra* gave light to the world (Jn 1.4b-5; see §60 [*Targ. Neof.* Gen. 1.3; *Targ. Neof.* Exod. 12.42; *Targ. Ps.-J.* Gen. 1.3]).

Every assertion regarding the *ensarkos logos* in the Prologue's final five verses, with the exception of the incarnation itself, is true of the targumic *memra*:

1. The *memra* 'tabernacled' among humankind (Jn 1.14a; see §62 [*Targ. Ps.-J.* Exod. 29.42b-45; *Targ. Ezek.* 43.7b-8; *Targ.* Zech. 2.5(9)]).
2. The *memra*'s glory was seen (Jn 1.14b; see §62 [*Targ. Isa.* 6.1, 5]; cf. §33 [LXX Exod. 25.8]).
3. The *memra* is full of grace and truth (Jn 1.14c, 16, 17; see §62 [*Targ. Ps.-J.* Exod. 29.42b-45; 34.5-6; *Targ. Isa.* 48.1; 51.1; *Targ. Jer.* 42.5]).
4. The Baptist bears witness to the *memra* (Jn 1.15a; see §63 [*Targ. Jer.* 42.5]) and to the fact that he (the *memra*) preceded him, not followed him (Jn 1.15b; see §56 [*Targ. Neof.* Gen. 1.1]).
5. Although one cannot see God, one can see the incarnate Word (Jn 1.14, 18; see §62 [*Targ. Isa.* 6.1, 5; cf. Jn 12.41] and §64 [*Targ. Onq.* Exod. 33.20]).

Twenty years ago Peder Borgen argued that the Prologue was organized as a targumic exegesis of Gen. 1.1-3.[1] He believes that three principal components have been drawn from Genesis: (1) the *Word*, which was in the beginning, was with *God* (vv. 1-2)[2]; (2) everything

---

1. P. Borgen, 'Observations on the Targumic Character of the Prologue of John', *NTS* 16 (1970), pp. 288-95.
2. The parallel with 'God', of course, is explicit. 'Word' is implied by the statement, 'God said'.

came into being through him (v. 3); and (3) he was the *life* and the *light* (vv. 4-5). This threefold structure is then elaborated and applied to Jesus in reverse order: (3′) John the Baptist was sent to witness to the *light* (vv. 6-9)[1]; (2′) although all things *came into being through him*, 'his own [created] things' did not receive him (vv. 10-13); and (1′) the *Word*, which had existed as the only-begotten *God* in the bosom of the Father, became flesh and dwelt among people (vv. 14-18). In other words, what could be said of the creative and light- and life-giving activity of the Word before and at the time of creation can now be said with reference to the incarnate Word: (1) whereas at the time of creation the Word lived with God (vv. 1-2), during his earthly sojourn the Word became flesh and lived among humans (vv. 14-18); (2) whereas it was through the Word that all things came into being (v. 3), at the time of the incarnation creation did not recognize or receive him (vv. 10-13); and finally, (3) whereas at the time of creation the Word was the light that shone in the darkness (vv. 4-5), during the incarnation he enlightened humanity (vv. 6-9).[2]

Borgen also points out that this chiastic exegetical structure occurs elsewhere in the targums and midrash which comment on Genesis 1–2. For example, according to one midrash (with principal elements italicized): 'Rabbi Abbahu said: "From the very beginning of the creation of the world the Holy One, blessed be he, foresaw [1] the *deeds of the righteous* and [2] the *deeds of the wicked*. Thus, [2′] 'Now the earth was formless and void' [Gen. 1.2] alludes to the *deeds*

---

1. The expected parallel to 'life' is missing in this section. However, the result clause, 'that they should have eternal life', is probably the unexpressed, but understood, completion of v. 7: 'in order that they should believe in him'. Such an idea finds explicit expression elsewhere (for example, 6.47; 11.25; 20.31). Note also that the one who believes in Jesus will not abide in darkness (12.46).

2. It should be noted that important elements from these three components find expression in the Gospel proper: (1) The Word lived ἐν ἡμῖν (v. 14, cf. 14.20: 'I in my Father and you in me and I ἐν ὑμῖν'), 'We beheld his glory' (v. 14, cf. 17.24: 'that they might behold my glory'), the 'only begotten' (v. 14, cf. 3.16: 'he gave his only begotten Son'), 'no one has seen God' (v. 18, cf. 14.7: 'you have seen him'); (2) 'he was in the world' (v. 10, cf. 17.11: 'I am no longer in the world'), 'the world did not know him' (v. 10, cf. 16.3: 'they have known neither the Father nor me'), 'those who believe in his name' (v. 12, cf. 2.23: 'many believed in his name'); and (3) witness/testimony (v. 7, cf. 5.36: 'I have the witness that is greater than that of John'), bear witness/testify (vv. 7-8, cf. 8.18: 'the Father who sent me bears witness'), light (vv. 7-9, cf. 8.12: 'I am the light of the world').

of the wicked; [1´] 'And God said, "Let there be light" [Gen. 1.3]'
alludes to the *actions of the righteous*"' (*Gen. R.* 2.5 [on 2.2-4]).[1]

Borgen further observes that the frequently raised objection that
'Word (of the Lord)' was no more than a periphrasis and not a bona
fide hypostasis, and therefore of little significance for the Johannine
Prologue, is met by observing the remarkable function of *logos* in
Philo. This is seen clearly in Philo's exegesis of Gen. 1.1-3: 'For the
model was the Word (λόγος) which contained his [God's] fulness—
[that is,] "light (φῶς)", for he says, "God said, 'Let light come into
being'" [Gen. 1.3]' (*Somn.* 1.13 §75).[2] 'He created the world through
the Word (λόγῳ)' (*Fug.* 18 §95).[3] 'But if there be any as yet unfit to
be called a Son of God, let him press to take his place under God's
First-born, the Word (ὁ πρωτόγονος αὐτοῦ λόγος), who holds elder-
ship among the angels, their ruler as it were. And many names are
his, for he is called, "the Beginning (ἀρχή)", "Name of God (ὄνομα
θεοῦ)", "Word (λόγος)", and the "Man after His Image (ὁ κατ'
εἰκόνα ἄνθρωπος)"' (*Conf. Ling.* 28 §146).[4] There is also the
remarkable statement in *Quaest. in Gen.* 2.62 (on Gen. 9.6), as noted
by Larry Hurtado:[5] 'Nothing mortal can be made in the likeness of the
most high One and Father of the universe but [only] in that of the

1. Translation based on H. Freedman, 'Genesis', in H. Freedman and
M. Simon (eds.), *Midrash Rabbah*, I (10 vols.; London: Soncino, 1983), pp. 18-19.
Another example may be found in *Targ. Ps.-J.* Gen. 3.24: 'Before God created the
world, [1] he created the *Law*, [2] he prepared the garden of Eden for the righteous
that they should eat and delight themselves with the fruit of the *tree*...and [3] he prepared Gehinnom for the *wicked*...and [3´] he prepared within [Gehinnom] flashing
sparks of fire and burning coals for the judgement of the *wicked*...[2´] Better is the
Law for the one who attends to it than the fruits of the *tree of life*—[1´] the *Law*
which the Word of the Lord has prepared in order that it may be kept, so that man
may live and walk by the paths of the way of the life of the world to come'; translation based on J. Bowker, *The Targums and Rabbinic Literature* (Cambridge:
Cambridge University Press, 1969), pp. 123-24. See Borgen, 'Targumic Character
of the Prologue of John', p. 293.

2. Borgen, 'Targumic Character of the Prologue of John', p. 290; *idem*, 'Philo
of Alexandria', in M.E. Stone (ed.), *Jewish Writings of the Second Temple Period*
(Philadelphia: Fortress Press, 1984), pp. 233-82, esp. pp. 273-74. Translation based
on F.H. Colson *et al.*, *Philo*, V (LCL; 12 vols.; Cambridge, MA: Harvard University
Press, 1929–53), p. 337.

3. Translation based on Colson *et al.*, *Philo*, V, p. 61.

4. Translation based on Colson *et al.*, *Philo*, IV, pp. 89, 91.

5. Hurtado, *One God, One Lord*, p. 45.

second God, who is his Logos (τὸν δεύτερον θεόν, ὅς ἐστιν ἐκείνου λόγος)'.[1] Finally, we should note the description in *Quaest. in Exod.* 2.68 (on Exod. 25.22), in which Philo says that God's *logos* (ὁ τοῦ θεοῦ λόγος) dwells in the tabernacle and brings peace by mediating between God and human beings.[2]

Have Borgen and others succeeded in demonstrating that the targumic *memra* clarifies the Johannine *logos*, or have they done no more than demonstrate the relevance of Philo's *logos*? Or, to rephrase the question: did the targumic practice of referring to God as the 'Word of the Lord' contribute to the distinctive functions of *logos* in either Philo or the Johannine Prologue?

memra and Jesus as *logos*

Philo's logos and the Targum's memra

Although comparison between the targumic *memra* and Philo's *logos* was at one time seriously entertained, especially in nineteenth-century studies, most scholars today appear persuaded that there is no relationship. Samuel Sandmel believes such a connection 'very tenuous' at best.[3] Sandmel's teacher, Edwin R. Goodenough, had earlier concluded that an attempt at such comparison 'is quite hopeless'.[4] Goodenough himself had cited George Foot Moore who had argued that connecting the targum's *memra* with Philo's *logos* is an 'erroneous opinion', for *memra* is nothing more than a 'phenomenon of translation, not a figment of speculation', as it is in Philo.[5] Moore had cited with approval the conclusion reached by Strack and Billerbeck that the 'expression "Memra of Adonai" was an empty, purely formal substitution for the

1. Translation is from R. Marcus, *Philo Supplement I: Questions and Answers on Genesis* (LCL; Cambridge, MA: Harvard University Press, 1979), p. 150.
2. Hurtado, *One God, One Lord*, p. 146 n. 13.
3. S. Sandmel, *Philo of Alexandria* (New York: Oxford University Press, 1979), p. 156.
4. E.R. Goodenough, *An Introduction to Philo Judaeus* (Oxford: Basil Blackwell, 1962), p. 76.
5. G.F. Moore, *Judaism in the First Centuries of the Christian Era*, I (3 vols.; Cambridge, MA: Harvard University Press, 1927–30), pp. 417-19; *idem*, 'Intermediaries in Jewish Theology', *HTR* 15 (1922), pp. 41-85. Moore also states (*Judaism*, I, p. 419) that *memra* is not found 'outside the Targums'. That may not be true, for G. Dalman (*The Words of Jesus* [Edinburgh: T. & T. Clark, 1902], p. 230) cites one example ('the Memra of Heaven') from *Seder Rab Amram* 1.52b.

Tetragrammaton'.[1] In view of these conclusions, Harry Wolfson's categorical statement was probably fair in his time: 'No scholar nowadays will entertain the view that [the targum's *memra*] is either a real being or an intermediary'.[2] But what of the origin of Philo's concept of *logos*? According to Goodenough, Philo's *logos* concept 'has no essential counterpart with anything in Jewish writings not influenced by Hellenism, in spite of the fact that Philo himself roots the conception so deeply in the Scriptures'.[3] Sandmel agrees, saying that Philo's use of *logos* has Greek (that is, Stoic) and Jewish (that is, personified Wisdom) 'ancestry'.[4] By this Jewish ancestry he basically means Hellenistic Judaism.

I do not think, however, that the matter is settled. There are some examples from the targums in which the *memra* appears very much to be an intermediary. (These examples will be discussed below.) Moreover, Martin McNamara has pointed out that Strack and Billerbeck, Moore, Goodenough and Wolfson did not have access to the *Neofiti* targum, in which there is a remarkable parallel between Exod. 12.42 and Jn 1.3 (see §60 above), and in which the word *memra* occurs in Gen. 1.1 and elsewhere in the creation account. McNamara further points out that because their surveys of the targumic materials were limited to *Onqelos* and *Pseudo-Jonathan* (where *memra* does not occur in Gen. 1–2), they were unaware of *memra*'s frequent occurrence in the creation accounts of Genesis.[5] Furthermore, the fact that Philo was influenced by Palestinian midrash[6] leaves open the very real possibility of his being influenced by other ideas of the academies and

---

1.   Moore, *Judaism*, I, p. 418 n. 1. For numerous examples, see Str–B, II, pp. 302-33 (the quotation is from p. 333); V. Hamp, *Der Begriff 'Wort' in den aramäischen Bibelübersetzungen: Ein exegetischer Beitrag zur Hypostasen-Frage und zur Geschichte der Logos Spekulation* (Munich: Filser, 1938). In his recent study A. Chester (*Divine Revelation and Divine Titles in the Pentateuchal Targumim* [Tübingen: Mohr (Paul Siebeck), 1986]) has affirmed Moore's position.

2.   H.A. Wolfson, *Philo*, I (2 vols.; Cambridge, MA: Harvard University Press, 1948), p. 287.

3.   Goodenough, *Philo Judaeus*, pp. 76-77.

4.   Sandmel, *Philo*, p. 98.

5.   McNamara, *Targum and Testament*, pp. 101-102.

6.   *EncJud*, XIII, p. 412: '[Philo] borrows from the Hebrew tradition not only a wealth of individual Midrashim, but also central midrashic concepts'. See also *JewEnc*, X, pp. 15-18; E. Stein, *Philo und Midrasch* (Giessen: Töpelmann, 1931).

the synagogues, such as the targumic *memra*.[1]

I suspect that Philo may very well have chosen *logos* and not *sophia* because of the former's use in the synagogue, as well as in Stoic circles.[2] But in choosing a word in use in the synagogue that would serve well his ideas of intermediacy, Philo exercised the liberty to define its character and functions as he chose. Philo's use of *logos* is no more limited to the functions of *memra* in the targums than it is limited by the functions of *logos* in Stoic thought. But the real question at hand, of course, is not the derivation of *logos* in Philo, but the derivation and meaning of *logos* in the Johannine Prologue.

The Johannine Prologue's logos and the Targum's memra

In the nineteenth century John's *logos* was frequently compared with the targumic *memra*.[3] But by the middle of the twentieth century such

---

1. J.A. Fitzmyer (*The Genesis Apocryphon of Qumran Cave I* [BibOr, 18a; Rome: Pontifical Biblical Institute Press, 2nd edn, 1971], p. 38) observes that *memra* does not occur in 11QtgJob or the targum-like 1QapGen (see 1QapGen 22.32 where אלהא substitutes for יהוה). He thinks that this may imply that the targumic *memra* was 'a device of a later date'. To this R. Le Déaut (in his review of Fitzmyer's 1966 edition in *Bib* 48 [1967], pp. 141-45) replies by suggesting that *memra* was used in targums intended for public readings, but would not be necessary in those like 11QtgJob which were evidently intended only for private, scholarly study. Fitzmyer (*Genesis Apocryphon*, p. 39) finds this suggestion 'quite plausible', but reminds us that this does not prove that the Cairo fragments, *Neofiti*, *Pseudo-Jonathan* or *Onqelos* date from the first century.

C.T.R. Hayward's attempt ('The Holy Name of the God of Moses and the Prologue of St John's Gospel', *NTS* 25 [1978], pp. 16-32) to find *memra* implied in the use of אהוה (or אהיה, as some emend the text) in 1QapGen 22.30 ('Now do not fear; I am with you; and I shall be [ואהוה] to you') is not compelling; see Chilton, *The Glory of Israel*, pp. 143-44 n. 31.

2. It is not necessary, of course, for this study to try to argue that Philo's use of *logos* had something to do with the use of *memra* in the targums. My concern is the relationship of *memra* with the use of *logos* in the Johannine Prologue. But because Philo's relationship to the Prologue is readily acknowledged, there is a natural tendency to assume that Philo's philosophical–theological background roughly approximates to that of the Prologue. Therefore, if it can be shown that Philo's *logos* concept has something to do with the targums' *memra*, then it is easier to assume that the Prologue's *logos* concept also has something to do with the targums' *memra*.

3. See for example B.F. Westcott, *An Introduction to the Study of the Gospels* (London: Macmillan, 4th edn, 1872), pp. 147-48; *idem, The Gospel according to St John* (repr.; Grand Rapids: Eerdmans, 1973 [1874]), pp. 2-3: 'The theological use of

comparison had been largely abandoned. Objections usually were (and still are) based on the observation that the vast majority of occurrences of *memra* in the targums seem to be little more than periphrasis for the divine name. Accordingly, C.K. Barrett thinks that the targumic *memra* as the background of *logos* in John is a 'blind alley',[1] while Edward Cook has recently opined that 'such a notion is certainly mistaken'.[2] But there are some targum scholars who do not agree.[3]

While it may be true that most occurrences of *memra* are periphrastic, three qualifications should be pointed out. First, sometimes *memra* is an independent agent. This is clearly seen in *Targ. Hab.* 1.12: 'Your Word (מימר) endures forever. O Lord, you created it [the Word] to administer judgment'. As does God, the *memra* has feeling: 'My Word (מימר) loathed you just as the Lord loathed Sodom and Gomorrah' (*Targ. Amos* 4.11). In another passage the targumic Word

the term appears to be derived directly from the Palestinian *Memra*, and not from the Alexandrian *Logos*'.

1. Barrett, *Gospel according to St John*, p. 153. See also Str–B, II, p. 333: *memra* is 'unsuitable to serve as a starting-point for the Logos of John'. J.A. Fitzmyer ('The Aramaic Language and the Study of the New Testament', *NTS* 20 [1974], pp. 382-407, esp. p. 396) has also expressed skepticism as to the value of the targums' *memra* for interpretation of *logos* in John's Prologue.

2. E.M. Cook, review of *The Targum Onqelos*, by B. Grossfeld, *CBQ* 53 (1991), p. 105.

3. Díez Macho, 'El Logos y el Espíritu Santo'; M. McNamara, '*Logos* of the Fourth Gospel and *Memra* of the Palestinian Targum (Ex 12.42)', *ExpTim* 79 (1968), pp. 115-17; *idem, Targum and Testament*, pp. 101-106; R. Le Déaut, 'Targumic Literature and New Testament Interpretation', *BTB* 4 (1974), pp. 243-89, esp. pp. 266-69; D. Muñoz León, *Dios Palabra: Memrá en los Targumim del Pentateuco* (Granada: Editorial Santa Rita, 1974) (summarized by L. Sabourin, 'The MEMRA of God in the Targums', *BTB* 6 [1976], pp. 79-85); *idem, Palabra y Gloria: Excursus en la Biblia y en la Literatura Intertestamentaria* (Verbum Gloriae 4; Madrid: Consejo Superior de Investigaciones Científicas Instituto 'Francisco Suárez', 1983); Hayward, 'The Holy Name of the God of Moses'; *idem,* 'Memra and Shekhina: A Short Note', *JJS* 31 (1980), pp. 210-13; Chilton, *The Glory of Israel*, pp. 143-44 nn. 30 and 31. Díez Macho and McNamara appeal primarily to *Targ. Neof.* and *Targ. Ps.-J.* Exod. 12.42. See also J.H. Charlesworth, 'The Jewish Roots of Christology: The Discovery of the Hypostatic Voice', *SJT* 39 (1986), pp. 19-41, esp. pp. 26-27; M. Black, *An Aramaic Approach to the Gospels and Acts* (Oxford: Clarendon Press, 3rd edn, 1967), p. 299: 'Perhaps we need not look beyond [the old Targum of] Palestine for the inspiration of the Logos doctrine of John'.

plays an intermediary role: 'I let myself be entreated through my Word (מימר) by those who did not inquire of me...by a people who do not pray in my name' (*Targ. Isa.* 65.1).[1] The ideas of administration and intermediacy occur in the Fourth Gospel in reference to Jesus, the incarnate Word. Jesus will administer judgment: 'For not even the Father judges anyone, but he has given all judgment to the Son' (Jn 5.22; cf. 5.27; 8.16; 9.39). The Son also functions as an intermediary, through whom people must approach God (Jn 14.6: 'no one comes to the Father except through me') or in his Son's name (Jn 15.16: 'Whatever you ask the Father in my name he will give you'; cf. 14.16; 16.23). The problem of what *memra* may or may not mean is taken up in the next point.

Secondly, John's usage need not be limited to the precise or even general function of *memra* in the targums. Bruce Chilton has rightly emphasized the point that *memra* has several different functions.[2] Scholarly discussion of the targumic *memra* is frequently not nuanced, often assuming that a fixed meaning underlies all or most occurrences. Chilton's comments are apposite: 'We have long since passed the point when all Targums may be supposed to adhere to a single sense of מימרא, be it sophisticated or otherwise';[3] 'Following the lead of [George Foot] Moore, we may say that מימרא is not a personal being, a being, a figment of speculation (so far Moore), or even (we now conclude) a systematic idea, consistent from Targum to Targum. What links the Targumim, in their usage of מימרא, is not a theological thought, but a theological *manner* of speaking of God'.[4] As an example, one finds in Chilton's helpful tabulation that *memra* occurs in Genesis, in reference to creating, eight times in *Neofiti* (cf. 1.9, 11, 16, 25, 27; 2.2; 14.19, 22) and not once in *Pseudo-Jonathan*.[5]

The simple fact that 'Word' appears as a periphrasis or name for God in Genesis 1–2 and elsewhere in reference to creation and to God's Shekinah dwelling among his people means that it could easily have been adopted by the Fourth Evangelist for his own use. Chilton

---

1. Chilton, *The Glory of Israel*, pp. 63-64.
2. B.D. Chilton, 'Recent and Prospective Discussion of *Memra*', in J. Neusner *et al.* (eds.), *From Ancient Israel to Modern Judaism: Intellect in Quest of Understanding* (BJS, 173; Atlanta: Scholars Press, 1989), pp. 119-37.
3. Chilton, 'Recent and Prospective Discussion of *Memra*', p. 123.
4. Chilton, 'Recent and Prospective Discussion of *Memra*', p. 131.
5. Chilton, 'Recent and Prospective Discussion of *Memra*', p. 133.

has observed that 'the general similarity of the memra-as-oath locution [in the *Isaiah Targum*] to the Johannine prologue, which also links the ideas of creation and witness (cf. vv. 1, 2, 4, 14-15), might also suggest that it was in use early on'.[1] The agency, if not hypostasis, of 'Word' in Philo and the presence of 'Word' in the targums, especially in Genesis 1–2, make it possible, perhaps even probable, that the *logos* in the Johannine Prologue (and elsewhere in the Fourth Gospel)[2] does reflect the targumic tradition.[3]

Thirdly, there is good reason to believe that God's self-identification in Rev. 1.4 ('the one who is and who was and who is coming [ὁ ὢν καὶ ὁ ἦν καὶ ὁ ἐρχόμενος]') approximates *memra*'s self-identification found in the targum: 'I am he who is and who was and I am he who will be (אנא הוא דהוי והוית ואנא הוא דעתיד למהוי)' (*Targ. Ps.-J.* Deut. 32.39). If the Apocalypse derives from the Johannine community, then we have evidence here that this community was familiar with the relatively rare tripartite form of the divine name.[4] Moreover, the identification of the wrathful Christ as 'the Word of God (ὁ λόγος τοῦ θεοῦ)' (Rev. 19.13) may very well be the Greek equivalent of the *memra* of God.

---

1. Chilton, *The Glory of Israel*, p. 63.
2. See B.D. Chilton, 'Typologies of *memra* and the Fourth Gospel', in P.V.M. Flesher (ed.), *Methods in the Study of the Targums: Suggestions and Explorations* (Atlanta: Scholars Press, forthcoming).
3. After his survey of several possible backgrounds, Brown (*Gospel according to John*, I, pp. 519-24) concludes that the targumic tradition, though not to the exclusion of other strands, lies behind the Prologue: '[Jesus] is the *Memra*, God's presence among men' (p. 524). Chilton ('Typologies of *memra* and the Fourth Gospel') differs from this conclusion in that he believes that it is more precise, indeed, more 'targumic', to speak of Jesus as the locus in which God's *memra* can dwell (which coheres with the targumic idea of the divine Shekinah) and through whom God's *memra* might speak. Chilton does not think that the Johannine Prologue intends to equate Jesus with the *logos*, as it came to be understood in patristic interpretation and theology. For another recent study that concludes that the targumic *memra*, especially as it is found in *Neofiti*, is the likely background against which the Johannine *logos* should be interpreted, see G. Anderson, 'The Interpretation of Genesis 1.1 in the Targums', *CBQ* 52 (1990), pp. 21-29, esp. pp. 27-29.
4. See the discussion in McNamara, *The New Testament and the Palestinian Targum to the Pentateuch*, pp. 97-112.

Targumic and Midrashic Tradition and the Prologue

The targums and midrash also supply the three important components, identified by Tobin, necessary to bridge the gap between Genesis 1–2 and the Johannine Prologue. First, with respect to the reality and function of the *logos*, it was noted that in one passage Sophia 'leaped out of heaven' to punish the Egyptians (Wis. 18.15). This parallels an important and frequent use of *memra* in the targums. In many passages the *memra* of the Lord is depicted as destroying Israel's enemies (for example, *Targ. Isa.* 30.27-33; 33.11-12).

With respect to the filial dimension of the *logos* in Philo and the Johannine Prologue, it may be pointed out that the rabbis spoke of Wisdom/Torah as a little child in God's presence (see §49 above). Although this is not in reference to the *memra*, the parallels between the attributes assigned to the *memra* and Wisdom/Torah are extensive (for example, §55, §56, §57, §58, §60, §64 and §65), such that it is probably accurate to say that what is true of one is true of the others (cf. Bar. 4.1: 'She [that is, Wisdom] is the book of the commandments of God, even the Law that endures forever'). That *memra* was identified with God, of course, is obvious.

Secondly, with respect to the antithesis between light and darkness found in Philo and in the Prologue, similar antitheses are found in rabbinic interpretation. Perhaps the most pertinent example comes from Rabbi Tanhuma (a third-century Palestinian Amora) who said, commenting on the opinion of Rabbis Yohanan and Simeon ben Laqish that Gen. 1.4 implies that God permanently divided light and darkness and put them into separate realms:

> I shall tell you what is the basis [in Scripture of the teaching of Yohanan and Simeon ben Laqish]: 'who creates light and makes darkness and makes peace' [Isa. 45.7]. When they [that is, light and darkness] went forth [into the world], God made peace between them [and assigned each to a separate domain]' (*y. Ber.* 8.6; cf. *Gen. R.* 3.6 [on 1.3-5]).[1]

The need to 'make peace' clearly implies conflict between light and darkness. The only way to make peace was to separate them. In a discussion on 'distinctions' Rabbi Zera is remembered to have said: 'He

---

1. Translation based on T. Zahavy, 'Berakhot', in J. Neusner (ed.), *The Talmud of the Land of Israel*, I (35 vols.; Chicago: University of Chicago Press, 1989), p. 298.

makes a distinction (הבדלה) between the holy and the profane, between light and darkness, between Israel and other nations, between the seventh day and the six working days. Why is this? He is merely enumerating the "distinctions"' (*b. Hul.* 26b).[1] Because of the use of the verb בדל (to separate or distinguish) in Gen. 1.4, the separation between light and darkness is one of several 'distinctions'. The important point to observe is that darkness parallels what is profane, the other nations and the six working days, while light parallels what is holy, Israel and the seventh day.

There are other examples that interpret light as symbolizing the righteous, such as Abraham, the Messiah and others, and darkness as symbolizing the wicked generation of Enosh, Esau, the Greek empire and the wicked in general (cf. *Gen. R.* 2.3 [on 1.2]; 2.4 [on 1.2]=*Pes. R.* 33.6;[2] *Gen. R.* 3.6 [on 1.3-5]; *Exod. R.* 1.20 [on 2.2]=*b. Sot.* 12a; *Exod. R.* 35.1 [on 26.15]= *b. Hag.* 12a; *b. Yom.* 38b; *Midr. Ps.* 27.1 [on 27.1]; *Elijah Zuta* §21=*Pes. R.* 36.1). Although many of the rabbinic expressions of this antithesis are ethical, conflict is still implied, especially in the one credited to Tanhuma, which approximates the antithesis presupposed in Jn 1.5.

Perhaps the most relevant rabbinic exegetical tradition has been exposed by Borgen.[3] He believes that the Johannine Prologue, especially vv. 4-5 and 6-9, has been modeled after the conception of light-giving Torah received through Moses.[4] Primordial light shone, until Adam sinned (*b. Hag.* 12a). Then followed darkness. But when Torah was received at Sinai the light once again shone (*2 Bar.* 17–18). Although Israel has once more been enveloped in darkness, in the age of the Messiah this light will once again shine (*Gen. R.* 2.3 [on 1.2]). In the Prologue this concept has been applied to the *logos*. It is in Jesus, not Moses, that the 'true light' will shine (Jn 1.9, 17).

With respect to life as the source of light in Philo's exegesis, these ideas are found in the targums as well. According to *Frag. Targ.* Gen. 1.3 (see §60), 'there was light in his Word', while according to *Targ. Neof.* Exod. 12.42 (see §60) the *memra* 'was the light and it shone'.

---

1. Translation based on E. Cashdan, 'Hullin', in I. Epstein (ed.), *The Babylonian Talmud*, XV (18 vols.; London: Soncino, 1978), p. 135.
2. In this midrash the 'hovering Spirit' of Gen. 1.2 is taken to be an allusion to Messiah, since according to Isa. 11.2 the 'Spirit is upon him'.
3. P. Borgen, 'Logos was the True Light', *NovT* 14 (1972), pp. 115-30.
4. Borgen, 'Logos was the True Light', p. 125.

Moreover, according to *Targ. Ps.-J.* Gen. 3.24 (see §59), interpreting the meaning of the 'tree of life', the *memra* prepared the Torah 'so that man may live and walk by the paths of the way of the life of the world to come'. In these passages we have the same ideas as in the Prologue and Philo. In the Word reside both light and eternal life.[1]

Thirdly, with regard to the identification of the *logos* with a specific human being, there is more to the incarnation idea of the Prologue than the identification of the Word with a particular person. Jn 1.14 states that the 'Word became flesh and dwelt among us'. The primary point of the Prologue, it seems to me, is not that Jesus is the Word, but that the Word became flesh and dwelt among humankind. The targums contain statements about the *memra* that seem to adumbrate this idea (see §62). For example, God delivered an unbelieving Israel lest they should ask, 'Where is he that caused the Word of his holy prophets to dwell among them?' (*Targ. Isa.* 63.11). Elsewhere the hope is expressed, 'May the Word of the Lord be among us as a true and faithful witness' (*Targ. Jer.* 42.5). The concept probably has its roots in the tradition of God's presence within the Tabernacle (cf. Exod. 40.34-38). According to the Hebrew text, God will meet Moses and the people of Israel at the Tabernacle and there he will dwell (שׁכן) among the people of Israel and be their God (Exod. 29.42b-45). According to Pseudo-Jonathan, God will appoint his Word to meet and speak with Moses and the people of Israel at the Tabernacle, where his Shekinah (שׁכינה) will dwell in their midst, and he will be their God. According to Ezekiel, just prior to the capture of Jerusalem and the destruction of the first Temple, the glory of God departed (Ezek. 10.18-19). But the prophet also foresaw the day when a new, purified Temple would be built, where God would 'dwell (שׁכן) in the midst of the people of Israel forever' (Ezek. 43.1-9). Following the exile, the prophets looked forward to the fulfillment of this hope. It was Zechariah's vision that God's glory would once again be present in Jerusalem (Zech. 2.5 [Hebr. v. 9]). God says to the daughter of Zion: 'I come and I will dwell (שׁכן) in the midst of you' (Zech. 2.10 [Hebr. v. 14]; cf. 2.11 [Hebr. v. 15]; 8.3). But according to the targum, 'My Word will be to her...like a wall of fire encircling her

---

1. In at least one midrash Prov. 20.27 ('The light of the Lord is the breath of humans') is linked with Gen. 2.7 ('And [God] breathed into his nostrils the breath of life, and the human became a living soul'); see *Midr. Tanḥ.* (B) Gen. 2.1 (on Gen. 6.9).

round about, and I will make my Shekinah dwell in her midst in honor' (*Targ. Zech.* 2.5 [targ. v. 9]).

Another targumic link to Jn 1.14 is the statement, 'we beheld his glory'. Gustaf Dalman, Alejandro Díez Macho and Martin McNamara have suggested that 'glory' (יקרא), another frequent periphrasis in the targums, may underlie this use of δόξα in the Johannine Prologue.[1] The targum has added these three words, *memra*, Shekinah and *yeqara* to the description of Isaiah's vision of God: 'I saw the *glory* of the Lord...And I said: "Woe is me! For...my eyes have seen the *glory* of the *Shekinah* of the eternal king, the Lord of hosts"...And I heard the voice of the *memra* of the Lord which said: "Whom shall I send..."' (*Targ. Isa.* 6.1-8).[2] This specific targumic reading may have particular relevance for the Fourth Gospel. At the turning point in John 12, where Jesus' public ministry of signs is acknowledged as having failed to produce widespread faith in Israel (cf. v. 37), the evangelist cites Isa. 53.1 and Isa. 6.10 as explaining Israel's inability to believe in Jesus. 'Isaiah said these things', the evangelist tells us, 'because [or when] he saw his [Christ's] glory, and he spoke concerning him' (Jn 12.38-41).[3] In view of these observations, I think that it is highly probable that targumic language and ideas, possibly Isaiah 6, are reflected in Jn 1.14.[4] In any event, the appearance and christological usage in the Fourth Gospel of the three words that the targums use to describe God's presence among humanity strongly suggest that Johannine Christology took shape in the context of the synagogue.

Finally, there are two other related points of coherence between Johannine language and theology and targumic tradition. First, Jesus' reference to himself as the Temple is significant: 'Jesus answered and said to them, "Destroy this Temple (ναός) and in three days I shall raise it up"...but that one was speaking concerning the Temple of his

---

1.   Dalman, *The Words of Jesus*, p. 231; Díez Macho, 'El Logos y el Espíritu Santo', pp. 381-96, esp. p. 389; McNamara, *Targum and Testament*, pp. 99-101.

2.   Translation is based on Chilton, *Isaiah Targum*, pp. 14-15. R. Middleton ('Logos and Shekina in the Fourth Gospel', *JQR* 29 [1933], pp. 101-33) was one of the first scholars to note the significance of the appearance of *memra*, Shekinah and *yeqara* in John and the targums.

3.   See Chilton, *The Glory of Israel*, p. 76; McNamara, *Targum and Testament*, p. 100; C.A. Evans, *To See and Not Perceive: Isaiah 6.9-10 in Early Jewish and Christian Interpretation* (JSOTSup, 64; Sheffield: JSOT Press, 1989), pp. 132-34, 214-15 n. 14.

4.   This question is probed further in Chapter 5.

body' (Jn 2.19-21). Chilton has pointed out that 'Shekinah and Temple are virtually identified' in the *Isaiah Targum*.[1] In John it is Jesus who is identified with the Temple (ὁ ναός). This identification with the Temple probably takes us back to Jesus as the Word. That is, Jesus, the *memra* (λόγος) of the Lord, has pitched his tent (σκηνοῦν), and represents God's dwelling place on earth (ἐν ἡμῖν), namely, the Temple (ναός) or Tabernacle (σκηνή). (Compare the language of 2 Macc. 14.35: 'O Lord of all...you were pleased that there be a temple for your habitation among us [ναὸν τῆς σῆς σκηνώσεως ἐν ἡμῖν].')

Assessing these texts and others Craig Koester believes that we can speak of a tabernacle theology lying behind the Fourth Gospel's Prologue.[2] He argues that the evangelist has combined the concept of God dwelling in the Tabernacle (or Temple), a concept based on Exodus, passages from the prophets (for example, Ezek. 37.27; Joel 3.17; Zech. 2.10), and Sirach 24, with the innovation of referring to the human body as a tabernacle or temple (for example, 1 Cor. 3.16, 17; 6.19; 2 Cor. 5.1, 4; 6.16; 2 Pet. 1.13, 14). Koester accordingly concludes that for the Fourth Evangelist 'tabernacle imagery was uniquely able to capture the idea that people encountered God's Word and glory in the person of Jesus'.[3]

Secondly, the idea of the 'place' that Jesus promises to 'prepare' for his disciples is probably influenced by language that we now find in the targum: 'In my Father's house are many lodgings; if it were not so, would I have told you that I go to prepare a place for you? If I go and prepare a place for you, I am coming again and shall receive you to myself that where I am you also should be' (Jn 14.2-3). According to the Hebrew the Lord tells Moses: 'My face will go with you and give you rest' (Exod. 33.14). But the passage reads in *Neofiti*: 'The glory of my Shekinah will lead among you, and I shall prepare a resting place for you'.[4]

---

1. Chilton, *The Glory of Israel*, p. 72.

2. C.R. Koester, *The Dwelling of God: The Tabernacle in the Old Testament, Intertestamental Jewish Literature, and the New Testament* (CBQMS, 22; Washington: Catholic Biblical Association, 1989), pp. 100-115.

3. C.R. Koester, *The Dwelling of God*, 115; cf. J. McCaffrey, *The House with Many Rooms: The Temple Theme of Jn. 14,2-3* (AnBib, 114; Rome: Pontifical Biblical Institute, 1988), pp. 222-24.

4. See M. McNamara, *Palestinian Judaism and the New Testament* (GNS, 4; Wilmington, DE: Michael Glazier, 1983), p. 240. Following the targumic reading,

Moses and Jesus as Agents of the Lord

Although Jesus is compared to several Old Testament figures, Moses appears to have offered the most informing paradigm for the evangelist's Christology.[1] Moses tradition, particularly that concerned with the signs and wilderness wanderings, has been put to good use throughout the Fourth Gospel.[2] In the final five verses of the Prologue (1.14-18) comparison is made between Jesus and the revered Lawgiver.[3] Whereas the Law, the Sinai Covenant, was given to Israel through Moses, grace and truth (probably meant to recall the 'grace and truth' of which God spoke when he passed before Moses in Exod. 34.6; cf. Jn 1.18) have been made available to all through Jesus Christ (cf. Jn 1.16-17). The Prologue's allusions to Moses, in effect, become

Rashi interprets this 'prepared place' as the 'place where the Shekinah is' (on Exod. 33.21).

1. According to W.A. Meeks ('The Divine Agent and his Counterfeit in Philo and the Fourth Gospel', in E. Schüssler Fiorenza [ed.], *Aspects of Religious Propaganda in Judaism and Early Christianity* [London and Notre Dame: University of Notre Dame Press, 1976], pp. 43-67) Philo views Moses as the intermediary between God and humankind *par excellence*. A similar view is found in the Fourth Gospel, but the evangelist presents Jesus in such an elevated manner that the synagogue rejects his Christology as heretical.

2. See R.H. Smith, 'Exodus Typology in the Fourth Gospel', *JBL* 81 (1962), pp. 329-42; T.F. Glasson, *Moses in the Fourth Gospel* (SBT, 40; London: SCM Press, 1963); W.A. Meeks, *The Prophet-King: Moses Traditions and the Johannine Christology* (NovTSup, 14; Leiden: Brill, 1967); M.-É. Boismard, *Moïse ou Jésus: Essai de christologie johannique* (BETL, 84; Leuven: Leuven University Press, 1988).

Again we have a significant lack of coherence between Johannine and Gnostic thinking. Whereas Moses serves as a model for the the former (even if surpassed by Jesus), the Lawgiver is denigrated in the latter. Four times in the *Apocryphon of John* we are told that what really happened is 'not the way Moses wrote [or said]' (II, 13.19-20; 22.22-23; 23.3-4; 29.6). In the *Second Treatise of the Great Seth* Moses is called a 'laughing-stock' (VII, 63.26). The authority of Moses is also likely questioned in the *Testimony of Truth* (IX, 48.15–50.11), but the fragmentary condition of the text makes it difficult to be certain. The Johannine community fully accepts the authority of Moses and his writings: 'If you had believed Moses, you would have believed me. For concerning me that one wrote' (5.46; cf. 1.45).

3. See especially A.T. Hanson, 'Jn 1,14-18 and Exodus 34', *NTS* 23 (1976), pp. 90-101; repr. in *The New Testament Intepretation of Scripture* (London: SPCK, 1980), pp. 97-109.

introductory to the many other comparisons drawn elsewhere.

Comparison with Moses does not in any way compete with comparison with the *logos*. These two elements are meant to be complementary in the Prologue. Indeed, the first element probably qualifies all other christological components found in the Fourth Gospel. For example, it is possible to assert that Jesus is the True Vine (as opposed to a fruitless vine), because he is God's *logos*. As God's *logos* he can be nothing else than the True Vine, or Good Shepherd, or the Light of the World. The two elements found in the Prologue's first five verses (*logos* and creation) and the last five verses (Moses and covenant) are actually combined in first-century traditions about Moses, as seen from the following statement attributed to the Lawgiver: 'But he designed and devised me, who [was] prepared from the beginning of the world, to be the mediator of his covenant' (*T. Mos.* 1.14). Here creation and covenant are juxtaposed and related to the person of Moses. (Moses is described as a mediator in *T. Mos.* 3.12 as well.)

One of the features of Johannine Christology that seems to relate closely the respective functions of *logos* and Moses is the idea of being sent into the world. We find this expressed several times in the Fourth Gospel using the word ἀποστέλλειν: 'God sent not his son to condemn the world' (3.17); 'he whom God sent speaks the words of God' (3.34); 'the Father has sent me' (5.36); 'you do not believe in the one whom that one sent' (5.38); 'that you believe in him whom he has sent' (6.29); 'the living Father has sent me' (6.57); 'I am from him, and he has sent me' (7.29); 'I did not come of myself, but he sent me' (8.42); 'whom the Father has sanctified and sent into the world' (10.36); 'that they might believe that you sent me' (11.42); and several times in the prayer of John 17 (vv. 3, 8, 18, 21, 23, 25). The same word is used of Jesus sending forth his disciples: 'I sent you to reap' (4.38). Similar statements are made employing πέμπειν (*passim*; in reference to the Paraclete cf. 14.26; 15.26; 16.7). The commissioning statement made by the risen Jesus employs both words: 'as the Father has sent (ἀποστέλλειν) me, I also send (πέμπειν) you' (20.21).[1] The noun ἀπόστολος occurs only once: 'Truly, truly, I say to you, a servant is not greater than his master; nor one sent (ἀπόστολος) greater than the one who sent (πέμπειν) him' (13.16).

---

1.   The usual distinction between ἀποστέλλειν and πέμπειν, with the former implying sending with a message and the latter simply being sent, does not hold in the Fourth Gospel.

What we have here is the language of agency. The Fourth Evangelist has presented Jesus as God's agent or *shaliach* (that is, שלוח or שליח, 'one who is sent', from שלח), who then commissions his disciples to carry on his ministry. The idea has its roots in the Old Testament, which speaks of the prophets being 'sent' with messages and assignments in behalf of God (1 Sam. 15.1; 2 Sam. 12.1; Isa. 6.8; 48.16; 61.1; Jer. 1.7; Ezek. 2.3; Mal. 3.1; 4.5; cf. Lk. 13.34). God's word (דבר/λόγος) is also sent into the world (cf. Ps. 107.20; 147.18). For Johannine Christology the most important examples are of Moses being sent: 'Come, I will send you to Pharaoh' (Exod. 3.10); 'this shall be a sign that I have sent you' (Exod. 3.12); 'The God of your fathers has sent me to you' (Exod. 3.13, 15); 'I AM has sent me to you' (Exod. 3.14); 'Moses told Aaron all the words of the Lord with which he had sent him, and all the signs which he had charged him to do' (Exod. 4.28); 'The Lord, the God of the Hebrews, sent me to you' (Exod. 7.16); 'all the signs and the wonders which the Lord sent him to do' (Deut. 34.11). In all of these examples שלח is used in the Hebrew, and ἀποστέλλειν in the LXX.

The primary function of the *shaliach* is to speak the message of God and to act as God's representative. There are numerous examples of dictional coherence between the Fourth Gospel and tradition concerning Moses in his role as God's agent.[1] Of first importance is establishing the claim that the agent speaks and acts in the name and authority of the one who has sent him. 1. God says to Moses: 'You will speak (λαλεῖν) to [Pharaoh] all that (πάντα) I command (ἐντέλλομαι) you' (Exod. 7.2).[2] Likewise, Jesus says to his disciples: 'I did not speak (λαλεῖν) from myself, but the Father who sent me has given commandment (ἐντολή) to me what I should say and what I should speak (λαλεῖν)' (Jn 12.49); and 'all (πάντα) that I have heard from my Father I have made known to you' (15.15). The expression attributed to Jesus, 'I did not speak from myself (ἐξ ἐμαυτοῦ)' (12.49), parallels Num. 16.28: 'that [the works] are not from myself (ἀπ' ἐμαυτοῦ)' and receives attention in halakic discussions of Moses. A pertinent illustration is found in Tannaic tradition: 'Moses said to them, "I am not speaking of myself—what I am saying to you

---

1. Although the parallels adduced here are with the LXX, this does not mean that other versions are necessarily excluded.
2. Similar language is found in the prophets: 'all (πάντας) that I should command (ἐντέλλομαι) you, you will speak (λαλεῖν)' (Jer. 1.7).

comes from the mouth of the Holiness"' (*Sifre Deut.* §5 [on 1.6]; cf.
Exod. R. 5.21 [on Exod. 5.21]; *b. Šab.* 87a). Peder Borgen has iden-
tified this idiom as an important element in the language of agency.[1]
(More examples from rabbinic writings will be considered below.) 2.
Jesus also claims to do the works of his Father: 'The works which the
Father has given me to complete—the works themselves which I do
(τὰ ἔργα ἃ ποιῶ)—testify (μαρτυρεῖν) concerning me that the
Father has sent me (με ἀποστέλλειν)' (Jn 5.36; cf. 7.3). Johannine
language once again echoes the language used to describe the com-
mission and accreditation of Moses. God commands Moses: 'You will
testify (διαμαρτυρεῖν) to them... and you will show them... the works
which they will do (τὰ ἔργα ἃ ποιήσουσιν)' (Exod. 18.20); and
Moses says to the people: 'the Lord sent me (ἀποστέλλειν με) to do
(ποιεῖν) all these works (τὰ ἔργα)' (Num. 16.28). Similarly, God
instructs Moses that the Levites are 'to work the works (ἐργάζεσθαι
τὰ ἔργα) of the Lord' (Num. 8.11, cf. 8.19). This language is recalled
when the Johannine Jesus is asked: 'What should we do that we should
work the works (ἐργαζώμεθα τὰ ἔργα) of God?' (Jn 6.28).

Secondly, it must be demonstrated that the agent knows the words
of the one who sent him and truly speaks in his name. The stories of
Moses and Jesus share several common elements that reflect this concern. 1. God promised Moses that he would raise up a prophet who
would speak his words (ῥήματα) in his name (ἐπὶ τῷ ὀνόματί μου)
(Deut. 18.18-19). As this expected prophet (cf. Jn 6.14; 7.40) Jesus
came in God's name: 'I have come in the name (ἐν τῷ ὀνόματι) of
my Father' (Jn 5.43); and he worked in God's name: 'the works which
I do in the name (ἐν τῷ ὀνόματι) of my Father' (10.25). 2. Of the
great Lawgiver it is said: 'Moses did (ποιεῖν) as (καθά) the Lord
commanded (ἐντέλλομαι) him' (Num. 27.22; cf. Lev. 16.34; Exod.
40.16). Similarly, Jesus says, 'I do (ποιεῖν) as (καθώς) the Father has
commanded (ἐντέλλομαι) me' (Jn 14.31; cf. 15.14). 3. God
promised Moses: 'I shall... teach you what you are about to speak
(λαλεῖν)' (Exod. 4.12); and Moses commanded the Israelites: 'You
will teach (διδάσκειν) them to your children, to speak (λαλεῖν) of
them while sitting at home...' (Deut. 11.19). Appropriately Jesus tells
his opponents: 'I speak (λαλεῖν) these things as the Father taught

1. P. Borgen, 'The Use of Tradition in Jn 12.44-50', *NTS* 26 (1979), pp. 18-35,
esp. pp. 31-34. An approximate expression is found in Tob. 12.18, which may attest
to the antiquity of the language.

(διδάσκειν) me' (Jn 8.28). Jesus speaks only what he has heard from the one who sent him into the world (8.26). 4. Moses said to the people: 'In this (ἐν τούτῳ) you will know (γινώσκειν) that the Lord sent me to do all these works, that [they are] not of myself' (Num. 16.28); 'In this (ἐν τούτῳ) you will know (γινώσκειν) that I am the Lord' (Exod. 7.17; cf. Exod. 29.46; 31.13). All of the words and phrases of these verses are echoed in the Fourth Gospel: 'In this (ἐν τούτῳ) all will know (γινώσκειν) that you are my disciples' (13.35); 'These have known (γινώσκειν) that you sent me (με ἀποστέλλειν)' (17.25); 'the works (τὰ ἔργα) themselves which I do (ποιεῖν)' (5.36; cf. 9.3-4; 10.25); 'that your disciples should behold the works (τὰ ἔργα) which you do (ποιεῖν)' (7.3; cf. Exod. 34.10: 'And all the people will see...the works (τὰ ἔργα) of the Lord...which I shall do (ποιεῖν) for you').

Thirdly, the instructions or commandments of the sender are summarized by his agent. In Deuteronomy Moses reminds the second generation of Israelites of 'all the commandments (ἐντολή) which I command (ἐντέλλομαι) you this day, to love (ἀγαπᾶν) the Lord' (Deut. 11.13); 'all these commandments which I command (τὰς ἐντολὰς ταύτας ἃς ἐγὼ ἐντέλλομαι) you to do (ποιεῖν) this day, to love (ἀγαπᾶν) the Lord your God' (Deut. 11.22). We are reminded of Jesus' 'new commandment': 'I give you a new commandment (ἐντολή), that you love (ἀγαπᾶν) one another' (Jn 13.34; 15.12, 17); 'If you love (ἀγαπᾶν) me, you will keep my commandments (ἐντολή)' (14.15); 'He who has my commandments (ἐντολή) and keeps them is the one who loves (ἀγαπᾶν) me' (14.21); 'if you do what I command (ποιῆτε ἃ ἐγὼ ἐντέλλομαι) you' (Jn 15.14).

Fourthly, the relationship between sender and agent is so close that in a certain sense the agent can be identified with the sender. We see this in Exod. 7.1 where God tells Moses: 'I have given you to Pharaoh as god (θεός)'; and perhaps also when Moses and Aaron say to the people: 'Your murmuring is not against us but against God' (Exod. 16.8). In the Fourth Gospel the *logos* is identified as θεός (1.1), while elsewhere the Johannine Jesus says, 'I and the Father are one' (10.30); and 'He who believes in me does not believe in me but in the one who sent me, and he who beholds me beholds the one who sent me' (12.44-45; cf. 14.1).[1]

---

1. Philo's interpretation of Moses is instructive at this point; see E.R. Goodenough, *By Light, Light: The Mystic Gospel of Hellenistic Judaism* (New

Fifthly, the *shaliach* was sometimes expected to perform signs confirming his claim that he spoke and acted for God.[1] We see this feature in the ministries of Moses and Jesus, with the Fourth Evangelist once again deriving his language from the Old Testament. At the beginning of his ministry Moses 'did (ποιεῖν) the signs (σημεῖα) before the people. And the people believed (πιστεύειν)' (Exod. 4.30b-31). We are reminded of the editorial statement that follows Jesus' first sign: 'This, the first of his signs (σημεῖα), Jesus did (ποιεῖν) at Cana...and his disciples believed (πιστεύειν) in him' (2.11). But at a later time in the ministry of Moses God becomes frustrated with an unbelieving Israel: 'How long will they not believe (πιστεύειν) in me, in spite of all the signs (σημεῖα) which I have done (ποιεῖν) among them?' (Num. 14.11). At the end of his ministry Moses says to Israel: 'You have seen all that the Lord has done (ποιεῖν) in the land of Egypt...those signs (σημεῖα) and great wonders. Yet the Lord (κύριος) has not given you a heart to know, and eyes to see, and ears to hear' (Deut. 29.2-4). Similarly, the Fourth Evangelist summarizes Jesus' public ministry of signs: 'Though he had done (ποιεῖν) so many signs (σημεῖα) before them, yet they did not believe (πιστεύειν) in him, in order that the word of Isaiah the prophet might be fulfilled, which he spoke: "Lord (κύριος), who has believed (πιστεύειν) our report?"...they were not able to believe (πιστεύειν), because again spoke Isaiah: "He has blinded their eyes and hardened their heart..."' (12.37; cf. Isa. 6.10). It is apparent that the Fourth Evangelist's understanding of faith, or the lack of it, is significantly informed by traditions relating to Moses, especially in reference to God's mighty works and 'signs'.[2]

Finally, God's messengers sometimes encountered resistance, even rebellion. During his ministry Moses had to endure a grumbling people. Most of this grumbling had to do with finding water and food in the wilderness. First there is murmuring for water: 'And the people murmured (διαγογγύζειν) against Moses, saying, "What shall we drink?"' (Exod. 15.24); then there is murmuring for bread: 'And all the synagogue (συναγωγή) of the sons of Israel murmured (διαγογγύζειν) against Moses and Aaron. And the sons of Israel said

Haven: Yale University Press, 1935), pp. 227-34.

1. For examples from the prophets, see Isa. 7.11, 14; Jer. 44.29; Ezek. 4.3.
2. See M.M. Thompson, 'Signs and Faith in the Fourth Gospel', *BBR* 1 (1991), pp. 89-108.

to them, "Would we had died...in the land of Egypt, when we...ate bread (ἄρτος) to satisfaction! For you have brought us out into this wilderness"...And the Lord said to Moses, "Behold, I shall rain upon you bread from heaven"' (Exod. 16.2-4). 'And the Lord spoke to Moses, saying, "I have heard the murmuring (γογγυσμός) of the sons of Israel. Speak to them, saying, '...in the morning you will be satisfied with bread"'' (Exod. 16.11-12). This passage is alluded to in John 6. The crowd says to Jesus: 'Our fathers ate the manna in the wilderness, as it is written, "He gave them bread from heaven to eat" [Ps. 78.24; cf. Exod. 16.15]' (Jn 6.31). When Jesus, teaching in a synagogue (συναγωγή), claims to be the 'true bread (ἄρτος) from heaven' (6.32, 35) and to be able to satisfy thirst and hunger (6.35), the 'Judeans murmured (γογγύζειν)' (6.41, 43). When Jesus reiterates that he is 'the bread of life' (6.48, 51) and that the bread is his flesh and the drink is his blood (6.51-56), food that the wilderness generation did not receive (6.58), the people again 'murmur (γογγύζειν)' (6.61). The rejection of Moses and Jesus is expressed elsewhere (5.45-47; 7.19). The Fourth Evangelist has not simply drawn a comparison, a sort of typology between Moses and Jesus who fed multitudes, he has emphasized the important point that Jesus has been 'sent' from heaven. Jesus is God's agent, an agent that is greater than Moses. Moses provided 'the food that perishes', whereas Jesus provides 'the food that remains forever' (6.27). Moses provided 'bread from heaven', which the wilderness generation ate and eventually perished never having entered the land of promise, but Jesus is himself the 'true bread from heaven' (6.32).

Representing what is probably a slightly later development of the *shaliach* idea, rabbinic usage parallels New Testament usage.[1] In a recent study Jan-Adolf Bühner concludes that rabbinic interpretation of Moses as God's *shaliach* offers further clarification of Johannine Christology.[2] Bühner argues that the Johannine portrait of Jesus as

1.   Aspects of the *shaliach* are brought out in the following sayings: 'a man's agent (שליח) is like to himself' (*m. Ber.* 5.5); 'Because of six New Moons messengers (שלוחין) go forth [to proclaim the time of their appearing]' (*m. Roš Haš.* 1.3); 'Rabban Gamaliel says: "The agent (שליח) of the congregation fulfills the obligation that rests upon the many"' (*m. Roš Haš.* 4.9). Prophets were regarded as agents; for example, God says to Jonah: 'I have other agents (שלוחין) like you' (*Mek.* on Exod. 12.1 [*Pisha* §1]).

2.   Bühner, *Der Gesandte und sein Weg.* For an independent review of rabbinic

one sent from heaven derives not from a Gnostic descending redeemer myth,[1] but rather owes its origin to a Jewish-rabbinic 'association of "prophet" and "angel"' as agents of God. Herein lies the basic religious 'presupposition of Johannine Christology of the "way of the Sent One"'.[2] His observation that the 'shaliach concept is encountered especially frequently in the Moses tradition'[3] is hardly surprising, given the already-observed emphasis in the Pentateuch on Moses as one sent by God. The following rabbinic interpretations of Moses appear to bear out at least this part of Bühner's thesis.[4]

Bühner discusses several passages from the rabbinic writings. The following four are representative. 1. Moses answers God: 'Lord of the world, you say to me: "Go to Egypt and lead the sons of Israel out of Egypt." Am I a שׁלׁיח?' (*Mek. SbY.* on Exod. 3.10-11).[5] 2. Moses says to God: 'You are the Lord of the world. Do you really wish that I be your שׁליח? "Behold, I am not a man of words" [Exod. 4.10]' (*Exod. R.* 3.14 [on Exod. 4.10]). 3. '"And this will be the sign for you that I have sent you": and by this will you be known as my שׁלׁיח, that I shall be with you, and all that you wish shall I do' (*Exod. R.* 3.4 [on Exod.

---

shaliach traditions, see C.K. Barrett, '*Shaliah* and Apostle', in E. Bammel *et al.* (eds.), *Donum Gentilicium: New Testament Studies in Honour of David Daube* (Oxford: Clarendon Press, 1978), pp. 88-102.

1. As, for example, is argued in Bultmann, *Gospel of John*, p. 50 n. 2: 'The characterisation of the Revealer or the revelation as "having been sent" by God is particularly striking in Gnosticism'. See also *idem*, 'Die Bedeutung der neuerschlossenen mandäischen und manichäischen Quellen', pp. 100-46, esp. pp. 105-106. For Bühner's criticisms, see *Der Gesandte und sein Weg*, pp. 24-47.

2. Bühner, *Der Gesandte und sein Weg*, p. 427. For his discussion of the principal texts and their interpretation, see pp. 270-373.

3. Bühner, *Der Gesandte und sein Weg*, p. 285. In what ways Moses functions as a *shaliach* is discussed by Bühner on pp. 285-313. See also the recent contribution to the discussion by O. Michel, 'Der aufsteigende und herabsteigende Gesandte', in W.C. Weinrich (ed.), *The New Testament Age*, II (2 vols.; Macon: Mercer University Press, 1984), pp. 335-61.

4. Bühner's conclusion (*Der Gesandte und sein Weg*, pp. 374-99) that the ascent–descent paradigm of the Fourth Gospel reflects 'angel of the Lord' traditions is less convincing. I am inclined to concur with Burkett's reservations (*Son of the Man*, pp. 35-37). 'Angel of the Lord' traditions may have contributed to Johannine Christology more generally. On Burkett's understanding of the ascent–descent paradigm, see Chapter 3 above.

5. The text is fragmentary; cf. J.N. Epstein and E.Z. Melamed, *Mekhilta D'Rabbi Sim'on b. Jochai* (Jerusalem: Mekize Nirdamim, 1955), p. 3.

3.12]). 4. 'The Torah, which the Holy One, blessed be He, gave to Israel, was given to them only through the hands of Moses, as it is written "between him and between the sons of Israel" [Lev. 26.46]; he appointed Moses to be שליח between the sons of Israel and God' (*ARN* A §1). Similar ideas also appear in the Samaritan writing, the *Memar Marqa*. 5. At the time of his departure the people reply to Moses: 'By your life, O apostle (שליח) of God, remain with us a little longer' (5.3). 6. 'He who believes in Moses, believes in his Lord' (4.7). 7. 'His words were from the words of his Lord' (4.7). 8. 'Your speech is the speech of God and He is the doer of all that you have manifested' (6.4). 9. 'Where is there any like Moses, apostle (שליח) of the True One, faithful one of the house of God, and his servant?' (6.3).

There are several important points of coherence with Johannine Christology. In all four of the rabbinic passages and two of the Samaritan passages (§5, §9) Moses is called *shaliach*, that is, one sent (by God). The Johannine Jesus is, of course, sent by God and in one passage may even be referred to as *shaliach* ('apostle'; cf. 13.16). God promises to be 'with' Moses (§3), which is commonly said of and by Jesus in the Fourth Gospel (for example, 3.2). God also promises Moses that he 'will do' whatever Moses should wish (§3). Similarly, Jesus promises his disciples that whatever they ask in his name his heavenly Father 'will do it' (14.13; cf. 15.7). The rabbinic statement that the Torah was 'given through the hands of Moses' (§4) parallels the Prologue's statement that Torah was 'given through Moses' (1.17). Statement §6 in *Memar Marqa* parallels the Johannine idea that to believe in Jesus is to believe in God (12.44; cf. 14.1). The identification of Moses' words and speech with those of the Lord (§7, §8) parallels many statements in the Fourth Gospel (for example, 3.34; 8.47; 12.49-50; 14.10). In statement §8 God is described as 'the doer of all that [Moses] manifested'. Similarly, Jesus tells his disciples that through his ministry 'the works of God might be manifest' (9.3-4). Perhaps it is only coincidental, but Jesus manifests the work of God by sending the blind man to wash in the pool called 'Sent' ('Siloam'/ 'Shiloach'; 9.7). Statement §9, which describes Moses as '*shaliach* of the true [God]', parallels Johannine Christology: 'I have not come of my own accord; he who sent me is true' (7.28); 'this is eternal life, that they know you the only true God, and Jesus Christ whom you have sent' (17.3). In sum, it appears that the Johannine portrait of Jesus as one sent from God, who speaks the words of God, who does the deeds of God, and who returns to the one who sent him seems to reflect Jewish *shaliach* traditions.

In a recent study Anthony Harvey has welcomed Bühner's study: 'The work of Bühner has offered a strong case for believing that [the Fourth Evangelist] was also familiar with the basic technicalities of the Jewish law of agency, and that he exploited this terminology in order to clarify the relationship of Jesus with his heavenly father'.[1] Harvey turns his attention to the question why the Fourth Evangelist stopped short of explicitly calling Jesus *shaliach* (which in Greek would be ἀπόστολος). In 13.16 ('the slave is not greater than his master, nor is the apostle greater than he who sent him') the evangelist probably has implied that Jesus is God's *shaliach*. Harvey suspects that it was because the evangelist wished to portray Jesus as the manifestation of God, hence the preference for the 'Son'. Harvey cites what could be an important passage in Josephus, who says that the office of the messenger (Josephus uses the word ἄγγελος) 'can bring God's presence (ἐμφάνεια) to human beings and reconcile enemies to one another' (*Ant.* 15.5.3 §136). Harvey wonders if the Fourth Evangelist has understood the office of the *shaliach* in a similar way and has applied it to his Christology accordingly. One thinks of Jn 14.21-22 where Jesus says that he will disclose (ἐμφανίζειν) himself to the one who loves him and keeps his commandments. The second part of Josephus' description, that of reconciliation, coheres with what the Johannine Jesus subsequently says: 'Peace I leave with you' (14.27).

Summary

The opening five verses of the Prologue offer an interpretation of Jesus against the backdrop of creation. He is God's *logos*, existing from eternity, through whom the cosmos came into existence. The Johannine *logos* appears to be informed principally from the function of 'word' in the Old Testament, as especially seen in the Wisdom writings such as Proverbs, Sirach and the Wisdom of Solomon, and in speculative tradition, such as what we have in Philo. Rabbinic midrash and interpretive traditions in the targums also cohere with certain interpretive features presupposed by the Prologue. In fact, it is possible

1. A.E. Harvey, 'Christ as Agent', in L.D. Hurst and N.T. Wright (eds.), *The Glory of Christ in the New Testament: Studies in Christology* (Oxford: Clarendon Press, 1987), p. 242.

that the Johannine *logos* may also represent a late first-century analogue of the targumic *memra*. This is not to say that the Johannine *logos* is identical to the targumic *memra*, or that the *memra* must be understood as a hypostasis. Rather, the coherence between the Prologue's *logos* and some of the functions of the *memra*, as variously presented in the targums, suggests that the former may reflect the latter, as it was coming to expression in the synagogue of the late first century.

The comparison between Jesus and Moses in the final five verses of the Prologue adumbrates a complex Moses/Sinai tradition that is developed throughout the Fourth Gospel. Although the text is never explicitly cited, Jesus is probably to be understood as the promised 'Prophet like Moses' (cf. Deut. 18.15-19).[1] Although like Moses in many ways—a giver of water, bread, and a new commandment—Jesus is superior to Moses. He is superior probably because it is through him that the *logos* speaks and acts. Like Moses, Jesus is presented as God's 'agent', a *shaliach* who speaks and acts with God's authority. But unlike Moses, Jesus is the *shaliach par excellence*, in whom God's Word, Torah, Wisdom and Glory have taken up residence and are revealed.

---

1. Pace H.A. Fischel ('Jewish Gnosticism in the Fourth Gospel', *JBL* 65 [1946], pp. 157-74), the Johannine usage of 'the Prophet' has nothing to do with Gnosticism.

Chapter 5

THE PROVENANCE OF JOHN AND THE PROLOGUE

In view of the parallels with Jewish–Hellenistic Wisdom writings and
related writings, such as those by Philo, including some targumic
elements, the most likely provenance of the Fourth Gospel and its
Prologue is the synagogue, and likely the synagogue of the Diaspora.
Further supporting evidence for the synagogue background is found
throughout the Gospel proper: (1) there is expression given to certain
rabbinic terms and methods; (2) there are important parallels with
specific targumic traditions and rabbinic midrashim; (3) explicit
reference is made to the expulsion of Christians from the synagogue;
(4) the use of the Old Testament appears to reflect an apologetic
designed to present Jesus as Israel's Messiah and to deflect skepticism
and criticism arising from the synagogue; (5) there are also important
parallels with Qumran that suggest that portions of the Johannine
tradition had their origin in Palestine. I will begin with the parallels
with Qumran and other Palestinian features. The first four topics will
then be considered in the order given above.

Parallels with Qumran and Other Palestinian Features

There are several significant parallels between the Fourth Gospel and
the writings discovered near Qumran. Probably the most important
parallels are those that express or presuppose dualism. The dualism
found in the Manual of Discipline has especially drawn scholarly
attention.[1] Contrasts between light and darkness, good deeds and evil

1. See especially J.H. Charlesworth, 'A Critical Comparison of the Dualism in
1QS 3.13–4.26 and the "Dualism" Contained in the Gospel of John', *NTS* 15
(1969), pp. 389-418; repr. in Charlesworth (ed.), *John and the Dead Sea Scrolls*,
pp. 76-106; J. Becker, 'Beobachtungen zum Dualismus im Johannesevangelium',
ZNW 65 (1974), pp. 71-87. Becker discusses the Prologue on pp. 73-78. For a

deeds, truth and falsehood are found in 1QS 3.13–4.26. A sample of the passage reads as follows:

> [God] allotted unto humanity two spirits that he should walk in them until the time of His visitation; they are the spirits of truth and perversity.[1] The origin of truth is in a fountain of light, and the origin of perversity is from a fountain of darkness. Dominion over all the sons of righteousness is in the hand of the Prince of light; they walk in the ways of light. All dominion over the sons of perversity is in the hand of the Angel of darkness; they walk in the ways of darkness (1QS 3.18-21).

Although Johannine and Qumranian dualism are not identical, there is significant similarity. Some of the most important parallels have been presented by James Charlesworth: 'Spirit of truth' (Jn 14.17; 15.26; 16.13; 1 Jn 4.6; cf. 1QS 3.18-19; 4.21, 23); 'Holy Spirit' (Jn 14.26; 20.22; cf. 1QS 4.21); 'sons of light' (Jn 12.36; cf. 1QS 3.13, 24, 25); 'eternal life' (Jn 3.15, 16, 36; 4.14, 36; 5.24; cf. 1QS 4.7); 'the light of life' (Jn 8.12; cf. 1QS 3.7); 'walk in darkness' (Jn 8.12; 12.35; cf. 1QS 3.21; 4.11); 'wrath of God' (Jn 3.36; cf. 1QS 4.12); 'eyes of the blind' (Jn 9.39-41; 10.21; cf. 1QS 4.11); 'full of grace' (Jn 1.14; cf. 1QS 4.4, 5); 'the works of God' (Jn 6.28; 9.3; cf. 1QS 4.4); 'men...for their works were evil' (Jn 3.19; cf. 1QS 4.10, 20).[2] To these a few others might be added: 'witness of the truth' (Jn 5.33; 18.37; cf. 1QS 8.6); 'do [or practice] the truth' (Jn 3.21; 1 Jn 1.6; cf. 1QS 1.5; 5.3; 8.2); 'walking in truth' (2 Jn 4; 3 Jn 3; cf. 1QS 4.6, 15); 'living water' (Jn 4.14; cf. CD 19.33-34); darkness overcome by light (Jn 1.5; 1 Jn 2.8; cf. 1QMyst 6).[3] Parallels such as these have led Herbert Braun to conclude that Johannine dualism can be understood

---

broader study on Johannine dualism, see O. Böcher, *Der johanneische Dualismus im Zusammenhang des nachbiblischen Judentums* (Gütersloh: Gerd Mohn, 1965).

1. The discussion of the two 'spirits of truth and perversity' (3.18-19) closely parallels 1 Jn 4.6: 'From this we know the spirit of truth and the spirit of error'.

2. Charlesworth, 'Dualism in 1QS 3.13–4.26', pp. 101-102. See also R.E. Brown, 'The Qumran Scrolls and the Johannine Gospel and Epistles', *CBQ* 17 (1955), pp. 403-19, 559-74; repr. in K. Stendahl (ed.), *The Scrolls and the New Testament* (New York: Harper & Row, 1957; London: SCM Press, 1958), pp. 183-207, esp. pp. 184-95.

3. Brown, 'The Qumran Scrolls and the Johannine Gospel and Epistles', pp. 196-99; M.-E. Boismard, 'The First Epistle of John and the Writings of Qumran', in Charlesworth (ed.), *John and the Dead Sea Scrolls*, pp. 156-65; W.S. LaSor, *The Dead Sea Scrolls and the New Testament* (Grand Rapids: Eerdmans, 1972), pp. 197-98.

as having derived from Palestine (as opposed to Syria or some other place where Gnostic dualism might have existed).[1] Several other parallels between Johannine and Qumranian diction and concepts have been observed. 1. The relationship between water and spirit (Jn 3.5; 7.37-38) may reflect Qumran's great interest in baptism and the Spirit: 'He will cleanse him of all wicked deeds by means of a Holy Spirit; like purifying waters He will sprinkle upon the Spirit of truth' (1QS 4.19-21; cf. Isa. 44.4).[2] 2. The respective manners in which Jesus and the Teacher of Righteousness (especially in 1QH) refer to themselves and to their distinctive missions have certain features in common.[3] 3. Otto Betz and others have pointed out the similarities between the Johannine paraclete and Qumran's 'Holy Spirit' (1QS 4.21), which is also called the 'Spirit of truth' (1QS 3.18; 4.21, 23).[4] 4. Johannine interpretation of Jesus' body as the Temple (Jn 2.19-21) resembles Qumran's concept of a spiritual temple: 'He has commanded a sanctuary of men to be built for Himself' (4QFlor 1.6).

In view of these similarities and parallels Charlesworth and others have seconded Braun's judgment that Palestine is the 'milieu which gave birth to John'.[5] This is not to say, however, that the Fourth

1. H. Braun, *Qumran und das Neue Testament*, I (2 vols.; Tübingen: Mohr [Paul Siebeck], 1966), p. 98.

2. Brown, *Gospel according to John*, I, p. 140; *idem*, 'The Qumran Scrolls and the Johannine Gospel and Epistles', pp. 202-203.

3. J.L. Price, 'Light from Qumran upon Some Aspects of Johannine Theology', in Charlesworth (ed.), *John and the Dead Sea Scrolls*, pp. 9-37, esp. pp. 30-37.

4. O. Betz, *Der Paraklet: Fürsprecher im häretischen Spätjudentum, im Johannesevangelium und in neu gefundenen gnostischen Schriften* (AGJU, 2; Leiden: Brill, 1963); A.R.C. Leaney, 'The Johannine Paraclete and the Qumran Scrolls', in Charlesworth (ed.), *John and the Dead Sea Scrolls*, pp. 38-61.

5. Charlesworth, 'Dualism in 1QS 3.13–4.26', p. 105. See also W.F. Albright, 'Recent Discoveries in Palestine and the Gospel of John', in Davies and Daube (eds.), *The Background of the New Testament and its Eschatology*, pp. 153-71; W.H. Brownlee, 'Whence the Gospel According to John?', in Charlesworth (ed.), *John and the Dead Sea Scrolls*, pp. 166-94, esp. pp. 179-85; G. Quispel, 'Qumran, John and Jewish Christianity', in Charlesworth (ed.), *John and the Dead Sea Scrolls*, pp. 137-55; J.A.T. Robinson, 'The New Look on the Fourth Gospel', in K. Aland *et al.* (eds.), *Studia Evangelica: Papers Presented to the International Congress on 'The Four Gospels' in 1957* (TU, 73; Berlin: Akademie Verlag, 1959), pp. 338-50; repr. in J.A.T. Robinson, *Twelve New Testament Studies* (SBT, 34; London: SCM Press, 1962), pp. 94-106; K. Schubert, *Die Gemeinde vom Toten Meer: Ihre Entsteh-*

Gospel was composed in Palestine. Scholars have rarely suggested that.[1] If that were the case, it would be hard to understand why the evangelist translated Hebrew and Aramaic words that would have been well known to Palestinians (for example, ῥαββί, 1.38; Μεσσίας, 1.41; 4.25; Κηφᾶς, 1.42; Σιλωάμ, 9.7; Γαββαθά, 19.13; Γολγοθά, 19.17; ῥαββουνί, 20.16). The evangelist's habit of translating such words indicates that his community was made up of people who did not know Hebrew and Aramaic and were not familiar with Palestine, particularly Jerusalem. (This linguistic knowledge also adds to the probability that the author was from Palestine.) As suggested above, the provenance of the composition of the Fourth Gospel was in all likelihood the synagogue of the Diaspora, although by the time the Gospel was written the Johannine community had already been put out of the synagogue (cf. 9.22; 12.42; 16.2; see discussion below). This suggestion is supported, furthermore, by the question posed in Jn 7.35: 'He is not about to go into the Diaspora of Greek-speaking people (οἱ Ἕλληνες) and teach them, is he?' (cf. 12.20).[2] Nigel Turner has concluded, moreover, that Johannine style is the 'Jewish Greek' of the LXX and the synagogue.[3]

---

ung und ihre Lehren (Munich: Reinhardt, 1958), pp. 131-33; ET *The Dead Sea Community: Its Origin and Teachings* (London: A. & C. Black, 1959), pp. 151-54. Schubert believes that 'Qumran research' has proven 'the Jewish origin of the Gospel of John conclusively' (p. 152). H.M. Teeple ('Qumran and the Origin of the Fourth Gospel', *NovT* 4 [1960], pp. 6-25) has disagreed with Schubert, arguing that the parallels with Qumran are insignificant, that Johannine traditions probably are not Palestinian, and that the author probably was a Gentile. Research of the last three decades, however, has moved closer to the position of Schubert.

1. It is usually assumed that it was written in the Diaspora; cf. Brownlee, 'Whence John?', pp. 187-91; Hengel, *The Johannine Question*, p. 110.

2. Commentators are divided as to what the evangelist means by the 'Greek-speaking' people, either Greek-speaking Jews or Greek-speaking Gentiles (or both).

3. N. Turner, *A Grammar of New Testament Greek. IV. Style* (Edinburgh: T. & T. Clark, 1976), pp. 64-79. See also G.D. Kilpatrick, 'What John Tells us about John', in A.S. Geyser *et al.* (eds.), *Studies in John* (NovTSup, 24; Leiden: Brill, 1970), p. 75-87, esp. pp. 79-87. Kilpatrick concludes that the Fourth Evangelist's Greek is the Greek of the LXX, not of the Hermetica. For studies that understand the language of the Prologue as an attempt to accommodate a Hellenistic audience, see Dodd, *Interpretation of the Fourth Gospel*, p. 296; A. Harnack, 'Über das Verhältnis des Prologs des vierten Evangeliums zum ganzen Werk', *ZTK* 2 (1892), pp. 189-231, esp. p. 230; G.W. MacRae, 'The Fourth Gospel and *Religionsgeschichte*', *CBQ* 32 (1970), pp. 13-24.

Independent and accurate knowledge of Jerusalem and its environs adds to our conviction that the author of the Fourth Gospel hailed from Palestine. The evangelist is familiar with Palestinian topography (3.22-23; 11.18). He knows that at the time of Jesus' ministry the Herodian Temple had been in construction for 46 years (2.20). He knows that Sychar is near Jacob's well (4.5-6). He knows of the hatred between Jews and Samaritans (4.9; 8.48). He knows that the Samaritan holy site is Mount Gerizim (4.20). He is familiar with issues relating to Jewish–Samaritan religious controversy (4.20-24).[1] He refers to Hanukkah ('feast of Dedication') and knows that it is celebrated in winter (10.22-23). Apparently he is also aware that on the last day of Sukkot ('feast of Tabernacles') water is poured out in front of the Altar (7.2, 14, 37-38).[2] The evangelist, furthermore, has knowledge of the principal figures involved in Jesus' arrest, interrogation and crucifixion. All of these facts lend to the conviction that the Johannine tradition does indeed derive from Palestine.[3] Although advanced thirty years ago, Dodd's conclusion that lying behind the Fourth Gospel is an ancient and independent tradition still seems wholly justified.[4]

---

1.   O. Betz, '"To Worship God in Spirit and in Truth": Reflections on John 4,20-26', in *Jesus, der Messias Israels: Aufsätze zur biblischen Theologie* (WUNT, 42; Tübingen: Mohr [Paul Siebeck], 1987), pp. 420-38, esp. pp. 423-29.

2.   For these points and others, see Hengel, *The Johannine Question*, p. 111.

3.   See Hengel, *The Johannine Question*, pp. 209-10 n. 15; J.A.T. Robinson, 'The Destination and Purpose of St John's Gospel', *NTS* 6 (1960), pp. 117-31; repr. in Robinson, *Twelve New Testament Studies*, pp. 107-25, esp. p. 124. According to W. Michaelis, *Einleitung in das Neue Testament* (Bern: Haller, 3rd edn, 1961), p. 123: 'It may now be said that the Palestinian character of the Gospel of John has become so clear that attempts to promote another provenance really should cease'.

An interesting alternative has been proposed by K. Wengst (*Bedrängte Gemeinde und verherrlichter Christus: Der historische Ort des Johannesevangeliums als Schlüssel zu seiner Interpretation* [BTSt, 5; Neukirchen–Vluyn: Neukirchener Verlag, 2nd edn, 1983]) who argues that the Johannine community was located in Trachonitis and Batanaea, which were ruled by King Agrippa II in the 80s, and was being intensely persecuted, even martryred, by Pharisees (cf. Jn 16.2). Several problems, however, attend this interpretation. Hengel (*The Johannine Question*, p. 115) thinks that this thesis is 'utterly improbable'.

4.   C.H. Dodd, *Historical Tradition in the Fourth Gospel* (Cambridge: Cambridge University Press, 1963), p. 423.

Rabbinic Terms and Methods

The general language of discipleship is characteristic of the academic and pedagogical world of first-century Judaism. The closest followers of Jesus are called 'disciples' (μαθηταί/תלמידים).[1] This language, of course, is quite common in the Synoptic Gospels (for example, Mt. 5.1; Mk 2.15, 18; Lk. 6.40), so one can hardly say that it is distinctive of the Fourth Evangelist (for example, Jn 2.12; 3.25; 6.3). There is, however, one expression that is. The Pharisees say to the former blind man: 'You are the disciple of that one; but we are disciples of Moses' (Jn 9.28). The claim to be 'disciples of Moses' (τοῦ Μωϋσέως μαθηταί), which with respect to the New Testament Gospels occurs only in John, was apparently characteristic of the Pharisees. In *b. Yom.* 4a one finds a *baraita* where the Pharisaic (as opposed to the Sadducean) scholars are called תלמידיו של משה.[2] Elsewhere God is blessed for having given the Torah 'through Moses our teacher (רבינו)' (*Sifre Deut.* §305 [on 31.14]; cf. *Lev. R.* 20.6 [on Lev. 16.1]; *Deut. R.* 8.6 [on Deut. 30.11-12]; *Eccl. R.* 7.5 §1). In the Gospels, especially in John, Jesus is also called rabbi (ῥαββί, cf. Mt. 23.7, 8; Jn 1.38, 49; 3.2, 26; 6.25) or rabbouni (ῥαββουνί, cf. Mk 10.51; Jn 20.16),[3] although the Judeans wonder 'how does he know letters not having learned (μανθάνειν)?' (Jn 7.15).

Pharisaic or early rabbinic exegesis is known to the Fourth Evangelist as well. Twice there is reference made to 'searching' the Scripture. The first occurrence is found on the lips of Jesus: 'You search (ἐραυνᾶτε) the Scriptures, because you suppose that in them you have life; these are what testify concerning me' (5.39). This comment refers to rabbinic interpretation known as 'midrash'.[4] The

1.   Both the Greek and the Hebrew come from the verb 'to learn' (μανθάνειν/ למד). From the Hebrew we have 'Talmud', that is, that which is to be learned.

2.   Barrett, *Gospel according to St John*, p. 362; Beasley-Murray, *John*, p. 158; Brown, *Gospel according to John*, p. 374; Carson, *Gospel according to John*, pp. 373-74; Dodd, *Interpretation of the Fourth Gospel*, pp. 77, 81; Lindars, *Gospel of John*, p. 348; Schnackenburg, *Gospel according to St John*, II, p. 251.

3.   Dodd, *Interpretation of the Fourth Gospel*, p. 77. See also *Targ. Ps.-J.* Deut. 32.3; 34.5, where several times we are told that 'Moses taught' the people of Israel various important laws, customs and rituals.

4.   Barrett, *Gospel according to St John*, I, p. 267; Beasley-Murray, *John*, pp. 78-79; Brown, *Gospel according to John*, I, p. 225; Carson, *Gospel according to*

principal purpose of searching the Scriptures was to find life. This idea is rooted in Scripture itself, for keeping the commandments of Torah meant life: 'You shall therefore keep my statutes and my ordinances, by doing which a man shall live' (Lev. 18.5; cf. Bar. 4.1-2). Hence, the principal aim of 'building a fence' around Torah (*Ab.* 1.1) was to gain life. According to Hillel, 'If a man...has gained for himself the words of the Law he has gained for himself life in the world to come' (*Ab.* 2.7).[1] The Johannine saying undoubtedly reflects this perspective, which evidently reached back well into the early first century, if not earlier, and apparently was not only held by Hillel, but by Jesus also. After the Law is summed up by the Two Great Commandments, Jesus tells the legist: 'Do this and you will live' (cf. Lk. 10.28). Because Jesus' answer was to a question that asked how to obtain eternal life (Lk. 10.25), it is probable that the eschatological

---

John, p. 263; Hoskyns, *Fourth Gospel*, I, p. 305. The Greek word ἐραυνᾶν in all probability reflects the very definition of 'midrash' itself (from שׁדר, 'to search'; with the noun מדרשׁ, literally a 'searching'). The verb דרשׁ occurs in a variety of contexts in the Old Testament meaning 'to seek', 'to inquire' or 'to investigate'. Scripture speaks of seeking God's will (2 Chron. 17.4; 22.9; 30.19; Ps. 119.10), making inquiry of God through prophetic oracle (1 Sam. 9.9; 1 Kgs 22.8; 2 Kgs 3.11; Jer. 21.2), or investigating a matter (Deut. 13.14; 19.18; Judg. 6.29; cf. 1QS 6.24; 8.26). The nominal form, מדרשׁ, occurs in the Old Testament twice meaning 'story', 'book' and possibly 'commentary' (2 Chron. 13.22; 24.27, cf. RSV). In later usage there is a shift from seeking God's will through prophetic oracle to seeking God's will through study of Scripture. In later traditions we are told that Ezra the scribe 'set his heart to search the Law of the Lord' (Ezra 7.10). Other texts convey similar meanings: 'Great are the works of the Lord, studied by all who have pleasure in them' (Ps. 111.2); 'I have sought thy precepts' (Ps. 119.45; cf. vv. 94, 155); 'Observe and seek out all the commandments of the Lord' (1 Chron. 28.8). Although this 'searching' of God's Law should not in these passages be understood as exegesis in a strict sense, it is only a small step to the later explicit exegetical reference of midrash: 'This is the study (מדרשׁ) of the Law' (1QS 8.15); 'The interpretation (מדרשׁ) of "Blessed is the man..." [cf. Ps. 1.1]' (4QFlor 1.14). Indeed, the Teacher of Righteousness is called the 'searcher of the Law' (CD 6.7). Philo urges his readers to join him in searching (ἐραυνᾶν = דרשׁ) Scripture (*Det. Pot. Ins.* 17 §57; 39 §141; *Cher.* 5 §14). In rabbinic writings midrash becomes standard and its practice as an exegetical method was consciously considered. For the seven rules (or *middot*) of Hillel the Elder cf. *t. Sanh.* 7.11; *ARN* (A) §37. All of these rules are represented in the Gospels.

1. In one midrash, Moses refers to 'the Torah, the whole of which is life' (*Deut. R.* 9.9 [on Deut. 31.14]).

interpretation found in the targum preserves an ancient interpretation of Lev. 18.5: 'if one practices them, he will live by them in the future world' (cf. *Targ. Onq.* Lev. 18.5; also in *Targum Pseudo-Jonathan*, but adding 'with the righteous ones'). This targumic paraphrase coheres with the midrash found in the Tannaic commentary on Leviticus, where it is reasoned that since people die in this life, 'live by them' must refer to life in the world to come (*Sifra Lev.* §193 [on 18.5]). Both the synoptic and Johannine traditions seem to reflect this understanding of the passage (cf. Jn 12.50). Thus, the Johannine statement, 'You search the Scriptures', is not merely a formal parallel with rabbinic exegetical method, but a reflection of a significant struggle between the Johannine community and the synagogue over soteriology. Is eternal life found in Torah or is it found in Christ?

The second example occurs in the context of a dispute among the religious leaders. Because he has defended Jesus, Nicodemus ('the teacher of Israel', according to Jn 3.10) is told, 'Search (ἐραύνησον) and see that a prophet does not arise from Galilee' (7.52). Once again this is a clear reference to the rabbinic practice of searching Scripture. In this instance the question at issue is the origin of a prophet (or 'the' prophet [Jn 7.40]), and probably, from the evangelist's point of view, the origin of the Messiah. Since literally this statement is incorrect (Jonah and Nahum were from Galilee, and Eliezer, a contemporary of the Fourth Evangelist, believed that every tribe of Israel had produced prophets; cf. *b. Suk.* 27b) Barrett thinks that what we have here is an indication of the evangelist's lack of acquaintance with Judaism.[1] On the contrary, I think that precisely the opposite is the case. The point of this inaccurate statement is to raise the question of the origin of Jesus. On one level, Bethlehem is hinted at (cf. Mic. 5.1[2e]; Jn 7.42), which conforms with at least one aspect of messianic expectation (cf. *Targ. Mic.* 5.1: 'from you shall come forth before me the Messiah'[2]). On another level, it hints at Jesus' heavenly origin. This is likely another instance of the evangelist's use of irony.[3]

There are also examples of early rabbinic modes of thought and

---

1. Barrett, *Gospel according to St John*, p. 333.

2. See also *Targ. Ps.-J.* Gen. 35.21; *y. Ber.* 2.4. The antiquity of the tradition is attested by Mt. 2.5-6.

3. Beasley-Murray, *John*, p. 121; Carson, *Gospel according to John*, pp. 332-33; Lindars, *Gospel of John*, p. 305. See P.D. Duke, *Irony in the Fourth Gospel* (Atlanta: John Knox, 1985).

typical expressions and issues. Claiming God as one's witness (Jn 5.32), which is an early practice (cf. Wis. 1.6; Rom. 1.9; 1 Thess. 2.5), is paralleled in the rabbinic writings (cf. *Ab.* 4.22; *Exod. R.* 1.15 [on Exod. 1.17]). When the disciples ask Jesus, 'Who sinned, this man or his parents?' (Jn 9.2), a question has been raised that was of interest to rabbis as well. In a few places the possibility of pre-natal sin is actually pondered (cf. *Gen. R.* 63.6 [on Gen. 25.22] and *Lev. R.* 27.6 [on Lev. 22.27], where speculation concerning the pre-natal struggle of Esau and Jacob is entertained). Jesus' asseveration that 'we must work the deeds of the one who sent me while it is day' (Jn 9.4) is similar to Rabbi Simeon ben Eleazar's admonition to work while one has opportunity and life (cf. *b. Šab.* 151b). Rabbi Tarphon's statement that 'the day is short and the task is great' (*Ab.* 2.15) should also be noted (cf. Jn 4.35). The words of the risen Jesus to doubting Thomas that they are blessed who do not see but believe (Jn 20.29) are similar to Rabbi Yohanan's rebuke of a skeptical student: 'Had you not seen, would you not have believed?' (*b. B. Bat.* 75a; cf. *b. Sanh.* 100a; *Midr. Ps.* 87.2 [on Ps. 87.3]; *Pes. R.* 32.4: 'Had I not beheld with mine own eyes what you are talking about, I still would not believe you'). Consider also the following saying: 'The proselyte who converts is more beloved than Israel when they stood at Mount Sinai. Why? Because, if they had not seen the thunder and lightning, the mountains trembling, and the noise of the trumpets, they would not have accepted the Torah. But this proselyte, who did not see one of them, came, resigned himself to the Holy One, and took upon himself the Kingdom of Heaven. Is there one of you more lovable than this one?' (*Midr. Tanḥ.* [B] Gen 3.6 [on Gen. 14.1]).[1]

There are instances in the Fourth Gospel of extended midrash. Peder Borgen has showed that the bread discourse in Jn 6.31-51 is a rabbinic-like midrash on Ps. 78.24, which is itself a reference to the giving of the manna (Exod. 16.4, 15; Num. 11.8).[2] He finds that the Fourth Evangelist has constructed his exegetical discourses according to the homiletical structures found in the midrashim (and in Philo as

1.　J.T. Townsend, *Midrash Tanhuma* (Hoboken, NJ: Ktav, 1989), p. 66.

2.　P. Borgen, 'Observations on the Midrashic Character of John 6', *ZNW* 54 (1963), pp. 232-40; *idem*, *Bread from Heaven: An Exegetical Study of the Concept of Manna in the Gospel of John and the Writings of Philo* (NovTSup, 10; Leiden: Brill, 1965).

well).[1] Several features commonly found in rabbinic midrash are present in the bread discourse.[2] Some of these details are particularly relevant for the concerns of the present study. For instance, Rabbi Joshua, on the meaning of Prov. 9.5 ('Come, eat of my bread' [= wisdom]), said: '"Bread" means the Torah' (*Gen. R.* 70.5 [on 28.20]). This interpretation coheres with the bread discourse: 'Moses has not given to you the bread from heaven, but my Father gives you the true bread from heaven' (6.32). (Further details will be pointed out below.) Borgen finds similar haggadic features in the Johannine Prologue.[3]

Another example of extended midrash may be found in John 12, which appears to be interpreting the Triumphal Entry through the lens of the Suffering Servant of Isaiah 52–53.[4] There are several points of convergence. 1. The language of glorification and exaltation (δοξάζειν in vv. 6, 23; ὑψοῦν in vv. 32, 34) probably owes its origin to the LXX's use of δοξάζειν and ὑψοῦν in the opening line of the Servant Song (Isa. 52.13), though some have pointed to the Aramaic version.[5] δοξάζειν is distinctive to the Greek version and may suggest that the evangelist either derived the word from the Isaianic passage or at least intends his readers to see the connection. In both Greek and Hebrew ὑψοῦν has the double meaning of (literal) elevation and (figurative) exaltation. Just as the Servant is to be lifted up and glorified, so Jesus is to be lifted up (both literally and

1. Borgen, *Bread from Heaven*, pp. 28-58.
2. Borgen, *Bread from Heaven*, pp. 59-98; cf. A. Finkel, *The Pharisees and the Teacher of Nazareth: A Study of their Background, their Halachic and Midrashic Teachings, the Similarities and Differences* (AGJU, 4; Leiden: Brill, 1964), pp. 149-59; G. Richter, 'Die alttestamentlichen Zitate in der Rede vom Himmelsbrot Jn 6,26-51a', in J. Ernst (ed.), *Schriftauslegung: Beiträge zur Hermeneutik des Neuen Testaments und im Neuen Testament* (Munich: Schöningh, 1972), pp. 193-279.
3. P. Borgen, 'Observations on the Targumic Character of the Prologue of John', *NTS* 16 (1970), pp. 288-95.
4. The targum, of course, presents Isa. 52.13–53.12 in an overtly messianic manner (cf. 52.13, 'Behold, my Servant, the Messiah'; cf. 53.10), although how early this interpretation can be assigned is problematic. See Chilton, *The Glory of Israel*, pp. 91-96. Chilton concludes that the portrait of the Servant as a victorious Messiah arose prior to Bar Kokhba. See Levey, *The Messiah: An Aramaic Interpretation*, p. 67. Levey (p. 70) finds 'messianic implications' in the LXX, Vulgate and Peshitta.
5. McNamara, *The New Testament and the Palestinian Targum to the Pentateuch*, pp. 145-49; *idem*, *Targum and Testament*, pp. 143, 163. Barrett (*Gospel according to St John*, p. 214) rightly looks to the LXX.

figuratively) and glorified. It is interesting to note that both occurrences of δοξάζειν (vv. 16, 23) and both occurrences of ὑψοῦν
(vv. 32, 34) are in the form of aorist passives, possibly suggesting
that what was regarded by Isaiah as a future event (the LXX has future
passives) has now, in the understanding of the Fourth Evangelist, been
fulfilled with the arrival of Jesus' 'hour'. It is in this connection that
for the first time Jesus is able to declare, 'the hour has come' (12.33).
2. Jesus' rejection, despite his signs, is explained in terms of quotations from two Isaianic passages (Isa. 53.1 and 6.10) in Jn 12.37-43.
Just as Isaiah's message was doomed to fall upon deaf ears and blind
eyes, so too would the Christian proclamation be received by the
Jewish people.[1] Despite the vision of Christ's glory (that is, Isa. 6.1-5;
cf. Jn 12.41), Isaiah prophesies an obdurate response (cf. Isa. 53.1;
6.9-10). 3. The anointing at Bethany (vv. 1-8) may be intended to
illustrate the 'anointing' of the Servant in Isa. 52.14, which in 1QIsa[a]
reads: 'As many were astonished at you, so I anointed his face more
than any man, and his body more than the sons of men'.[2] 4. The
crowd which went out (ἐξῆλθον) of Jerusalem to greet Jesus (12.12-
13) may fulfill the exhortation in Isa. 52.11 to go out (ἐξέλθατε) of
Jerusalem. 5. The jubilant shouting of the people (Jn 12.13) could be
viewed as a fulfillment of Isa. 52.8-9. The return of the Lord to Zion,
as described in Isaiah, could be seen as fulfilled in the return of Jesus
to Jerusalem which he has previously visited. When the people see
Jesus they see the Lord (cf. Jn 12.45, 'the one who sees me sees the
one [that is, the Lord] who sent me'). 6. Hailing the approaching Jesus
as 'king' (see Jn 12.13 where 'king of Israel' is added to the Ps. 118
citation, and Jn 12.14 where Zech. 9.9 is quoted) correlates with Isa.

1.   I might add that it is interesting to note that whereas the New Testament (that
is, all four Gospels and the book of Acts) quotes or paraphrases all or parts of Isa.
6.9-10, thus deriving support from the text for its theologies, Nag Hammadi quotes
it twice and is offended by what it says (cf. *Ap. John* [NHC II, *1*] 22.25-29; *Testim.
Truth* [NHC IX, *3*] 48.8-13). The Gnostics reject this God—a God who would blind
the eyes of his people—identifying him as the evil demiurge that created the physical
cosmos.
2.   W.H. Brownlee (*The Meaning of the Qumran Scrolls for the Bible, with
Special Attention to the Book of Isaiah* [New York: Oxford University Press, 1964],
pp. 204-215) has argued that the term משחת in MT Isa. 52.14 is ambiguous and may
mean either 'marring' or 'anointing'. Both משח ('mar') and משח ('anoint') could have
been seen in משחת (cf. Dan. 9.26). He is convinced that antiquity must be granted to
the reading preserved in 1QIsaiah[a].

52.7 which announces to Zion: 'Your God is King!'[1] The LXX uses the future βασιλεύσει ('He will be king', or 'He will reign'), which lends the passage more readily to the idea of fulfillment. 7. When the Greeks or foreign Jews (Ἕλληνες), who have come to worship at the feast, request to see Jesus (Jn 12.20-21) Isa. 52.10 may here be echoed: 'The Lord has bared his holy arm in the sight of all nations; that all the ends of the earth may see [LXX: 'will see'] the salvation of our God'.[2] Recall too that the name *Jesus* was understood to mean 'the Lord saves' (cf. Mt. 1.21).

Targumic and Midrashic Traditions

There are several areas where Johannine elements and targumic and rabbinic features converge. Of course, in making use of targumic and rabbinic materials one must bear in mind the criteria for assessing documents that postdate the New Testament. (See the discussion of these criteria in Chapters 1 and 4 above.) At this point we shall briefly consider several examples of similar interpretation and several passages that betray a knowledge of Pharisaic or early rabbinic customs and rulings.

Targumic Traditions
There are potentially numerous examples of targumic diction and concepts in the Fourth Gospel. 1. When Jesus' brothers say to him, 'reveal yourself to the world' (Jn 7.4), we may have echoed here the targumic idea of the revelation of the Messiah: 'the King Messiah is destined to reveal himself at the end of days' (*Targ. Ps.-J.* Gen. 35.21; cf. *Targ. Zech.* 3.8; 4.7; 6.12; *Targ. Song* 8.1; *Targ. 1 Chron.* 3.24).[3] 2. The idiom 'taste of death' (Jn 8.52), which is not found in the Hebrew or Greek versions of the Old Testament, is found in the

---

1. The Hebrew reads מלך, 'is king' or 'reigns'.
2. For further discussion of these parallels, see C.A. Evans, 'Obduracy and the Lord's Servant: Some Observations on the Use of the Old Testament in the Fourth Gospel', in C.A. Evans and W.F. Stinespring (eds.), *Early Jewish and Christian Exegesis* (Homage, 10; Atlanta: Scholars Press, 1987), pp. 221-36, esp. pp. 232-36. Recently J. Beutler ('Greeks Come to See Jesus (Jn 12,2f)', *Bib* 71 [1990], pp. 333-47, esp. pp. 335-37) has reached a similar conclusion.
3. McNamara, *Targum and Testament*, p. 140.

targums (cf. *Frag. Targ.* and *Targ. Ps.-J.* Deut. 32.1).[1] 3. In response
to Jesus' cry that the Father glorify his name, 'A voice came from
heaven, "I have glorified it and I shall glorify it again"' (Jn 12.28).
Traditions of the *bat qol* occur in rabbinic writings (cf. *Ab.* 6.2; *t.
Soṭ.* 13.2; *b. Ker.* 5b; *Lev. R.* 6.5 [on Lev. 5.1]; other examples are
considered below), as well as in the targums. But the form and context
of this Johannine example coheres with what is found in the targums:
on the day that Moses died 'a voice fell from heaven', enjoining the
people to behold the great Lawgiver, a man to whom the 'glory of the
Shekinah of the Lord was revealed' (*Targ. Ps.-J.* Deut. 34.5; cf. Jn
12.28).[2] The antiquity of the *bat qol* tradition is witnessed by Josephus
(cf. *Ant.* 13.10.3 §282). 4. Jesus' statement that 'there are many
dwelling places in my Father's house' (Jn 14.2) probably reflects
targumic language: 'The glory of my Shekinah will accompany among
you and will prepare a resting place for you' (*Targ. Neof.* Exod.
33.14; cf. *Targ. Neof.* Gen. 46.28; *Targ. Onq.* and *Neof.* Deut.
1.33).[3] The antiquity of the idea is attested by *1 En.* 39.4-8. 5. The
expression 'cup (of death)' (Jn 18.11), is found in the targums:
'Joseph...put his trust in flesh...which will taste the cup of death'
(*Frag. Targ.* and *Targ. Neof.* Gen. 40.23).[4] 6. The Fourth Gospel's
reference to 'blood and water' that issued forth from the side of Jesus
(19.34) may have been intended as an echo of the tradition that blood
and water issued forth from the rock which Moses struck, a tradition
preserved in the targums (cf. *Targ. Ps.-J.* Num. 20.11).[5]

Several other words and phrases should be noted: *memra*, 'Shekinah/
Dwelling' and 'glory' (Jn 1.14, and the discussion in Chapter 4);
'from the beginning' (Jn 8.44; 15.27; 1 Jn 1.1); 'come and see'
(Jn 4.27); 'sign' (Jn 12.37; 20.30); 'hour (of affliction)' (Jn 12.27);
and to 'bear witness to the truth' (Jn 5.33). All of these words and

---

1. The expression also occurs in Mk 9.1.

2. McNamara, *Targum and Testament*, pp. 113-14. Other examples of the *bat
qol* in the targums include *Targ. Neof.* Gen. 22.10; 38.25-26.

3. Reim, 'Targum und Johannesevangelium', p. 10; McNamara, *Targum and
Testament*, p. 142.

4. R. Le Déaut, 'Targumic Literature and New Testament Interpretation', *BTB* 4
(1974), pp. 243-89, esp. p. 246.

5. Le Déaut, 'Targumic Literature', p. 277. With some hesitation Carson
(*Gospel according to John*, p. 624) mentions Numbers 20 and Exod. 17.6 as
possibly alluded to, though he does not mention the Targum.

phrases constitute typical targumic language.[1]

Johannine comparisons of Jesus with the patriarchs and major Old Testament figures parallel in exegetically significant ways midrashic traditions found in the targumim. Several examples are apparent. 1. Jn 1.26 ('There stands in your midst one whom you do not recognize') and 7.27 ('whenever the Messiah should come no one knows whence he is') may reflect the targumic idea of the hidden Messiah: 'And you, O Messiah of Israel, who have been hidden away because of the sins of the congregation of Zion, the kingdom shall come to you' (*Targ. Mic.* 4.8; cf. *Targ. Zech.* 4.7; 6.12).[2] It is interesting to observe that according to this targumic reading the Messiah has been hidden because of Israel's sins. This aspect coheres with the Johannine Baptist's proclamation that the Coming One will take away the 'sin of the world' (Jn 1.29).

2. When Jesus says that his disciples will see 'heaven opened and the angels of God ascending and descending on the Son of Man' (Jn 1.51), we have coherence with the kind of interpretation preserved in *Frag. Targ.* and *Targ. Neof.* Gen. 28.12 (cf. *Gen. R.* 68.12 [on Gen. 28.12]), in which it is said that the angels ascended and descended upon Jacob (rather than upon the stairway).[3]

3. Jesus' statement that he will build the 'Temple' (Jn 2.19) may

1. Reim, 'Targum und Johannesevangelium', p. 12; McNamara, *Targum and Testament*, pp. 104, 142-44.

2. Translation based on K.J. Cathcart and R.P. Gordon, *The Targum of the Minor Prophets* (ArBib, 14; Wilmington, DE: Michael Glazier, 1989), p. 120. According to Justin Martyr (*Dialogue with Trypho* 8.4; 110.1) the second-century Jew Trypho believed that 'Messiah, even if he be born and actually exist somewhere, is an unknown'. Ideas about the Messiah hidden away apparently existed at least by the end of the first century, as seen in *4 Ezra* 13.51-52: 'no one on earth can see my Son or those who are with him, except in the time of his day', and in *1 En.* 48.6: 'the Chosen One...was concealed in the presence of [the Lord of the Spirits] prior to the creation of the world'. Barrett (*Gospel according to St John*, p. 322), Beasley-Murray (*John*, p. 110), Brown (*Gospel according to John*, I, p. 53), Hoskyns (*Fourth Gospel*, I, p. 361), and Lindars (*Gospel of John*, p. 293) believe that these passages are relevant for the interpretation of the Fourth Gospel. Carson (*Gospel according to John*, pp. 317-18) has doubts. Bultmann (*Gospel of John*, p. 296 n. 4) believes that the Gnostic myth of the mysterious origin of the Revealer is what lies behind Jn 7.27.

3. J.H. Neyrey, 'The Jacob Allusions in Jn 1.51', *CBQ* 44 (1982), pp. 586-605. See also McNamara, *Targum and Testament*, pp. 146-47; C. Rowland, 'Jn 1.51, Jewish Apocalyptic and Targumic Tradition', *NTS* 30 (1984), pp. 498-507.

represent an adaptation of the targumic tradition that Messiah will build the Temple (cf. *Targ. Isa.* 53.5; *Targ. Zech.* 6.12-13),[1] a tradition that probably arose following the destruction of the Second Temple.[2]

4. The exchange between Jesus and the woman at the well of Jacob offers another example of coherence with targumic tradition. Jesus' promise to provide living water that will spring up into eternal life (Jn 4.12-13) is probably a deliberate comparison to the haggadah which claimed that the well surged up during the twenty years that Jacob lived in Haran (*Frag. Targ.* and *Targ. Neof.* Gen. 28.10).[3]

5. The conversation with the Samaritan woman, in which the woman mentions the patriarch Jacob and her fathers' tradition that worship was to take place on Mount Gerizim, concludes with Jesus' statement that the Father seeks 'true worshippers' (Jn 4.20-25). This dialogue is reminiscent of *Targ. Neof.* Deut. 6.5 where Jacob is cited as an example of faithful worship, with Moses adding: 'Follow the true worship of your fathers'.[4]

6. Comparison of Jesus with the 'true bread' in part likely reflects tradition attested in *Neofiti* and *Pseudo-Jonathan*.[5] *Targ. Neof.* Exod. 16.15 reads: 'He [that is, Moses] is the bread which the Lord has given you to eat'.[6] Geza Vermes believes that *Neofiti* has pulled together interpretive traditions partly attested in Josephus, Philo and rabbinic tradition (where manna is variously identified with Moses, Wisdom, Torah or the *logos*).[7] The earliest and fuller attestation is found in

1. Reim, 'Targum und Johannesevangelium', p. 10.

2. Chilton, *Glory of Israel*, pp. 94-96.

3. J.H. Neyrey, 'Jacob Traditions and the Interpretation of Jn 4.10-26', *CBQ* 41 (1979), pp. 419-37. See also A. Jaubert, 'La symbolique du puits de Jacob', in *L'homme devant Dieu* (Théologie, 56; Paris: Aubier, 1963), pp. 63-73; McNamara, *Targum and Testament*, pp. 145-46.

4. McNamara, *Targum and Testament*, pp. 126-27.

5. B.J. Malina, *The Palestinian Manna Tradition: The Manna Tradition in the Palestinian Targums and its Relationship to the New Testament Writings* (AGSU, 7; Leiden: Brill, 1968).

6. G. Vermes, 'He is the Bread: Targum Neofiti Ex. 16.15', in E.E. Ellis and M. Wilcox (eds.), *Neotestamentica et Semitica* (Edinburgh: T. & T. Clark, 1969), pp. 256-63, esp. p. 262.

7. Vermes, 'He is the Bread', pp. 259-62. Philo's identification of the manna as ὁ λόγος θεοῦ (*Leg. All.* 3.59 §§169-70) would, of course, be compatible with Johannine Christology.

John 6, where the manna has been identified with Jesus.[1] According to *Targ. Ps.-J.* Exod. 16.15, which reads differently, Moses describes the manna as 'the bread which had been laid up for [Israel] from the beginning in the heavens on high'. Not only is the bread from 'heaven', which is the idea of Ps. 78.24 (quoted in Jn 6.31), but it is 'from the beginning', which is what the Fourth Evangelist says of the Word (Jn 1.1).

7. The vitriolic exchange between Jesus and the Pharisees (Jn 8.39-47), especially where Jesus calls his opponents descendants of the Devil, who was 'a murderer from the beginning' (v. 44), probably betrays acquaintance with targumic interpretation of the Cain and Abel story (Gen. 4.1-16).[2] According to *Targ. Ps.-J.* Gen. 4.1 and 5.3 Cain was not the son of Adam, but rather was the son of the evil angel Sammael, also known as Satan.[3] Moreover, the statement, 'whenever that one should speak the lie' (v. 44), is likely an allusion to the Devil and his lie in Gen. 3.4 (see also 1 Jn 3.11-15). According to *Targ. Ps.-J.* Gen. 3.4-6 the serpent of the Garden of Eden is none other than Sammael (cf. *3 Bar.* 4.8; 9.7). Nils Dahl and Günter Reim have noted that the Pharisees' wish to stone Jesus (Jn 8.59) was probably understood as a

---

1. Vermes, 'He is the Bread', p. 263.

2. Reim, 'Targum und Johannesevangelium', 9; *idem*, 'Joh. 8.44—Gotteskinder/ Teufelskinder: Wie antijudaistisch ist "Die wohl antijudaistischste Äusserung des NT"?', *NTS* 30 (1984), pp. 619-24; N.A. Dahl, 'Der Erstgeborene Satans und der Vater des Teufels (Polyk. 7.1 und Joh 8.44)', in U. Eickelberg *et al.* (eds.), *Apophoreta* (BZNW, 30; Berlin: Töpelmann, 1964), pp. 70-84, esp. p. 78; Le Déaut, *Message*, pp. 41-42, 44; McNamara, *The New Testament and the Palestinian Targum to the Pentateuch*, pp. 156-60. A similar interpretation (that is, that Cain is a son of the Devil, while Seth is a son of light) is found in Samaritan tradition; cf. A.F.J. Klijn, *Seth in Jewish, Christian and Gnostic Literature* (NovTSup, 46; Leiden: Brill, 1977), pp. 29-33. The antiquity of the Jewish practice of categorizing antagonists and apostates as sons of the Devil (or Beliar/Belial), as opposed to sons of God (or light), is attested by Qumran (cf. 1QS 1.18, 24; 2.5, 19; 1QM 1.1, 5, 13; 4.2; 11.8; 13.2, 4, 11; 14.9; 15.3; 18.1; 1QH 2.16, 22; 3.28, 29, 32; 4.10, 13; 5.25; 6.21; 7.3; CD 4.13, 15; 5.18; 8.2), the *Testaments of the Twelve Patriarchs* (cf. *T. Reub.* 4.11; 6.3; 7.2; *T. Iss.* 6.1; *T. Dan* 1.7; 3.6; 5.6; 6.3; *T. Jos.* 20.2; *T. Benj.* 6.1; 7.1-2), the *Lives of the Prophets* (cf. 4.6, 20; 17.2), and the New Testament itself (cf. 2 Cor. 6.15).

3. J.R. Díaz, 'Targum Palestinense y Nuevo Testamento', *EstBíb* 21 (1962), pp. 337-42; ET 'Palestinian Targum and the New Testament', *NovT* 6 (1963), pp. 75-80; Le Déaut, *Message*, pp. 40-41 n. 95; Bowker, *The Targums and Rabbinic Literature*, pp. 126, 136.

parallel to the manner in which Cain murdered Abel. According to
Targ. Ps.-J. Gen. 4.8 the former 'drove a stone into the forehead' of
the latter and killed him.[1] Jesus' comment implies that the attitudes
and actions of his opponents are like those of Cain, whose real father
was the Devil.[2]

8. According to the targums, Abraham saw Israel's future, its
domination by the four world powers, the final downfall of Rome
(*Frag. Targ.* Gen. 15.12; cf. *Targ. Isa.* 43.12: 'I declared to Abraham
your father what was about to come...just as I swore to him between
the pieces'), and the day of judgment, including Gehenna prepared for
the wicked (*Frag. Targ.* Gen. 15.17).[3] This tradition coheres with
Jesus' statement: 'Abraham your father rejoiced to see my day' (Jn
8.56). Speculations that Abraham was granted visions of the future are
early, as seen in the *Apocalypse of Abraham* and the *Testament of
Abraham*, both of which probably originated in Hebrew and in Palestine in the first century (cf. *4 Ezra* 3.14; *2 Bar.* 4.4). (See also the
midrashic traditions noted below.) The statement that Abraham
'rejoiced' may also reflect targumic language (cf. *Targ. Onq.* Gen.
17.17).

9. Failure to believe in Jesus, despite his many signs, is explained by
appeal to Isa. 53.1: 'Lord, who has believed in our report? To whom
has the arm of the Lord been revealed?' (Jn 12.37-38). Although the
Fourth Evangelist has quoted the LXX in this instance, his application
of the passage to Jesus may indicate that the messianic interpretation
of Isaiah 52–53, as seen in the targums (cf. *Targ. Isa.* 52.13; 53.10),
was known to him.[4]

10. When the Fourth Evangelist states that 'Isaiah said this when [or
because] he saw his glory' (Jn 12.41, following the quotation of Isa.
6.10 in Jn 12.40) the Aramaic paraphrase of Isa. 6.1 and 6.5 is probably in view: 'I saw the glory of the Lord' (instead of the reading, 'I

---

1. Reim, 'Targum und Johannesevangelium', p. 9.

2. Reim ('Joh. 8.44–Gotteskinder/Teufelskinder', p. 624) rightly concludes that
Jn 8.44 is not anti-Semitic, but one of the most misunderstood and misapplied
statements of the New Testament.

3. Reim, 'Targum und Johannesevangelium', p. 11; McNamara, *Targum and
Testament*, pp. 144-45.

4. On the antiquity of the messianic interpretation of Isaiah 52–53, see Chilton,
The Glory of Israel, pp. 86-96.

saw the Lord', as found in the Hebrew and Greek).[1]

11. The Fourth Evangelist cites Zech. 12.10 ('they will look on him whom they pierced') as fulfilled in the piercing of Jesus' side (Jn 19.34-37). Only in the targums (at least according to Codex Reuchlinianus) is this passage paraphrased in an overtly messianic sense: 'And they will look to me and will inquire of me why the gentiles pierced the Messiah son of Ephraim'.[2] According to *b. Suk.* 52a this was the interpretation of Rabbi Dosa (second century), which if correct would argue for its antiquity.[3]

Midrashic Traditions

There are several interpretive points of convergence between the Fourth Gospel and midrashic traditions. 1. Jesus' statement that he and his Father are continuously working (Jn 5.17) coheres with the rabbinic interpretation of Gen. 2.2-3 (cf. *Gen. R.* 11.10 [on Gen. 2.3]; *Exod. R.* 30.9 [on Exod. 21.1]). The antiquity of this interpretation is attested in Philo (cf. *Leg. All.* 1.3 §6; *Cher.* 26 §87-90). 2. The bread discourse in John 6 reveals points of coherence with early rabbinic interpretation of manna traditions (cf. *Mek.* on Exod. 16.4 [*Vayassa'* §3]; *Gen. R.* 70.5 [on Gen. 28.20]; *Exod. R.* 25.2 [on Exod. 16.4]). Again, at points there is convergence with Philo's interpretation (cf. *Vit. Mos.* 1.36 §201-202; 2.48 §267). 3. The enigmatic saying in Jn 7.37-39 ('rivers of living water will flow from his belly...now this he spoke concerning the Spirit') may be clarified in part by the equation of the well that waters the flock with God's Spirit (cf. *Gen. R.* 70.8 [on Gen. 29.1]).[4] 4. When the Johannine Jesus states that Abraham saw his day and rejoiced (Jn 8.56), we could have here an allusion to interpretations of Gen. 15.10-11, where the dismembered animals were thought to symbolize the Messiah's coming victory (*Gen. R.* 44.22 [on

1.   Barrett, *Gospel according to St John*, p. 432; Brown, *Gospel according to John*, I, pp. 486-87; Carson, *Gospel according to John*, p. 449; Schnackenburg, *Gospel according to St John*, II, p. 416; McNamara, *Targum and Testament*, pp. 99-100; Chilton, *The Glory of Israel*, p. 76.

2.   Reim, 'Targum und Johannesevangelium', p. 9; *idem*, *Studien*, pp. 54-55.

3.   See Cathcart and Gordon, *The Targum of the Minor Prophets*, p. 218 n. 28. The identification of the Messiah as the 'son of Ephraim' may represent late tradition, but this does necessarily mean that the messianic interpretation of Zech. 12.10 is itself late.

4.   See G.M. Burge, *The Anointed Community: The Holy Spirit in the Johannine Tradition* (Grand Rapids: Eerdmans, 1987), p. 92 n. 183.

Gen. 15.18]; *Midr. Tan.*, *Hayye Sarah* §6 [on Gen. 24.1]; *PRE* §28).
According to Philo, Abraham experienced prophetic ecstasy (cf.
Quaest. in Gen. 3.9 [on Gen. 15.12]). According to *T. Levi* 18.14
Abraham, Isaac, and Jacob will rejoice in the eschaton. The word
'rejoice' (ἀγαλλιᾶν) used here is the same as that used by the Fourth
Evangelist (cf. *Jub.* 14.21; 15.17). 5. Jesus' interpretation of Ps. 82.6
('I said, "You are gods"') in Jn 10.31-39 reflects midrashic interpretation of the giving of the Law at Sinai (cf. *Mek.* on Exod. 20.19
[*Bahodesh* §9]; *Sifre* §329 [on Deut. 32.20]; *b. 'Abod. Zar.* 5a).[1] Had
the Israelites obeyed the covenant, instead of worshiping the golden
calf, they could have become immortal 'gods, sons of the Most High',
but because of their sin they 'will die like mere mortals' (Ps. 82.6-7).
6. The heavenly voice (φωνὴ ἐκ τοῦ οὐρανοῦ) of Jn 12.28 is probably to be understood as a *bat qol* (cf. *t. Soṭ.* 13.3: 'A *bat qol* came
forth and said to them, "There is a man among you who is worthy to
receive the Holy Spirit, but his generation is unworthy of such an
honor". They all set their eyes upon Hillel the Elder'; cf. *b. Soṭ.* 48b;
b. Yom. 9b).[2] It is interesting to note that some of the people thought
that 'it had thundered (βροντὴν γεγονέναι)' (Jn 12.29), which may
recall 1 Sam. 7.10: 'and the Lord thundered (ἐβρόντησε) with a great
voice (φωνῇ)' (cf. 1 Sam. 12.18). 7. When the Fourth Evangelist, in
contrast to the Synoptics (cf. Mt. 27.32; Mk 15.21; Lk. 23.26), says
that Jesus himself bore his cross (Jn 19.17), it is possible that a
parallel with early traditions of the Binding of Isaac is being drawn.
Isaac carried the cross (or stake) on which he was to be sacrificed (cf.
Gen. R. 56.3 [on Gen. 22.6]).[3]

---

1.   J.S. Ackerman, 'The Rabbinic Interpretation of Psalm 82 and the Gospel of
John: Jn 10.34', *HTR* 59 (1966), pp. 186-91; A.T. Hanson, 'John's Citation of
Psalm LXXXII: John X.33-36', *NTS* 11 (1965), pp. 158-62; *idem*, 'John's Citation
of Psalm LXXXII Reconsidered', *NTS* 13 (1967), pp. 363-67; J.H. Neyrey, 'I said
"You are Gods": Psalm 82.6 and John 10', *JBL* 108 (1989), pp. 647-63.
2.   Barrett, *Gospel according to St John*, p. 425; Carson, *Gospel according to
John*, p. 441; Dodd, *Interpretation of the Fourth Gospel*, p. 267 n. 1; Lindars,
Gospel of John, p. 432.
3.   So Barrett, *Gospel according to St John*, p. 548. The typology is made
explicit in *Barn.* 7.3. See also Carson, *Gospel according to John*, p. 609. For further
discussion and additional examples, see J. Bonnet, *Le 'midrash' de l'Evangile de
Saint Jean* (St-Etienne: Hénaff, 2nd edn, 1982).

Customs and Halakot

Drawing upon the work of John Christopher Thomas and others,[1] I note several passages which indicate that the Fourth Evangelist was familiar with first-century Pharisaic or early rabbinic customs and halakic traditions. 1. The reference to the 'six stone water pots according to the cleansing custom of the Jews' (Jn 2.6) coheres with purity traditions concerned with Lev. 11.29-38. Since contaminated clay pots were to be destroyed, stone pots (regarded as unsusceptible to uncleanness) were preferred. In the various early traditions that treat the subject (cf. *m. Kel.* 5.11; *m. Beş.* 2.3; *m. Par.* 3.2) the status of stone utensils is never questioned. Thomas rightly comments: 'Their unsusceptibility to uncleanness is presumed. John reflects an understanding of such subtleties which suggests his familiarity with Pharisaic and/or emerging rabbinic practices'.[2] 2. The evangelist's explanatory remark, 'for Jews do not mix with Samaritans' (Jn 4.9), once again betrays acquaintance with first-century Jewish customs. Following David Daube, Thomas suggests that the only plausible rendering of συγχρῶνται is 'mix [food or drink]'.[3] That is, the comment has nothing to do with Jews being in the company of Samaritans; rather, it refers to Jews' reluctance to share vessels with Samaritans. A few mishnaic passages, which Jacob Neusner thinks are early,[4] seem to reflect the thinking that lies behind the evangelist's comment: 'Rabbi Eliezer used to say, "One who eats the bread of Samaritans is like one who eats pork"' (*m. Šeb.* 8.10; cf. *m. Ber.* 8.8; *m. Nid.* 4.1). 3. The Sabbath controversy in the Fourth Gospel (cf. Jn 5, 9) also coheres with first-century Pharisaic or early rabbinic perspectives.

---

1. J.C. Thomas, 'The Fourth Gospel and Rabbinic Judaism', *ZNW* 82 (1991), pp. 159-82.

2. Thomas, 'The Fourth Gospel and Rabbinic Judaism', p. 165.

3. D. Daube, *The New Testament and Rabbinic Judaism* (repr.; New York: Arno, 1973 [1956]), p. 379: 'The conclusion is obvious. Unless John applies the verb in a way recurring nowhere else—and it may be repeated that this is just possible—it must signify either "to use something together with another person", or "to use two things together"...or simply "to use something"...The result is that, in all probability, the prefix is stressed together with another person: Jews do not use vessels together with Samaritans, most definitely not with Samaritan women'. Cited by Thomas, 'The Fourth Gospel and Rabbinic Judaism', p. 167.

4. J. Neusner, *Judaism: The Evidence of the Mishnah* (Chicago: University of Chicago Press, 1981), p. 53. See also Thomas, 'The Fourth Gospel and Rabbinic Judaism', pp. 167-69.

When the healed lame man carried his bed from one domain to another (Jn 5.8-18), he was apparently in violation of oral Sabbath law (cf. *m. Šab.* 11.1-2). Similarly, the making of clay to anoint the eyes of the blind man (Jn 9.6, 14-16) may also have violated oral Sabbath laws that existed in the first century (cf. *m. Šab.* 7.2 [kneading]; 22.6 [anointing, kneading for purposes of healing]).[1] Jesus' allusion to the practice of his opponents to circumcise on the Sabbath (Jn 7.14-24) also probably reflects first-century tradition preserved in the Mishnah (*m. Šab.* 19.1, 3).[2] 4. Thomas also points to the controversy regarding Jesus' witness to himself (Jn 5.31-47; 8.13). Jesus' argument that others bear witness to him (such as God the Father, John the Baptist, Moses and the Scriptures themselves) probably reflects early rabbinic halakah based on Num. 35.30, Deut. 17.6 and 19.15 (cf. *m. Yeb.* 15.1-2; *m. Ket.* 1.6-9). Neusner regards these mishnaic traditions as deriving from the Yamnian period.[3] 5. In Jn 7.49 the Pharisees refer to the crowd that does not know the Torah as 'accursed'. This appears to be a typical attitude toward the common people. According to Hillel 'an ignorant man cannot be holy' (*Ab.* 2.6). A similar view was apparently held by Hanina ben Dosa (cf. *Ab.* 3.11). 6. The point of order raised by Nicodemus, 'Our Torah does not judge a person unless it should first hear from him what he is doing, does it?', coheres with legal opinion held in the first century and later (cf. Josephus, *Ant.* 14.9.3 §167; *War* 1.10.6 §209; *Exod. R.* 21.3 [on Exod. 14.15]: 'Unless flesh and blood [that is, mortals] hear the pleas that one can put forward, they are not able to give judgment').[4] 7. The threat of stoning for blasphemy (Jn 8.59; 10.31-32)

---

1.   The Sabbath controversy in the Fourth Gospel is likely an indication of disputes between the Johannine community and the synagogue over Torah and halakic interpretation. The contrast between Moses and Jesus in Jn 1.17 probably presupposes this controversy; cf. E. Grässer, 'Die antijüdische Polemik im Johannesevangelium', *NTS* 11 (1964), pp. 74-90.

2.   J. Neusner (*A History of the Mishnaic Law of Appointed Times. Part One: Sabbath* [SJLA, 34; Leiden: Brill, 1981], pp. 65-66) assigns this tradition to Yamnia or earlier.

3.   J. Neusner, *A History of the Mishnaic Law of Women. Part One: Yebamot* (SJLA, 33; Leiden: Brill, 1980), pp. 71, 87-88.

4.   Barrett, *Gospel according to St John*, p. 332; Carson, *Gospel according to John*, p. 332.

may also reflect first-century oral tradition (cf. *m. Sanh.* 7.4).[1]
8. The notation that Lazarus had been dead for four days and now
'stinks' (Jn 11.39) probably presupposes the belief that after three
days the spirit of the deceased has departed and the body has suffered
irreversible corruption (cf. *m. Yeb.* 16.3; *b. Yeb.* 120a; *Lev. R.* 18.1
[on Lev. 15.1-2]; *Eccl. R.* 12.6 §1).[2] 9. Caiaphas's statement that 'it is
expedient for one person to die in behalf of the people and not the
whole people perish' (Jn 11.50) is similar to a later saying attributed
to Rabbi Judah: 'they should surrender one person to them and not be
all slain' (*Gen. R.* 94.9 [on Gen. 46.26-27]).[3] 10. Jesus' prediction that
a time will come when the one who kills one of his disciples will
suppose that he is offering a sacrifice to God (Jn 16.2) parallels the
rabbinic comment, 'if a man sheds the blood of the wicked it is as
though he had offered a sacrifice' (*Num. R.* 21.3 [on Num. 25.13]; cf.
m. Sanh. 9.6).[4] 11. The Jewish leaders' involvement with Pilate
coheres at two points with Jewish custom. First, their refusal to enter
the governor's praetorium in order to avoid ritual defilement and
disqualification from partaking in the Passover (Jn 18.28) goes beyond
the requirement of Scripture (cf. Num. 9.10-12), but likely reflects
the practice articulated in *m. Ohol.* 18.7: 'Dwelling places of the
Gentiles [in the land of Israel] are unclean'. Again Neusner suspects
that this tradition is quite early, perhaps even earlier than the first
century.[5] Secondly, the Jewish leaders' statement that 'it is not lawful'
for them to put someone to death (Jn 18.31) agrees with Josephus
(*War* 2.8.1 §117)[6] and coheres with the rabbinic tradition that capital

---

1. Barrett, *Gospel according to St John*, p. 352; Carson, *Gospel according to John*, pp. 358, 396.

2. Barrett, *Gospel according to St John*, p. 401; Carson, *Gospel according to John*, p. 411.

3. Barrett, *Gospel according to St John*, p. 406.

4. Barrett, *Gospel according to St John*, pp. 484-85. Carson (*Gospel according to John*, p. 531) rightly cautions against assuming that Jn 16.2 and the sentiment expressed in *Num. R.* 21.3 represented widespread practice and policy.

5. J. Neusner, *A History of the Mishnaic Law of Purities. Part Twenty-Two: The Mishnaic System of Uncleanness* (SJLA, 6; Leiden: Brill, 1977), pp. 55, 116.

6. Although it is not certain, I think that this is the explanation of the incident Josephus describes in *Ant.* 20.9.1 §§197-203. The high priest Ananus, son of Ananus (or Annas, cf. Jn 18.13, 24), taking advantage of the death of the Roman governor, executed James the brother of Jesus. When Albinus the new governor arrived, he removed Ananus from office, 'because *it was not lawful* for Ananus to

judgment was taken away from the Sanhedrin forty years before the destruction of the Second Temple (*y. Sanh.* 1.1; 7.1; *b. Šab.* 15a; *b. 'Abod. Zar.* 8b).[1] 12. Finally, the reference to the 'preparation of the Passover' (19.14) translates ערב־הפסח (cf. *b. Sanh.* 43a—in reference to Jesus' execution!)[2] and further clarifies the priests' refusal to enter the praetorium.

Expulsion from the Synagogue

In three passages the Fourth Gospel makes explicit mention of being expelled from the synagogue: 'if some one should confess him as Christ, he should be expelled from the synagogue (ἀποσυνάγωγος γένηται)' (9.22; cf. v. 34: 'and they cast him out'); 'on account of the Pharisees they were not confessing him lest they should be expelled from the synagogue (ἀποσυνάγωγοι γένωνται)' (12.42); and 'they will make you synagogue outcasts (ἀποσυναγώγους ποιήσουσιν)' (16.2). Principally on the basis of these texts Louis Martyn developed his classic portrait of the Johannine community in relation to the synagogue of the first century.[3] He concluded that the expulsion passages should be understood in the light of the Talmudic tradition that speaks of the revision of the twelfth benediction of the *Amidah*, in

convene the Sanhedrin without [the governor's] consent' (my emphasis). It is likely that the offence was in convening the Sanhedrin for purposes of carrying out capital judgment, something reserved for the Roman governor.

1. Reference to 'forty years' is problematic. Given the homiletical nature of the discussion (that is, the various times in its history that the Sanhedrin was exiled) this number should perhaps not be taken literally. As to the oft raised doubts about the Fourth Evangelist's reliability in having the religious leaders state that capital judgment was not permitted them, it should be pointed out that the charge being brought against Jesus was treason against Rome, hardly a matter for the Jewish Sanhedrin to deal with. If the Synoptic portrait can be accepted, that the Jewish leaders feared the Passover multitude (cf. Mk 11.18, 32; 12.12), then it is logical that the leaders would have wished the Romans, rather than themselves, to dispose of Jesus. Better the Romans take the blame. Hence the Jewish leaders were not interested in Pilate's offer (Jn 18.31).

2. See Dodd, *Historical Tradition*, pp. 109-10; Barrett, *Gospel according to St John*, p. 545.

3. J.L. Martyn, *History and Theology in the Fourth Gospel* (Nashville: Abingdon Press, 2nd edn, 1979). See also Barrett, *Gospel according to St John*, pp. 361-62; Beasley-Murray, *John*, pp. 152-54.

order to expel Christians and others suspected of heresy (cf. *b. Ber.* 28b-29a):

> Our rabbis taught: Simeon ha-Pakuli arranged the eighteen benedictions in order before Rabban Gamaliel in Jabneh. Rabban Gamaliel said to the Sages: 'Can any one among you frame a benediction relating to the Minim?' Samuel the Lesser arose and composed it. The next year he forgot it and he tried for two or three hours to recall it, but they did not remove him. Why did they not remove him, seeing that Rab Judah has said in the name of Rab: 'If a reader made a mistake in any of the other benedictions, they do not remove him, but if in the benediction of the Minim, he is removed, because we suspect him of being a Min'?— Samuel the Lesser is different, because he composed it.[1]

This revision may be represented primarily by the insertion of the following words: 'Let the Nazarenes (הנצרים) and the Minim be destroyed in a moment, and let them be blotted out of the Book of Life[2] and not be inscribed together with the righteous'.[3] Although some scholars have questioned Martyn's identification of the Johannine *Sitz im Leben* with that described in *Berakot*,[4] he remains convinced that

---

1. Translation based on M. Simon, 'Berakoth', in Epstein (ed.), *Babylonian Talmud*, I, p. 175.

2. It is important to observe the interest shown in the Apocalypse with regard to who is and who is not written in the Book of Life (Rev. 17.8; 20.12, 15; 21.27). When one also observes the polemic against the 'synagogue of Satan' (cf. Rev. 2.9; 3.9) one may wonder if the Seer's affirmations regarding whose names are written in the Book of Life constitute a direct response to the imprecation of the revised twelfth benediction. (Again, it is assumed that the Apocalypse derives from the Johannine community.)

3. Martyn, *History and Theology*, p. 58. For the Hebrew text of the Palestinian rescension of the *Amidah* (or *Shemoneh Esreh*), see G. Dalman, *Die Worte Jesu* (Leipzig: Hinrichs, 1898), pp. 299-301. The insertion is not found in the Babylonian rescension; cf. Dalman, *Die Worte Jesu*, p. 303.

4. W.A. Meeks, '"Am I a Jew?" Johannine Christianity and Judaism', in J. Neusner (ed.), *Christianity, Judaism and Other Greco-Roman Cults* (SJLA, 12; Leiden: Brill, 1975), pp. 163-86. The principal problem that Meeks has with Martyn's interpretation has to do with the proposed linkage between the *Birkat ha-Minim* and the Johannine community. For the view that there never was an anti-Christian 'blessing', see R. Kimelman, '*Birkat Ha-Minim* and the Lack of Evidence for an anti-Christian Jewish Prayer in Late Antiquity', in E.P. Sanders *et al.* (eds.), *Jewish and Christian Self-Definition*, II (3 vols.; Philadelphia: Fortress Press, 1980–82), pp. 226-44, 391-403. W. Horbury ('The Benediction of the Minim and Early Jewish–Christian Controversy', *JTS* 33 [1982], pp. 19-61) has argued that the

the *Birkat ha-Minim* 'was issued under Gamaliel II and that it is in some way reflected in Jn 9.22'.[1]

Whether or not one is inclined to accept Martyn's hypothesis, it must be acknowledged that having been cast out of the synagogue for confessing Jesus as the Christ (Jn 9.22) is clearly what lies at the heart of the Johannine community's concerns. If this community's Christology had been shaped by Gnostic mythology, one might expect that the grounds for expelling Christians from the synagogue would reflect these ideas; but they do not. Christians are expelled for confessing Jesus as 'the Christ'.[2]

twelfth benediction was a later attempt to strengthen earlier expulsion mechanisms. Although skeptical of Martyn's hypothesis, Carson (*Gospel according to John*, pp. 371-72) suspects that bans and expulsions may very well date to the time of the Jesus movement itself. This is a point that needs to be looked at carefully.

1.   Martyn, *History and Theology*, pp. 54-55 n. 69; *idem*, 'Glimpses into the History of the Johannine Community', in de Jonge (ed.), *L'Evangile de Jean*, pp. 149-75. Martyn's hypothesis has been adopted in an attempt to understand the nature and context of Johannine polemic by R.A. Whitacre, *Johannine Polemic: The Role of Tradition and Theology* (SBLDS, 67; Chico, CA: Scholars Press, 1982).

For older studies that concluded that the Fourth Gospel originated in the context of the synagogue, see G.A. Box, 'The Jewish Environment of Early Christianity', *The Expositor* 12 (1916), pp. 1-25, who finds the Fourth Gospel thoroughly Jewish; K. Bornhäuser, *Das Johannesevangelium: Eine Missionschrift für Israel* (BFCT, 2.15; Gütersloh: Bertelsmann, 1928), who also believed that John was written to evangelize Jews; W. Wrede, *Charakter und Tendenz des Johannesevangeliums* (Tübingen: Mohr [Paul Siebeck], 2nd edn, 1933), who understood the Johannine *Sitz im Leben* as involving serious dispute with the synagogue; E.R. Goodenough, 'John a Primitive Gospel', *JBL* 64 (1945), pp. 145-82, who emphasizes the Jewish background of the Fourth Gospel; W. van Unnik, 'The Purpose of St John's Gospel', in Aland *et al.* (eds.), *Studia Evangelica*, pp. 382-411, who concludes: 'The purpose of the Fourth Gospel was to bring the visitors of a synagogue in the Diaspora (Jews and Godfearers) to belief in Jesus as the Messiah of Israel' (p. 410); and Robinson, 'The Destination and Purpose of St John's Gospel', pp. 124-25, who concludes that the Fourth Gospel 'is composed, no doubt, of material which took shape as teaching *within* a Christian community *in Judaea* and under the pressure of controversy with "the Jews" of that area. But in its present form it is, I believe, an appeal to those *outside* the Church, to win to the faith that Greek-speaking *Diaspora Judaism* to which the author now finds himself belonging as a result (we may surmise) of the greatest dispersion of all, which has swept from Judaea Church and Synagogue alike' (his emphasis). Also see G. Reim, 'Johannesevangelium und Synagogengottesdienst— ein Beobachtung', *BZ* 27 (1983), p. 101.

2.   It should be noted here that there is a singular lack of coherence between this

One might reply by saying that the Johannine confession was an offence to the synagogue because it included the claim that Jesus was equal to God (cf. Jn 5.18; 10.33). It must be admitted that this aspect of Johannine Christology is coherent with Gnostic mythology. However, the history of Jewish polemic against Christian and Gnostic beliefs in 'two powers' in heaven does not support this view. Alan Segal, whose primary interests have little to do with the Fourth Gospel, has found that the evidence suggests that Johannine and Pauline Christology, in which Jesus is viewed as a heavenly power alongside of God ('ditheism'), is based upon the Old Testament and Jewish speculations about Wisdom and other intermediaries. The earliest polemical traditions in the rabbinic writings is against this form of the 'two powers' heresy. These two powers are understood as allies or partners. The rabbinic traditions that polemicize against Gnostic views of the two powers are later and appear to presuppose the earlier traditions. The two powers in these contexts are adversaries (with the God of the Old Testament denigrated as the evil demiurge). Segal concludes that the traditional view that Gnosticism emerged after Christianity and was dependent upon the Christologies of Paul and John is supported by the polemic found in the rabbinic writings.[1]

confession and typical Gnostic disparagement of Jewish messianic ideas. According to the Johannine community, the 'liar' and 'antichrist' is he who 'denies that Jesus is the Christ' (1 Jn 2.22). It is generally assumed that the 'antichrist' who denies the Messiahship of Jesus refers to an early form of Gnostic Christianity. It is not easy to explain, then, how Gnostic mythology could give rise to an expression of Christology that in its simplest form ('Jesus is the Christ') coheres with Judaism but not with Gnosticism; cf. M. de Jonge, 'The Use of the Word χριστός in the Johannine Epistles', in *Studies in John*, pp. 66-74. It is not impossible to explain, of course, but it does rather increase the burden of proof for those who find the origin of Johannine Christology in Gnostic mythology.

1.   A.F. Segal, *Two Powers in Heaven: Early Rabbinic Reports about Christianity and Gnosticism* (SJLA, 25; Leiden: Brill, 1977). Segal comments that concepts such as *memra*, Shekinah and *yeqara* 'formed the background out of which [ditheistic] heresy arose' (p. 183). See also P. Borgen, 'God's Agent in the Fourth Gospel', in J. Ashton (ed.), *The Interpretation of John* (London: SPCK; Philadelphia: Fortress Press, 1986), pp. 67-78, 75: 'It is therefore quite probable that the ideas of heavenly agents in Gnostic/Mandaean literature similarly have been influenced by Jewish principles of agency and Jewish ideas of heavenly figures. In that case the gnostic agents do not explain the background of God's agent in the Fourth Gospel, as Bultmann thinks. The Fourth Gospel rather gives a clue to the

Use of the Old Testament

The surest method of ascertaining the *Sitz im Leben* of the Johannine community lies, in my judgment, in assessing the function of the Old Testament in the Fourth Gospel. It will be shown that what we have in this Gospel is a christological apologetic that is not only rooted in the Jewish Scriptures but which also presupposes Jewish assumptions and thinking. It is an apologetic that is designed primarily to assure those within the community that their faith in Jesus as the Christ is not misplaced and secondarily to persuade those outside of the community that their criticisms and objections are without force. Moody Smith has rightly argued that the scriptural apologetic of the Fourth Gospel is basically what we should expect in a document designed to defend Christianity in a Jewish context.[1] It will be seen that such a scriptural apologetic is foreign to Gnostic thinking and the formation of its various 'Christologies'.[2] The point that will be underscored is that made in

Jewish background of the gnostic/Mandaean mythology'. Also see W.A. Meeks, 'The Man from Heaven in Johannine Sectarianism', *JBL* 91 (1972), pp. 44-72. Both G. MacRae ('The Jewish Background of the Gnostic Sophia Myth', *NovT* 12 [1970], pp. 86-101) and J.T. Sanders (*The New Testament Christological Hymns: Their Historical Religious Background* [SNTSMS, 15; Cambridge: Cambridge University Press, 1971], p. 139) conclude that Jewish wisdom provided the point of entry for Gnostic redeemer myths. But it is not clear that such myths existed *prior* to Christianity (as Sanders, p. 132, supposes).

1.   D.M. Smith, 'The Setting and Shape of a Johannine Narrative Source', *JBL* 95 (1976), pp. 231-41; repr. in *Johannine Christianity: Essays on its Setting, Sources, and Theology* (Columbia: University of South Carolina Press, 1984), pp. 80-93, esp. pp. 84-90. R.T. Fortna (*Gospel of Signs: A Reconstruction of the Narrative Source Underlying the Fourth Gospel* [SNTSMS, 11; Cambridge: Cambridge University Press, 1970], pp. 228-30) has argued that the 'narrative' source (that is, the signs plus the Passion) employed by the Fourth Evangelist had been composed with the synagogue in view. W. Nicol (*The Semeia in the Fourth Gospel: Tradition and Redaction* [NovTSup, 32; Leiden: Brill, 1972], pp. 48-68) has come to a similar conclusion with regard to the more traditional *semeia* source. Although certainly in agreement with these scholars' emphasis on the synagogue, I am inclined to view the Fourth Gospel itself, as opposed to its putative sources, as designed with the criticisms and objections of the synagogue in mind.

2.   Robinson ('Sethians and Johannine Thought', pp. 643-62, esp. p. 659) has rightly pointed out the logical fallacy of assuming that if a text has been influenced by the Old Testament, it therefore cannot have been influenced by Gnosticism (or something else). The Old Testament, especially the early chapters of Genesis, per-

the first paragraph of this chapter: the most likely provenance of the Fourth Gospel is the synagogue, especially the synagogue of the Diaspora.[1]

John formally quotes the Old Testament several times and alludes to it many more times, revealing a familiarity with the LXX, the Hebrew, and the targums.[2] Major Old Testament themes, moreover, are interwoven throughout the Gospel. Jesus is presented as the Messiah, the Servant of the Lord, the King of Israel and the Prophet (probably in

---

meates several of the Gnostic writings, and therefore could, at least in theory, have been mediated to another source, such as the Fourth Gospel, through Gnostic traditions. The point that is being made in this chapter is that the Old Testament and the way it was interpreted in Jewish circles—circles which give little or no evidence of acquaintance with Gnostic ideas—explain the principal features of Johannine Christology, making appeal to Gnostic mythology redundant and probably anachronistic as well. Years ago C.K. Barrett ('The Old Testament in the Fourth Gospel', *JTS* 48 [1947], pp. 155-69, esp. p. 168) was correct when he concluded that 'the whole body of the OT formed a background, or framework, upon which the new revelation rested'.

1. Pace Barrett, *John and Judaism*, p. 19. Of course, I do not mean that the Johannine community at the time of the writing of the Fourth Gospel still existed within the confines of the synagogue. Passages such as 9.22, 12.42 and 16.2, as well as the heated polemical exchanges such as those in John 8, indicate that the community had been put out of the synagogue. What I mean is that the Fourth Gospel reflects the thinking of the synagogue. Although differing sharply in their respective assessments of Jesus, the Johannine community and the synagogue share much common ground. In fact, the only differences between the Johannine community and the synagogue that I can discern have to do with Jesus. At all other points there is agreement. Even with respect to the Sabbath controversies in John 5 and 9, the point of contention had to do with Jesus' activity on the Sabbath, not whether or not Jewish Sabbath law was valid. In this regard, the Fourth Evangelist is closer to the Jewish point of view than are the Markan and Lukan evangelists. On this point I am in essential agreement with J.L. Martyn, *The Gospel of John in Christian History* (New York: Paulist Press, 1978), pp. 100-101.

2. C.K. Barrett, 'The Old Testament in the Fourth Gospel', *JTS* 48 (1947), pp. 155-69; R.J. Humann, 'The Function and Form of the Explicit Old Testament Quotations in the Gospel of John', *LTR* 1 (1988–89), pp. 31-54; A.T. Hanson, *The Prophetic Gospel: A Study of John and the Old Testament* (Edinburgh: T. & T. Clark, 1991). In a recent study B.G. Schuchard (*Scripture within Scripture: The Interrelationship of Form and Function in the Explicit Old Testament Citations in the Gospel of John* [SBLDS, 133; Atlanta: Scholars Press, 1992], pp. xvii, 151) concludes that the LXX (or 'Old Greek', as Schuchard would have it) lies behind all of the evangelist's explicit citations of the Old Testament.

the sense of the new Moses, based on Deut. 18.15-19). There are references to Abraham (8.31-58), Isaac (3.16; cf. Gen. 22.2, 12), and Jacob (4.5-6, 12). There are numerous references to Moses and the exodus (1.17; 5.46; 6.31-32, 49 [manna in wilderness]; 7.38 [water from rock?]; 3.14 [bronze serpent]; 1.14 [the Tabernacle], 17 [the Sinai covenant]).[1] The book of Isaiah, as well as legendary Isaianic tradition, plays an important role in the Fourth Gospel.[2]

The function of the Old Testament in the Fourth Gospel, as seen in the formal quotations, is not ad hoc but is systematic and progressive, showing that Jesus' public ministry (1.29–12.36a) conformed to scriptural expectations and requirements, while his Passion (12.36b–19.37) fulfilled scriptural prophecies. This progression is clearly indicated by the Scripture quotation formulas.

In a previous study I argued that the quotation formulae in the Fourth Gospel do not assist us in identifying pre-Johannine sources[3] but in recognizing the evangelist's understanding of how Jesus' ministry and rejection relate to Scripture (which is never introduced as 'fulfilled' in the public ministry, but is always introduced as 'fulfilled' in the Passion).[4] The quotation formulae appear in John as follows, with cited Scriptures noted in parentheses:

| 1.23 | ἔφη (Isa. 40.3): 'he said' |
| 1.45 | ὃν ἔγραψεν Μωϋσῆς ἐν τῷ νόμῳ καὶ οἱ προφῆται (no citation): 'of whom Moses wrote in the law, and [of whom] the prophets [spoke]' |

---

1. W.A. Meeks, *The Prophet-King: Moses Traditions and the Johannine Christology* (NovTSup, 14; Leiden: Brill, 1967).

2. F.W. Young, 'A Study of the Relation of Isaiah to the Fourth Gospel', *ZNW* 46 (1955), pp. 215-33. In a recent study W. Carter ('The Prologue and John's Gospel: Function, Symbol and the Definitive Word', *JSNT* 39 [1990], pp. 35-58) explains that the reason that the Fourth Gospel asserts that Abraham, Moses and Isaiah (about whom there were revelatory traditions) saw Jesus, the *logos*, was in order to present Jesus as the supreme revelation of God. Such an emphasis makes the best sense in the context of the synagogue.

3. Pace A. Faure, 'Die alttestamentlichen Zitate im 4. Evangelium und die Quellenscheidungshypothese', *ZNW* 21 [1922], pp. 99-122. Faure has not been followed.

4. For further explanation of the function of the Scripture quotation formulae in John, see C.A. Evans, 'On the Quotation Formulas in the Fourth Gospel', *BZ* 26 (1982), pp. 79-83.

2.17	ἐμνήσθησαν...ὅτι γεγραμμένον ἐστιν (Ps. 69.9): 'they remembered that it was written'
5.46	περὶ γὰρ ἐμοῦ ἐκεῖνος (Μωϋσῆς) ἔγραψεν (no citation): 'for concerning me that one [Moses] wrote'
6.31	καθώς ἐστιν γεγραμμένον (Ps. 78.24): 'just as it is written'
6.45	ἔστιν γεγραμμένον ἐν τοῖς προφήταις (Isa. 54.13): 'it is written in the prophets'
7.42	ἡ γραφὴ εἶπεν ὅτι (2 Sam. 7.12; Mic. 5.2): 'the Scripture said that'
8.17	καὶ ἐν τῷ νόμῳ δὲ τῷ ὑμετέρῳ γέγραπται ὅτι (Deut. 17.6; 19.15): 'and it is written in your law that'
10.34	ἔστιν γεγραμμένον ἐν τῷ νόμῳ ὑμῶν ὅτι (Ps. 82.6): 'it is written in your law that'
12.14	καθώς ἐστιν γεγραμμένον (Zech. 9.9): 'just as it is written'
12.16	ἐμνήσθησαν ὅτι ταῦτα ἦν ἐπ᾽ αὐτῷ γεγραμμένα (alluding to Zech. 9.9 and other passages): 'they remembered that these things were written of him'
12.38	ἵνα ὁ λόγος Ἡσαΐου τοῦ προφήτου πληρωθῇ ὃν εἶπεν (Isa. 53.1): 'in order that the word of Isaiah the prophet, which he spoke, should be fulfilled'
12.39	πάλιν εἶπεν Ἡσαΐας (Isa. 6.10): 'again Isaiah said'
13.18	ἵνα ἡ γραφὴ πληρωθῇ (Ps. 41.9): 'in order that the Scripture be fulfilled'
15.25	ἵνα πληρωθῇ ὁ λόγος ὁ ἐν τῷ νόμῳ αὐτῶν γεγραμμένος ὅτι (Ps. 35.19): 'in order that the word which is written in their law be fulfilled'
17.12	ἵνα ἡ γραφὴ πληρωθῇ (no citation): 'in order that the Scripture be fulfilled'
18.9	ἵνα πληρωθῇ ὁ λόγος ὃν εἶπεν ὅτι (in reference to Jn 6.39): 'in order that the word which he spoke be fulfilled'
18.32	ἵνα ὁ λόγος τοῦ Ἰησοῦ πληρωθῇ ὃν εἶπεν (in reference to Jesus' words; cf. Jn 3.14; 8.28; 12.33): 'in order that the word of Jesus which he spoke be fulfilled'
19.24	ἵνα ἡ γραφὴ πληρωθῇ ἡ λέγουσα (Ps. 22.18): 'in order that the Scripture be fulfilled which says'
19.28	ἵνα τελειωθῇ ἡ γραφή (Ps. 22.15): 'in order that the Scripture be fulfilled'
19.36	ἵνα ἡ γραφὴ πληρωθῇ (Exod. 12.10, 46; Num. 9.12; Ps. 34.20): 'in order that the Scripture be fulfilled'
19.37	καὶ πάλιν ἑτέρα γραφὴ λέγει (Zech. 12.10): 'and again another Scripture says'

In Jn 1.23–12.16 Scripture is regularly introduced or alluded to with 'it is written', or the like, while in 12.38–19.37 it is regularly introduced with the formula 'in order that [the Scripture or what was spoken] be fulfilled'. The one exception in 19.28, which employs the synonym τελειωθῇ, probably reflects tradition[1] or the attempt to match the formula with Jesus' dying words, 'It is finished (τετέλεσται)' (19.30; cf. v. 28).[2] The formulae in 12.39 and 19.37 are not exceptions, but are to be understood as extensions of the respective formulae in 12.38 and 19.36 (as is also indicated by the presence of the linking word πάλιν).

This segregation of fulfillment formulae appears to be deliberate.[3] How is it to be explained? Whereas in the first half of the Gospel Jesus performs his many 'signs' and conducts his ministry 'just as it is written', in the second half of the Gospel Jesus' rejection and crucifixion take place 'in order that Scripture be fulfilled'. Far from proving that Jesus was not Israel's Messiah (as is implied by such a statement as, 'We have heard from the Law that the Messiah remains forever' [12.34]), his rejection and death fulfilled Scripture and so proved that he really was the Messiah. The Fourth Evangelist has offered his contemporaries an apologetic that was meant to demonstrate the scriptural truth of the Christian message[4] and to summon people to 'faith in God, mediated through the person of Jesus'.[5]

What we have here is an apologetic designed to answer significant objections to Christian faith, which in all likelihood were raised in the

1. Bultmann, *Gospel of John*, p. 675 n. 2 (though with a Gnostic slant).
2. Carson, *Gospel according to John*, pp. 620-21.
3. Humann ('Old Testament Quotations', p. 50), Carson (*Gospel according to John*, p. 612), and Schuchard (*Scripture within Scripture*, p. 86 n. 5) agree. Matthew offers an instructive comparison. Among the various Old Testament passages that this evangelist quotes and introduces as having taken place 'in order that it be fulfilled' is Zech. 9.9: 'Tell the daughter of Zion, Behold, your king is coming...' (cf. Mt. 21.4-5). The Fourth Evangelist quotes the same passage and also applies it to the Triumphal Entry, but he does not introduce it as fulfilled (cf. 12.14-15), for it falls outside of the 'fulfillment' half of his Gospel (12.37–19.37). Like many of the quotations in the first half (1.23–12.16), the Johannine evangelist introduces Zech. 9.9 with the words 'as it is written'. See also J.J. O'Rourke, 'John's Fulfilment Texts', *ScEccl* 19 (1967), pp. 433-43; *idem*, 'Explicit Old Testament Citations in the Gospels', *Studia Montis Regii* 7 (1964), pp. 37-60.
4. This view has been recently accepted by Carson, *Gospel according to John*, pp. 450, 612; *idem*, 'John and the Johannine Epistles', in Carson and Williamson (eds.), *It is Written*, pp. 245-64, esp. pp. 247-49; and Beutler, 'Greeks Come to See Jesus', p. 337.
5. M.M. Thompson, 'Signs and Faith in the Fourth Gospel', *BBR* 1 (1991), pp. 89-108, esp. p. 108.

synagogue. Proclaiming the teachings and 'signs' of Jesus would probably have had little effect among educated Jews, unless an explanation of Jesus' rejection and death could be offered, an explanation grounded in the Scriptures of Israel.[1] Moody Smith reasons cogently that the Fourth Evangelist's use of Scripture in the second half of this Gospel 'presupposes a Jewish audience and probably arose out of the necessity to preach and defend the gospel by showing that the death of Jesus took place according to God's will'.[2]

If some of the liberation movements of the first century had messianic overtones, and I believe that some of them did,[3] it is clear that there were Jews who hoped for a violent overthrow of Roman authority in Israel. Seen against these hopes Jesus' crucifixion at the hands of the Romans, tinged with the mockery of the *titulus* that proclaimed him 'king of the Jews' (Jn 19.19-22), could hardly have been viewed by the Diaspora synagogue in any other light than as evidence of Jesus' utter failure. Jesus' apparent defeat at the hands of the Romans, along with with his rejection by the religious authorities of Jerusalem, would have made Christian proclamation of Jesus' Messiahship in the context of the synagogue ludicrous. An apologetic that would have any hope of persuading Jews that Jesus really was Israel's Messiah would have to explain both the religious rejection and

1. Summarizing rabbinic tradition regarding Simon ben Kosiba (or bar Kochba), Moses Maimonides says: 'Rabbi Aqiba, the greatest of the sages of the Mishnah, was a supporter of King Ben Kozeba, saying of him that he was King Messiah. He and all the contemporary sages regarded him as the King Messiah, until he was killed for sins which he had committed' (*Mishneh Torah, Melakhim* 11.3). Simon's death at the hands of the Romans ended speculation that he might be Israel's Messiah. It is hard to imagine that any other conclusion regarding Jesus— apart from a very persuasive account of his death and resurrection in terms of scriptural fulfillment—would have been drawn by Jewish religious authorities. For rabbinic traditions relating to Simon ben Kosiba, see *y. Ta'an.* 4.5; *Lam. R.* 2.2 §4; *b. Giṭ.* 57a-b; *b. Sanh.* 93b. For early Christian traditions about Simon, see Justin Martyr, *Apol.* 31.6; Eusebius, *Hist. Eccl.* 4.6.2.

2. Smith, 'Setting and Shape', p. 88; cf. Schuchard, *Scripture within Scripture*, pp. 151-56.

3. So also R.A. Horsley and J.S. Hanson, *Bandits, Prophets, and Messiahs: Popular Movements at the Time of Jesus* (San Francisco: Harper & Row, 1985), pp. 88-134. It is probable that both Menahem and Simon bar Giora (in the first war with Rome) made messianic claims of one sort or another, while it is virtually certain that Simon ben Kosiba (in the second war with Rome) claimed to be Israel's Messiah.

the apparent political defeat. This apologetic, moreover, would have to be scripturally grounded, if it were to make any significant headway against the objections of the synagogue's teachers of Scripture. Although due allowance must be made for its obvious apologetic slant, the question with which Justin Martyr credits Trypho the Jew very likely approximates the misgivings many Jews would have entertained when hearing Christian claims:

> Then Trypho remarked, 'Be assured that all our nation awaits the Messiah; and we admit that all the Scriptures which you have quoted refer to him. Moreover, I also admit that the name of Jesus by which the son of Nun was called, has inclined me very strongly to adopt this view. But we are in doubt about whether the Messiah should be so shamefully crucified. For whoever is crucified is said in the Law to be accursed, so that I am very skeptical on this point. It is quite clear, to be sure, that the Scriptures announce that the Messiah had to suffer; but we wish to learn if you can prove it to us whether by suffering he was cursed' (*Dialogue with Typho* 89.1).

> 'Lead us on, then,' [Trypho] said, '*by the Scriptures*, that we may also be persuaded by you; for we know that he should suffer and be led as a sheep. But prove to us whether he must also be crucified and die such disgraceful and dishonorable death, cursed by the Law. For we cannot bring ourselves even to consider this' (*Dialogue with Typho* 90.1 [my emphasis]).

Of course, Jews were not alone in mocking the Christian proclamation that the crucified Galilean was none other than Israel's King and God's Messiah. According to Origen, Celsus regarded as absurd the notion that someone betrayed, abandoned, captured and executed could be regarded as God and Savior. The whole notion is preposterous (Origen, *Contra Celsum* 2.9, 35, 68; 6.10, 34, 36).[1] To make any headway at all, especially in a Jewish context, a Christian apologetic would have to explain the circumstances of the Passion and would have to show how the Passion was in keeping with scriptural expectation.

The most obvious political part of the Fourth Evangelist's apolo-

---

1. See M. Hengel, *Crucifixion in the Ancient World and the Folly of the Message of the Cross* (Philadelphia: Fortress Press, 1977), pp. 1-10; *idem*, 'Christological Titles in Early Christianity', in J.H. Charlesworth (ed.), *The Messiah: Developments in Earliest Judaism and Christianity* (Minneapolis: Fortress Press, 1992), pp. 425-48, esp. pp. 425-30.

getic is seen in Jesus' statement that his 'kingdom is not of this world', which is why his 'servants' did not put up a struggle at the time of his arrest (18.36). In other words, no battle was fought and no war was lost. It had not been Jesus' intention to confront Pilate and Roman power in a bid to establish a kingdom 'of this world'. Closely related to this point is Jesus' statement that Pilate's authority to execute him did not lie with the Roman governor, but had been ordained by heaven (19.10-11). Not only is Jesus' kingdom not of this world (hence, it is of heaven), even his execution had not been 'of this world'. Both aspects of this political apologetic are rooted in the evangelist's Christology. Jesus is not from the world (cf. 1.1; 3.13, 17, 31; 6.62). Through the cross he has departed from the world to return to his Father (12.32-34; 13.3, 36; 14.28-29; 17.11), paving the way for his disciples to follow him (13.36; 14.3). Because he has fulfilled his mission, to 'bear witness to the truth' (18.37), he can say, 'I have overcome the world' (16.33). (Jesus' disciples can make the same claim; cf. 1 Jn 4.3-5; 5.4-5.) Jesus has not been defeated by Rome; he has defeated the forces of darkness that drive Rome and the world as a whole (1.5). His mission has not gone awry; it has been accomplished. Therefore, in dying Jesus can say, 'It is finished' (19.30).[1]

The Fourth Evangelist attempts to answer the religious objections to Christian proclamation by interpreting Jesus' death as predicted, even ordained of heaven. He accomplishes this in two ways. First, he quotes Scripture that predicts Jewish unbelief (Jn 12.38, quoting Isa. 53.1) and Scripture that implies that spiritual obduracy was God's will (Jn 12.39-40, quoting Isa. 6.10). In other words, Jesus' rejection and death are not evidence of divine rejection, but are evidence of the fulfillment of the divine plan.[2] It is important to note that these are the first Old Testament quotations introduced by means of the fulfillment

---

1. M. Hengel ('The Old Testament in the Fourth Gospel', *HBT* 12 [1990], pp. 19-41, esp. pp. 33-34) makes the intriguing suggestion that Jesus' statement, 'It is finished', alludes to the creation references in the Prologue. In other words, Jesus has completed (on the sixth day no less!) a new work of creation.

2. Evans, *To See and Not Perceive*, pp. 129-35. See H. Schneider, '"The Word Was Made Flesh": An Analysis of the Theology of Revelation in the Fourth Gospel', *CBQ* 31 (1969), pp. 344-56, who relates the Fourth Gospel's rejection motif to the Prologue, esp. 1.14.

formula.[1] These quotations provide the framework for the quotations that follow and provide the theological backdrop against which the whole of the Johannine Passion story should be read.[2] Secondly, the evangelist interprets Jesus' death as his 'hour of glorification' (12.23, 28; 13.31-32; 17.5). He achieves this primarily by the play on 'lift up' (literally meaning lifting up on the cross; figuratively meaning exaltation) and its conjunction with 'glorify', as he finds these words in the Suffering Servant Song (cf. LXX Isa. 52.13). The glory of the *logos* is manifested in the whole of Jesus' ministry (Jn 1.14) and reaches its climax in the lifting up on the cross (12.16), the first step in Jesus' return to his Father. Consequently, according to the theology of the Fourth Evangelist, far from disqualifying his claims, the crucifixion of Jesus provides a vital link in his descent–ascent pattern.[3] It is for this reason that the evangelist twice says that Jesus 'signified by what death he was to die' (12.33; 18.32). The *manner* of death, that is, being lifted up on the cross, becomes part of the apologetic itself.

It is also important to understand that according to the evangelist this 'glory' is the glory which the prophet Isaiah saw and of which he spoke (Jn 12.41). The coordination of the quotations of Isa. 53.1 (Jn 12.38) and Isa. 6.10 (Jn 12.40) suggests that what was *seen* was the 'glory' which the prophet beheld in his famous vision of Isaiah 6 and what was *spoken* were the words of the Suffering Servant Song.[4] That

1. See R. Schnackenburg ('Zur christologischen Schriftauslegung des vierten Evangelisten', in H. Baltensweiler and B. Reicke [eds.], *Neues Testament und Geschichte* [Tübingen: Mohr (Paul Siebeck), 1972], pp. 167-77, esp. pp. 170-71) and M.J.J. Menken ('Die Form des Zitates aus Jes 6,10 in Joh 12,40', *BZ* 32 [1988], pp. 189-209) for proper appreciation of the evangelist's work in quoting and contextualizing the Isaiah passages. See also E.D. Freed, *Old Testament Quotations in the Gospel of John* (NovTSup, 11; Leiden: Brill, 1965), p. 88.

2. Schnackenburg, 'Zur christologischen Schriftauslegung', pp. 176-77. Beutler ('Greeks Come to See Jesus', pp. 345-46) concludes that the 'Suffering Servant seems to be the leading figure behind the christology of John 12'.

3. This important feature has been treated by G.C. Nicholson, *Death as Departure: The Johannine Descent–Ascent Schema* (SBLDS, 63; Chico, CA: Scholars Press, 1983). Nicholson rightly underscores the significance of the 'lifted up' sayings for Johannine Christology. Being lifted up is Jesus' first step in his return to heaven, and it is the counterpart to his descent. The concept of lifting up is clearly based on the glorification and lifting up of the Suffering Servant and not on some myth of descending–ascending revealer/redeemer.

4. The fact that Isaiah 6 and 52–53 have several words and themes in common (such as glory and being lifted up) would have encouraged the linkage of the sort

is to say, when (or because) Isaiah saw God's *glory* he spoke about God's *servant*, who is none other than the *logos* who became flesh and tabernacled among us (Jn 1.14).[1]

There is another very important aspect of the Fourth Evangelist's understanding of the death of Jesus that must not be overlooked. The report that Jesus' legs were not broken (19.31-34) makes it possible to quote Exod. 12.46 (or Num. 9.12) as 'fulfilled': 'A bone of him [or "it", referring to the Passover lamb][2] will not be broken' (Jn 19.36). There are several details in the context of this passage that suggest that the evangelist has interpreted and portrayed Jesus as the Passover lamb:[3] (1) Jesus is killed on the eve of Passover (18.28, 39; cf. *b. Sanh.* 43a);[4] (2) Jesus is sentenced to death by Pilate at noon, the hour at which the slaughter of the Passover lamb begins (19.14); (3) there is mention of hyssop (19.29), which plays a part in the observance of Passover (Exod. 12.42); (4) three times reference is made to the 'preparation of the Passover' (19.14, 31, 42), which could imply emphasis; (5) the blood that flowed from Jesus' side (19.34) may have been intended to correspond with the blood of the Passover rite (Exod. 12.22; cf. *m. Pes.* 5.5, 8 and *m. Ohol.* 3.5 where the blood of

found in the Fourth Gospel; see Evans, 'Obduracy and the Lord's Servant', pp. 230-32.

1. See Schnackenburg, 'Zur christologischen Schriftauslegung', 175-76. I think that C.K. Barrett ('The Prologue of St John's Gospel', in Barrett, *New Testament Essays* [London: SPCK, 1972], pp. 27-48, esp. p. 47) is correct when he says the emphasis of Jn 1.14 falls not on the first statement, 'and the Word became flesh', but rather on the last, 'and we beheld his glory'. On the meaning of δόξα in the Fourth Gospel, see G. Kittel and G. von Rad, 'δοκέω, δόξα, κτλ', *TDNT*, II, pp. 232-55, esp. pp. 242-51; G.B. Caird, 'The Glory of God in the Fourth Gospel: An Exercise in Biblical Semantics', *NTS* 15 (1969), pp. 265-77; T.C. de Kruije, 'The Glory of the Only Son (John i 14)', in Geyser *et al.* (eds.), *Studies in John*, pp. 111-23; M. Pamment, 'The Meaning of *doxa* in the Fourth Gospel', *ZNW* 74 (1983), pp. 12-16.

2. In the LXX 'lamb' is ἀμνός in Exod. 12.5 (according to A), but πρόβατον in 12.21.

3. See Brown, *Gospel according to John*, II, pp. 952-53; G.A. Barton, '"A Bone of Him Shall Not Be Broken", John 19.36', *JBL* 49 (1930), pp. 13-19; J.M. Ford, '"Mingled Blood" from the Side of Christ (John xix. 34)', *NTS* 15 (1969), pp. 337-38; G.L. Carey, 'Lamb of God and Atonement Theories', *TynBul* 32 (1981), pp. 97-122.

4. See A. Jaubert, 'The Calendar of Qumran and the Passion Narrative in John', in Charlesworth (ed.), *John and the Dead Sea Scrolls*, pp. 62-75.

the Passover sacrifice and the blood that gushes out of a man who has been crucified is called 'mingled blood'); and (6) Jesus' unbroken legs and the quotation of Exod 12.46 as 'fulfilled' (19.33, 36) seem fairly clear indications that Passover lamb imagery is intended.[1]

There are other indications as well. At the outset of his ministry the Baptist had declared Jesus to be 'the lamb (ἀμνός) of God who takes away the sin of the world' (1.29). This is probably an allusion to the Suffering Servant (Isa 53.7),[2] who like a lamb (ἀμνός) is delivered up to death on account of his people's sin (Isa. 53.4, 5, 6, 8, 10, 12).[3] This coheres with the context of John 12, where the Servant will be glorified by being lifted up on the cross. This atoning aspect of Jesus' death is alluded to just prior to ch. 12 when Caiaphas the high priest says that it is expedient that Jesus die 'for the people' (11.49-50). The

1. So Carson, *Gospel according to John*, p. 627; Freed, *Old Testament Quotations*, p. 114; Hengel, 'The Old Testament in the Fourth Gospel', p. 34; Hoskyns, *Fourth Gospel*, II, pp. 634-35; O'Rourke, 'John's Fulfilment Texts', pp. 439-40, 443; Schnackenburg, *Gospel according to St John*, III, p. 292 (with some hesitation).

2. Lindars, *Gospel of John*, p. 109; Schnackenburg, *Gospel according to St John*, I, pp. 298-300. The allusion is clear enough, given Jn 19.31-36. There is no need to appeal to confusion involving the Aramaic word טליא, which can mean either 'lamb' or 'servant', as was argued by C.F. Burney, *The Aramaic Origin of the Fourth Gospel* (Oxford: Clarendon Press, 1922), pp. 104-108. For criticism of this view, see Bultmann, *Gospel of John*, p. 96 n. 3; Dodd, *Interpretation of the Fourth Gospel*, pp. 235-36. Even less likely is the suggestion of A. Negoïtsa and C. Daniel ('L'Agneau de Dieu est le Verbe de Dieu [Ad Jo. i 29 et 36]', *NovT* 13 [1971], pp. 24-37) that lying behind the Baptist's declaration is a play on *imra*, meaning 'lamb' or 'word'.

3. See Brown (*Gospel according to John*, I, pp. 58-63) and Carson (*Gospel according to John*, pp. 149-51) for the various interpretations of what the words attributed to the Baptist could mean. Carson thinks that the two images of apocalyptic lamb and the lamb of Isa. 53.7 are in view. Beasley-Murray (*John*, pp. 24-25) argues for the former (though not necessarily to the exclusion of the lamb of Isa. 53 or the lamb of the Passover), primarily on the basis of Revelation 5 (which, it should be pointed out, uses ἀρνίον, instead of ἀμνός). The problem with the apocalyptic lamb image is that there is no indication of such imagery in the Fourth Gospel. But there are numerous indications of sacrificial imagery, the most obvious being the reference to Jesus' blood and the fulfillment of the commandment not to break the bones of the Passover lamb. According to Barrett (*Gospel according to St John*, p. 176): 'Probably John's primary reference is to the Paschal lamb'. I am inclined to think that the evangelist has presented Jesus as the Suffering Servant, who as 'lamb' (Isa. 53.7) has been interpreted as the Passover lamb.

evangelist interprets this statement as divine prophecy (11.51) indicating that Jesus was to die 'for the nation' and for 'the scattered children of God' (11.52). (The latter expression again points to the synagogue of the Diaspora.) Caiaphas's statement and the evangelist's interpretation of it conclude the public ministry of signs (chs. 2–11) and prepare for the transition from signs to passion in John 12. As the Suffering Servant Jesus dies the death of a Passover lamb.[1] But Jesus accomplishes more than either the Servant or the Passover lamb. The evangelist wishes to interpret Jesus' death against this imagery, but does not limit the significance of his death to this imagery.

Whereas the Servant 'bears' (φέρειν) the sin of his people, Jesus 'takes away' (αἴρειν) the sin of the world. The evangelist has both *intensified* and *widened* the scope of the efficacy of the Servant's suffering. He has intensified it in that Jesus removes sin, he does not merely bear it. This is an important element in Johannine soteriology and hamartiology (cf. 1 Jn 1.7; 2.2; 3.5; 4.10). In removing sin, he makes it possible to abide in him without 'sinning' (cf. 1 Jn 2.1; 3.6, 9; 5.18). The evangelist has widened the efficacy of the Servant's suffering by claiming that it is in behalf of the world, and not only in behalf of his people. This too is in step with the evangelist's soteriology (cf. Jn 3.16; 1 Jn 2.2; 4.14).

Commentators have pointed out that the Passover lamb had nothing to do with sacrifice for sin[2] (and for this reason some question whether the Passover lamb is the appropriate background for the Baptist's statement in Jn 1.29 and 36). But that point is without force when it is remembered that Christians a generation before the writing of the Fourth Gospel were already speaking of Jesus as the Passover lamb that had been 'sacrificed' (as seen for instance in 1 Cor. 5.7). The Passover lamb is appropriate for Johannine Christology because,

1. The possibility that the Fourth Evangelist interpreted Jesus as the Passover lamb is increased when it is observed that such an interpretation predates the Fourth Gospel by three or four decades, as is witnessed by Paul: 'Christ our Passover is sacrificed' (1 Cor. 5.7; cf. 1 Pet. 1.19). The implication in this context is that Christ's paschal sacrifice requires that evil (that is, the 'old leaven') be replaced by sincerity and truth (that is, the 'unleavened bread'). Toward the end of the second century the date and character of Passover observance for Christians of Asia Minor were clearly influenced by the Fourth Gospel; cf. Eusebius, *Hist. Eccl.* 5.24.1-18.

2. For a discussion of the various objections that have been raised, see Barrett, *Gospel according to St John*, p. 176; Brown, *Gospel according to John*, I, pp. 61-63.

in reference to the first Passover, its blood spelled the difference between life and death. Those covered by its blood were spared; those who were not covered by its blood were not. It is probable that the Fourth Evangelist was thinking along similar lines. The blood of Jesus, God's Son, gives life (Jn 6.53-56) and cleanses believers from all sin (1 Jn 1.7). 'By his amalgamation of Old Testament ideas John indicates that the death of Jesus was a new and better sacrifice.'[1]

Summary

The point of all of this is that the Christology of the Fourth Evangelist is fundamentally indebted to the language, concepts and institutions of the Old Testament and first-century Judaism. Portrayed as a heavenly agent, with many parallels to Moses traditions, Jesus performs signs and proclaims his teaching in a way that coheres with (but does not fulfill) the Scriptures. When he is finally rejected (formally noted at Jn 12.37), despite the many significant signs, Scripture can now be introduced as 'fulfilled'. It is in rejection and death—death by means of being 'lifted up' on a cross—that the Johannine Jesus truly fulfills what the prophets had spoken and what Moses had commanded. Because he has been lifted up, he may be understood as the glorified Suffering Servant, whose glory Isaiah beheld. Because his bones were not broken and his blood flowed freely, he may be understood as the Passover lamb 'who takes away the sin of the world'. Johannine Christology's indebtedness to the Scriptures of Israel can hardly be exaggerated.[2]

This apologetic has been produced in dialogue with a synagogue that has questioned and finally rejected Christian claims. It has come as no surprise then to find the Fourth Gospel permeated by the language, exegesis and presuppositions of the synagogue. What we have here is a complex apologetic that presupposes much of what the synagogue pre-supposes. The Scriptures, various interpretive traditions and customs, and the general belief that 'salvation is of the Jews' (4.22)—another

---

1. Barrett, *Gospel according to St John*, p. 177.
2. Hengel ('The Old Testament in the Fourth Gospel', pp. 34-35) rightly comments that 'it is clear that Johannine scriptural proof within the framework of the gospel's dominating Christology has a greater significance than has generally been recognized'.

remarkably *un*-Gnostic dogma![1]—are held as common ground. The Fourth Evangelist is attempting to persuade those within his community, as well as those outside of it, that belief in Jesus does not contradict these sacred and authoritative traditions and institutions. On the contrary, Jesus has fulfilled them, enabling the evangelist to assert that 'the Messiah, the Son of God is Jesus' (20.31).[2]

The Johannine Prologue coheres with these observations.[3] In it Jesus

1. The author of the *Tripartite Tractate* speaks of the 'heresies' which exist among the Jews (NHC I, 112.20-22). The Jews serve as a poor example in the *Gospel of Thomas* (NHC II, 40.23-26 [log. §43]). According to the author of the *Gospel of Philip*: '[As] Christian [people], we [do not descend] from the Jews' (NHC II, 75.30-34).

2. See Carson, 'John and the Johannine Epistles', p. 258.

3. In my opinion scholars have exaggerated the differences between the Prologue and the body of the Fourth Gospel. There are only two differences that call for comment. First, the Prologue, unlike the body of the Gospel, is cast into poetic form. Secondly, in the Prologue, but not in the body of the Gospel, there is explicit reference to the *logos*. Neither of these differences, however, warrants treating the Prologue as having a distinct or foreign origin. Its poetic style is certainly no indication of non-Johannine origin. Compare 1 John which contains poetic elements (cf. 1 Jn 2.12-14). As to the second point, while it is true that the *logos* is mentioned only in the Prologue, Jesus acts and teaches as God's 'Word' throughout the Gospel proper. On this point, see B.D. Chilton, 'Typologies of *memra* and the Fourth Gospel', in P. Flesher (ed.), *Methods in the Study of the Targums: Suggestions and Explorations* (Atlanta: Scholars Press, forthcoming). As to language (that is, vocabulary, syntax, style) and concepts, the Prologue is thoroughly Johannine.

Several older studies rightly emphasized the Prologue's relationship to the Gospel, for example, Hoskyns, *Fourth Gospel*, I, p. 130: 'The Prologue...is not so much a preface to the Gospel as a summary of it'. See also T.E. Pollard, 'Cosmology and the Prologue of the Fourth Gospel', *VC* 12 (1958), pp. 147-53, esp. p. 149. For more recent assessments of the Prologue's literary relationship to the Gospel, see H. Thyen, 'Aus der Literatur zum Johannesevangelium', *TRu* 39 (1975), pp. 53-69, 222-52, esp. p. 223: the Prologue is 'a directive to the reader how the entire Gospel should be read and understood'; E.L. Miller, *Salvation-History in the Prologue of John* (NovTSup, 60; Leiden: Brill, 1989), pp. 2-10; Carter, 'The Prologue and John's Gospel', p. 43: the Prologue is interwoven with the concerns and context of the Gospel as a whole; A. Dettwiler, 'Le prologue johannique (Jean 1,1-18)', in Kaestli *et al.* (eds.), *La communauté johannique*, pp. 185-203: the Prologue is closely linked to the Gospel as a whole, for it speaks directly to the issue of Jesus' identity, the issue with which the Gospel as a whole grapples. On the numerous parallels between the Prologue and the body of the Gospel, see J.A.T. Robinson, 'The Relation of the Prologue to the Gospel of St John', *NTS* 9 (1963), pp. 120-29; repr. in *Twelve More New Testament Studies* (London: SCM Press, 1984), pp. 65-

is presented as the fleshly dwelling of the *logos*, that which has existed with God from eternity and that which enlightens the world. As such Jesus represents the fulfillment of eschatological hopes that God (or perhaps his 'extensions' such as Word, Glory, Wisdom or Spirit) would someday 'tabernacle' among humankind. As the human tabernacle in which the glory of God could be witnessed Jesus conducts his ministry as God's agent, an aspect of his ministry clarified by *shaliach* traditions associated with Moses. He does the work of his Father and speaks only what he has heard from him. He says and does nothing from his own accord. But Jesus is an agent vastly superior to Moses, for unlike Moses who only beheld glimpses of God's glory, Jesus *is* God's glory. Unlike Moses, who perhaps visited heaven (either at Sinai or at death), Jesus came from heaven and returned to heaven, having 'finished' his work.

Seen against this Jewish and scriptural background, the possibility that the Fourth Evangelist's Christology has been influenced by a Gnostic myth is by no means excluded, but such a possibility does appear rather remote. There does not appear to be any significant component of Johannine Christology that could be clarified more helpfully by Gnostic mythology than by the scriptural and interpretive traditions I have considered.

76, esp. p. 68; Carson, *Gospel according to John*, p. 111; C.H. Giblin, 'Two Complementary Literary Structures in Jn 1.1-18', *JBL* 104 (1985), pp. 87-103. For an interpretation of the so-called 'Baptist interpolations' as connecting links, see M.D. Hooker, 'John the Baptist and the Johannine Prologue', *NTS* 16 (1970), pp. 354-58. Recently O. Cullmann ('The Theological Content of the Prologue to John in its Present Form', in R.T. Fortna and B.R. Gaventa [eds.], *The Conversation Continues: Studies in Paul and John* [Nashville: Abingdon Press, 1990], pp. 295-98, esp. p. 298) has said: 'As an integrating element in the theological framework of the Gospel of John lying before us it [the Prologue] is in fact indispensable'.

Chapter 6

COMMENTS ON METHOD

In this final chapter I would like to offer a few comments that relate to scholarly criticism of the Fourth Gospel. Some of these comments will summarize findings in previous chapters. Others will touch upon subjects not treated in this book, but which do have a bearing on the wider issue of the Fourth Gospel's provenance. The concern of this book, as stated in the Preface, is as much with method as it is with specific conclusions. The comments that follow will speak, first, to the problem of assessing 'parallels' as an aid in exegesis and in determining a document's provenance and, secondly, to some historical factors that often do not play a significant role in Johannine studies.

Assessing Parallels

It is difficult to understand why Robinson and others persist in arguing that Gnostic writings, such as those found in Nag Hammadi, provide the closest and most natural background against which Johannine theology, and especially the Prologue, should be studied. The biblical and interpretive parallels adduced above in Chapters 3 and 4 enjoy several advantages over the Gnostic parallels that have been presented.

1. All of the biblical parallels (that is, §1–§42) antedate the Fourth Gospel. This, of course, cannot be said with any certainty with respect to the *Trimorphic Protennoia* or other Gnostic writings that yield potential parallels. If the language and ideas of the Prologue can be traced to writings known to have been in existence at the time of the composition of the Fourth Gospel, then on critical grounds it makes little sense to look for parallels in documents that are late or, at best, of uncertain date. Indeed, there is the distinct likelihood that the *Trimorphic Protennoia* actually borrows from the Fourth Gospel, as

well as from other New Testament writings. The reference to Protennoia revealing herself 'in their tents as the Word' (NHC XIII 47.13) is probably an instance of direct dependence upon Jn 1.14. How many other elements depend directly or indirectly on the Fourth Gospel?

2. The exegetical traditions presupposed by the Fourth Evangelist also point to a Jewish context. Johannine interpretation of the various biblical passages quoted or alluded to in the Gospel and Epistles coheres with Jewish (and Jewish Christian) interpretive traditions (§43–§54). (Indeed, in some instances Johannine interpretation differs sharply from Gnostic interpretation of the Old Testament.) What is especially significant is the observation that the Old Testament has supplied the raw materials out of which the Fourth Evangelist has formulated his Christology. Even the feature most commonly associated with Gnostic mythology—that of a divine being's descent and ascent—is grounded on two or three Old Testament passages and coheres with Wisdom and *logos* speculations current in first-century Jewish circles. Another feature which some have thought points to Gnosticism in the Fourth Gospel—dualism—is attested at Qumran, but there its expression is significantly different from typical Gnostic expressions of dualism.

3. Parallels adduced from targumic and midrashic sources (that is, §55–§65) strongly suggest that the provenance of the Fourth Gospel is the synagogue. This suggestion receives support when it is observed that Old Testament characters and themes that receive emphasis in targumic or rabbinic traditions play central roles in major teachings in this Gospel. The references to being expelled from the synagogue (9.22; 12.42; 16.2) only add further confirmation. In contrast, the *Trimorphic Protennoia* and other Gnostic writings are of uncertain origin and provenance, and there is little evidence to suggest that they derive from groups that had more than incidental contact with the synagogue.

4. The point that Carsten Colpe has made with reference to the disparity of the Wisdom traditions, in supposed contrast to their concentration in a single source, such as the *Trimorphic Protennoia*, is overdrawn. After all, most of the Wisdom parallels come from a single source: the Old Testament, and from a single context: the Jewish synagogue. Verses scattered among the pages of three or four tractates within the Jewish–Christian canon of Scripture (though, of

course, hardly 'canonized' at the end of the first century) should not be viewed as 'disparate'. Moreover, the exegesis of Philo demonstrates how the 'link' between Genesis and the theology of the Johannine Prologue can be found in a single individual.

5. Even the most promising parallels between the Fourth Gospel and Gnostic writings are not close enough to clarify Johannine Christology significantly. The oft-made claim that Gnostic soteriology (or 'Christology') shares a common root with New Testament Christology is highly suspect. Pheme Perkins has rightly concluded that the Gnostic writings of Nag Hammadi 'developed their picture of the Savior from traditions quite different from those which underlie NT christological assertions'.[1] She also avers that the 'I am' statements of the Fourth Gospel do not derive from the traditions that came to expression in Gnostic works which contain the *sophia* myth. The findings in the present study comport with Perkins's conclusions.

An important critical axiom of biblical research expects proposed theories to aid in the task of exegesis. The parallels with Sirach and related Jewish Wisdom writings, including some of the exegetical traditions found in the targums, provide such aid. The parallels with *Trimorphic Protennoia* do not. Comparison with the *Trimorphic Protennoia* leads us to suspect that it was part of the broader milieu out which of the Prologue emerged (that aspect of Colpe's conclusion with which I agreed[2]), but it fills in no missing pieces of the puzzle— certainly not that part of it that can be dated with any confidence before the end of the first century. Sirach 24 and related Jewish Wisdom traditions, however, do clarify the picture.

6. Neither has the related, and equally persistent, claim that the Christology (or 'redeemer myth') of the *Trimorphic Protennoia* and other Gnostic writings is pre-Christian and lies behind the theology of the Fourth Gospel been demonstrated. There is simply no firm

---

1. P. Perkins, 'Gnostic Christologies and the New Testament', *CBQ* 43 (1981), pp. 590-606, quotation from p. 606. For further discussion, see *idem*, 'New Testament Christologies in Gnostic Transformation', in B.A. Pearson (ed.), *The Future of Early Christianity* (Minneapolis: Fortress Press, 1991), pp. 433-41.

2. Evans, 'On the Prologue of John', pp. 395-401, esp. p. 399 and p. 401 n. 28. Sanders ('Nag Hammadi, Odes of Solomon', p. 66) rightly speaks of a motif that 'evolves in related but different directions' in the Johannine Prologue and the *Trimorphic Protennoia*. He places this motif 'on the edge of Jewish wisdom speculation'. I would place it well within Jewish speculation.

evidence that this is the case.[1] Years ago A.D. Nock made the prudent comment: 'Certainly it is an unsound proceeding to take Manichaean and other texts, full of echoes of the New Testament, and reconstruct from them something supposedly lying back of the New Testament'.[2] Despite caveats such as this, Robinson and his supporters continue to assume the existence of a pre-Christian redeemer myth as though it were self-evident.

One final point should be made with regard to the utilization of parallels and the search for the Prologue's exegetical and theological background. In his recently published study of the Johannine Prologue, E.L. Miller claims that the

> attempts to trace [the *logos*] concept to some pre-Johannine milieu such as the *dabar* and *hochma* traditions of the Old Testament and Apocrypha, or wisdom speculations of later Jewish literature, or Greek philosophical strains, or Gnosticism, and the like, are utterly misplaced and in the end serve only to dilute and confuse the original meaning and power of John's Logos.[3]

This is an odd statement and there are at least three problems with it. First, these diverse backgrounds are hardly on the same footing. Whereas one or two of these proposed backgrounds may clarify Johannine thought, one or two others could be misleading. It is therefore important to ascertain which is relevant and which is not. Secondly, attempts to uncover the pre-Johannine antecedents are hardly 'misplaced', but are prerequisites to any exegesis. By definition exegesis is concerned with full context, and that includes the theological and literary antecedents to any passage. (Unless we imagine that an author wrote in a vacuum.) Thirdly, other than obviously wrongheaded attempts (such as those of Bultmann and his successors), these attempts do not 'dilute and confuse the original meaning'. An 'original

1. M. Hengel, *Son of God* (Philadelphia: Fortress Press, 1976), p. 33: 'In reality there is no gnostic redeemer myth in the sources which can be demonstrated chronologically to be pre-Christian'. See also Yamauchi, *Pre-Christian Gnosticism*, pp. 163-69, 243-45; Talbert, 'The Myth of a Descending–Ascending Redeemer in Mediterranean Antiquity', pp. 418-40.

2. A.D. Nock, *Essays on Religion and the Ancient World*, II (2 vols.; Cambridge, MA: Harvard University Press, 1972), p. 958; cited by Hengel, *Son of God*, p. 34.

3. E.L. Miller, *Salvation-History in the Prologue of John: The Significance of John 1:3/4* (NovTSup, 60; Leiden: Brill, 1989), p. 1.

meaning' cannot be ascertained apart from background study.

Without disputing the merits of Miller's interpretation of Jn 1.1-5, it is still necessary to inquire into the question of how the evangelist and his community would have interpreted *logos* and its relation to the obvious allusion to Genesis 1. Our concern is with the complex of ideas associated with the whole Prologue, not just with an original christological hymn (whatever its makeup). Miller is apparently not aware of this inconsistency. When he says that Gnostic and Philonic interpretations of πάντα 'assume a philosophical-theological frame of reference which is hardly appropriate for the first verses of John' (particularly Jn 1.3),[1] he has made a background judgment (which I think in this case is accurate). Miller is correct to say that the Johannine concept of *logos* cannot be reduced to what the *logos* meant to groups or persons outside the Johannine community. But it must also be affirmed that it cannot be adequately understood apart from comparative study. The problem does not lie with searching for the exegetical and theological background, the problem lies with defining and applying proper historical criteria for assessing the relevance or irrelevance of literary parallels.[2]

Historical Factors

Finally, there are two other matters that should be addressed: authorship, and the pre-Johannine Jesus tradition. Curiously enough, these factors are often treated as if they were of minimal importance, if treated at all.

Authorship
Perhaps one of the most inexplicable aspects of Johannine scholarship is the lack of interest in the question of authorship.[3] Martin Hengel,

---

1. Miller, *Salvation-History in the Prologue of John*, p. 73.
2. R. Kysar ('The Background of the Prologue of the Fourth Gospel: A Critique of Historical Methods', *CJT* 16 [1970], pp. 250-55) addresses this problem in his comparison of the methods of Bultmann and Dodd.
3. This is particularly so in German scholarship, as Hengel (*The Johannine Question*, p. 136 n. 3) has pointed out. There are some good discussions in English commentaries such as those by Barrett, *Gospel according to St John*, pp. 100-34; Brown, *Gospel according to John*, I, pp. lxxxvii-cii; and Carson, *Gospel according to John*, pp. 68-81.

who has reopened the question of the authorship of the Johannine
Gospel and Epistles, castigates Johannine scholars who treat the question as either too remote for critical investigation or as irrelevant and
out of step with modern thinking. He quotes a recent comment by
Robert Fortna as illustrative:

> I intended at first to entitle this work *The Evangelist John and His
> Predecessor*...Why then avoid speaking of the former in the title?
> Because...the provisional title was sexist, most obviously in the posses-
> sive pronoun 'his' but also in using the traditional name 'John'. The femi-
> nist movement in biblical studies has convinced me that these conventions,
> supposedly innocent in intent and justified by the canon, must be given
> up. Just as we have no idea of the Evangelist's identity and name, so also
> of his or her gender. And like all of the Gospels, that according to 'John'
> is in fact anonymous, its apostolic attribution added roughly a century
> after it was written and on spurious grounds. We cannot know even the
> degree of likelihood that the writer was a male. So the custom of calling
> 'him' by the traditional name 'John' ought to be abandoned.[1]

To this Hengel replies, 'Nevertheless, I think it is time to speak out
against this or similar "progress" towards an ahistorical nirvana'.[2] I
concur. Fortna's comment might be politically correct in today's
academic climate, but it is hardly fair to the ancient sources. It is
simply inaccurate to say that 'we have no idea of the Evangelist's identity and name'. On the contrary, we do. The widely spread tradition
of the second-century church was that the author's name was 'John'.[3]
Admittedly the question of *which* John—the Apostle or the Elder—
was a matter of dispute and some confusion. Late second-century
assertions that the Gospel was a forgery (assertions motivated because
of its exploitation by followers of Montanus) imply that Johannine
authorship was already well known. Similarly, the claim by some that
it had been authored by Cerinthus was a reckless attempt to discredit
this Gospel whose theology had been exploited by second-century
Gnostic groups. Despite these vulnerabilities, the Fourth Gospel, along
with its Johannine tradition of authorship, continued to enjoy wide

---

1.   R.T. Fortna, *The Fourth Gospel and its Predecessor* (Philadelphia: Fortress
Press, 1988) xi, cited by Hengel, *The Johannine Question*, pp. 136-37 n. 3.
2.   Hengel, *The Johannine Question*, p. 137 n. 3.
3.   See Papias, *Frags.*; Irenaeus, *Ep. ad Flor.*; *Adv. Haer.* 2.22.5; 3.1.1; 3.3.4;
Muratori Canon, pp. 9-16; Eusebius, *Hist. Eccl.* 3.23.3-4; 3.31.3; 3.39.3-4; 4.14.3-
8; 5.8.4; 5.20.4-8; 5.24.2-3. Second-century MSS also attest Johannine authorship; cf.
$\mathfrak{P}^{45}$, $\mathfrak{P}^{72}$.

recognition.[1] Hengel's study—refreshing for its reliance on facts and common sense (as opposed to unsubstantiated and subjective hypotheses)—concludes that the author was John (not the son of Zebedee or one of the other apostles), of priestly family, who as a very young man had followed Jesus, and who became known in Asia Minor as the 'beloved disciple'.

Hengel's conclusion is consistent with the findings of this book. The internal evidence suggests that the author was a Palestinian Jew, familiar with Judea and Jerusalem, who wrote in a Diaspora context in a way that is best understood against the background of the late first-century synagogue. Hengel's examination of the external evidence leads to the same conclusion. In my judgment scholars who uncritically make and accept assertions that the authorship of the Fourth Gospel is unknown and irrelevant undermine the exegetical task. Exegesis based on this kind of thinking lacks a historical orientation and is in danger of becoming docetic, in that it only appears to be genuine historical-literary exegesis.

Pre-Johannine Jesus Tradition

Years ago Bultmann rightly recognized that Jesus' logia were viewed as Wisdom sayings (especially in Q).[2] He went astray, however, in supposing that the Old Testament 'myth of divine Wisdom' (such as seen in Prov. 1.20-33)[3] paralleled the hypothetical 'myth of the Primal Man'.[4] Unfortunately there was no evidence for the existence of a first-century Primal Man myth and therefore of any parallel with Wisdom mythology. Nevertheless, assuming Bultmann to be correct, even if lacking adequate documentation, Robinson has tried to trace a trajectory in which one moves 'from God's Sophia to the gnostic redeemer'.[5]

---

1. See Hengel, *The Johannine Question*, pp. 1-23.
2. R. Bultmann, *History of the Synoptic Tradition* (Oxford: Basil Blackwell, 1972), pp. 69-108.
3. For a discussion of the antecedents of the Old Testament myth of divine Wisdom, see H. Conzelmann, 'Die Mutter der Weisheit', in E. Dinkler (ed.), *Zeit und Geschichte: Dankesgabe an Rudolf Bultmann zum 80. Geburtstag* (Tübingen: Mohr [Paul Siebeck], 1964), pp. 225-34. Conzelmann gives special attention to Sirach 24. He suspects that a major influence was ancient Egyptian wisdom.
4. Bultmann, *History of the Synoptic Tradition*, pp. 114-15.
5. J.M. Robinson, 'LOGOI SOPHON: On the Gattung of Q', in Robinson and Koester, *Trajectories through Early Christianity*, pp. 71-113, quotation from p. 113 n. 95.

Following Bultmann's lead, Robinson believes that the trajectory began with the personification of Wisdom,[1] which in Christian circles came to be identified with Jesus himself. Once this identification was made, it was natural that under the influence of Gnostic ideas (such as those attested in the *Trimorphic Protennoia*) Jesus came to be understood as the heavenly redeemer of the Gnostic myth.[2] Stated in these terms one can hardly object. This basic sequence of development is probably correct. What creates the problem is *where* in this trajectory Bultmann and Robinson locate the Christologies of Paul and John. According to them the Gnostic myth penetrated the Wisdom Christology trajectory *before* Paul and the Fourth Evangelist formulated their respective theologies. Robinson quotes Kurt Rudolph with approval: 'In my opinion Paul and the anonymous author of the Gospel of John presuppose a gnostic-type doctrine of the redeemer'.[3] For the reasons already presented in this book there is insufficient evidence (and certainly no need) to explain Pauline and Johannine Christologies in terms of a Gnostic myth. It is doubtful that such a myth existed in the first century. It is more likely that such a myth took shape in the second century and was dependent in differing degrees upon Old Testament Wisdom and New Testament Christology and various speculations—Jewish and Christian—that had grown up around them.

The trajectory proposed by Bultmann and Robinson is also faulty because it has not adequately taken into account the Old Testament antecedents and the interpretive speculations that accompanied them. One such antecedent had to do with ideas about God dwelling on earth or in Israel. This trajectory begins with the Mosaic dictum that God had chosen to 'dwell' in Israel (Exod. 25.8), which is taken up in the later prophets' hope that the day will come when God will again 'dwell' in Israel (Joel 3.17; Zech. 2.10), and eventually comes to be related to Wisdom traditions that describe Wisdom (and Word) sojourning and dwelling among people. It is this combination of Wisdom seeking a place of habitation on earth and the dwelling of God among human beings that is presupposed by the Johannine

---

1. U. Wilckens, 'σοφία, κτλ', *TDNT*, VII, pp. 507-509; and G. Fohrer on Wisdom in the Old Testament ('σοφία, κτλ', *TDNT*, VII, pp. 489-92).

2. Robinson, 'LOGOI SOPHON', pp. 104-105, 112-13.

3. Robinson, 'The Johannine Trajectory', p. 263. This position has been repeated recently by Koester, 'Les discours d'adieu de l'évangile de Jean', pp. 269-80.

Prologue, particularly v. 14: 'and the Word became flesh and taber-nacled among us, and we beheld his glory'. In this statement these two themes converge: Wisdom who was commanded to 'tabernacle' among the children of Jacob (Sir. 24.8) and the 'glory' of God which filled the 'tabernacle' (Exod. 40.31). These are the traditions presupposed by the Fourth Evangelist, not a Gnostic myth of a Primal Man.[1]

To what degree did the activities and teachings of the historical Jesus fit into and contribute to this Jewish Wisdom/tabernacle trajectory? The very style of Jesus' teaching and ministry (cf. Mt. 11.19 = Lk. 7.35) probably suggested to his earliest followers a fusion of Jesus as Wisdom incarnate with the prophetic hope of God's dwelling among his people. There are several sayings in Q, whose contents represent the earliest extant material, that strongly suggest that Jesus was understood as God's Wisdom.[2] Consider Lk. 10.21-22 (= Mt. 11.25-27) where Jesus thanks God that he has revealed his Son to 'babes' (νήπιοι), rather than to the wise and learned.[3] The saying is reminiscent of Wis. 10.21 where we hear that 'Wisdom opened the mouth of the dumb, and made the tongues of babes (νήπιοι) eloquent'. To this context the Matthean evangelist adds the related saying:

---

1. The Johannine Prologue represents a logical extension of the Wisdom/tabernacle trajectory. It contains nothing that is foreign to it. On the other hand, the *Trimorphic Protennoia*, in its extant form, represents a Gnostic reinterpretation of this trajectory. When stripped of its secondary Gnostic and Christian elements, along the lines suggested by Turner ('Trimorphic Protennoia', pp. 512-13), it contributes nothing that was not by the end of the first century in circulation in the complex and diverse Jewish wisdom traditions.

2. See J.S. Kloppenborg, *The Formation of Q: Trajectories in Ancient Wisdom Collections* (Studies in Antiquity & Christianity; Philadelphia: Fortress Press, 1987), pp. 171-263; R.A. Piper, *Wisdom in the Q Tradition: The Aphoristic Teaching of Jesus* (SNTSMS, 61; Cambridge: Cambridge University Press, 1989).

3. Bultmann (*History of the Synoptic Tradition*, p. 160), among others, accepts the authenticity of Mt. 11.25-26. More recently, J.A. Fitzmyer (*The Gospel according to Luke X–XXIV* [AB, 28a; Garden City, NY: Doubleday, 1985], p. 870) has opined: 'I am inclined to regard the substance of these sayings as authentic'. W. Grimm (*Jesus und das Danielbuch* [ANTJ, 6.2; Frankfurt am Main: Peter Lang, 1984], pp. 48-49, 97-100) agrees, arguing that the historical Jesus polemicized against the Danielic view that wisdom was for the learned and the professional (cf. Dan. 1.17; 2.21).

Come (δεῦτε) to me (πρός με) all who labor (κοπιᾶν) and are heavy laden, and I will give you rest (ἀναπαύειν). Take my yoke (ζυγός) upon you and learn from me, for I am meek and lowly in heart, and you will find rest (ἀνάπαυσις) for your souls (ψυχή). For my yoke (ζυγός) is easy and my burden is light (Mt. 11.28-30).[1]

We are reminded of Wisdom's summons: 'Come to me (πρός με)' (Sir. 24.19; cf. Prov. 9.5); 'Come (δεῦτε), therefore, let us enjoy the good things...' (Wis. 2.6); 'Come (δεῦτε), O children, listen to me, I will teach you the fear of the Lord' (LXX Ps. 33.12 [34.11]). Especially interesting is Sir. 51.23-27: 'Draw near to me (πρός με), you who are untaught... Put your neck under the yoke (ζυγός), and let your soul (ψυχή) receive instruction; it is to be found close by. See with your eyes that I have labored (κοπιᾶν) little and found for myself much rest (ἀνάπαυσις)'.[2] These sayings hint that Jesus may have understood himself as God's Wisdom (or as Wisdom's messenger). This suspicion is confirmed when he claims to be 'greater than Solomon' (Lk. 11.31 = Mt. 12.42), Israel's famous patron of Wisdom.[3] In light of these passages and others Hengel has concluded that Jesus understood himself as the messianic teacher of wisdom, indeed as Wisdom's envoy.[4]

---

1. A few scholars have regarded Mt. 11.28-30 as authentic dominical tradition; cf. E. Klostermann, *Das Matthäusevangelium* (HNT, 4; Tübingen: Mohr [Paul Siebeck], 4th edn, 1971), p. 102; A.M. Hunter, 'Crux Criticorum—Matt. 11.25-30', *NTS* 8 (1962), pp. 241-49; S. Bacchiocchi, 'Matthew 11.28-30: Jesus' Rest and the Sabbath', *AUSS* 22 (1984), pp. 289-316. Others have contested this view; cf. R.H. Gundry, *Matthew: A Commentary on his Literary and Theological Art* (Grand Rapids: Eerdmans, 1982), p. 219; C. Deutsch, *Hidden Wisdom and the Easy Yoke: Wisdom, Torah and Discipleship in Matthew 11.25-30* (JSNTSup, 18; Sheffield: JSOT Press, 1987), p. 51; W.D. Davies and D.C. Allison, *The Gospel according to Matthew VIII–XVIII* (ICC; Edinburgh: T. & T. Clark, 1991), p. 293. If the substance of Mt. 11.28-30 does indeed go back to Jesus, there can be little question that the tradition has been heavily edited (cf. Davies and Allison, *Matthew*, pp. 287-91). But if inauthentic, Mt. 11.28-30 does reflect aspects of Jesus' manner of speaking and acting as Wisdom's envoy.

2. See J.D.G. Dunn, *Christology in the Making: A New Testament Inquiry into the Origins of the Doctrine of the Incarnation* (London: SCM Press, 1980), pp. 163-64.

3. Bultmann (*History of the Synoptic Tradition*, pp. 112-13) accepts the saying as authentic.

4. M. Hengel, 'Jesus als messianischer Lehrer der Weisheit und die Anfänge der Christologie', in J. Leclant *et al.* (eds.), *Sagesse et Religion: Colloque de*

It is this self-understanding on the part of Jesus that probably explains why *sophia* speculations became part of Christology. But Bultmann wondered how to account for the shift from *sophia* to *logos*:

> But now the question arises why a figure encountered in Jewish writings as *Wisdom* should be called *Logos* in the Prologue. The assumption that the evangelist made the change of his own accord is far from obvious... there is at best an indirect allusion to the 'Word' in Gen. 1. In fact most scholars assume that he has borrowed the Logos concept from elsewhere...which makes one think of *Alexandrian-Jewish speculation*... But a direct dependence on Philo can, I believe, be excluded. There is nothing *specifically* Philonic in the Prologue, even if the phrase 'the Word was God'...be traced to Philo's idea of the Logos as a 'second God'...[1]

It should be remembered that in Sirach 24 Sophia describes herself as having issued forth from the mouth of the Most High (v. 3), while in the Wisdom of Solomon Sophia becomes *logos* (18.15). In Bar. 4.1 Sophia is explicitly identified with God's Torah (which is often referred to as God's Word).[2] But apart from these examples which could explain the Johannine shift, a fallacy lies behind Bultmann's discussion. Why must the Johannine *logos* be identical to Philo's *logos* and give evidence of 'direct dependence'? Is there no room for even a small measure of creativity? In this case very little creativity is required. The Jesus tradition goes a long way toward adumbrating the possibilities that lay before the Fourth Evangelist: Jesus proclaims the word, he becomes the Word; Jesus speaks wisdom, he becomes Wisdom.[3] In view of these tendencies, is it really necessary to find a detailed paradigm or myth in order to understand how the Fourth Evangelist could have conceived of Jesus as God's Word incarnate and of his origins and ministry in terms of Wisdom ideas?

Strasbourg, Octobre 1976 (Paris: Bibliothèque des Centres d'Etudes Supérieures Spécialisés, 1979), pp. 147-88, esp. pp. 163-66, 180-88. See also B. Witherington, *The Christology of Jesus* (Minneapolis: Fortress Press, 1990), pp. 51-53, 221-28, 274-75; B.L. Mack, 'The Christ and Jewish Wisdom', in Charlesworth (ed.), *The Messiah: Developments in Earliest Judaism and Christianity*, pp. 192-221, esp. pp. 210-15.

1. Bultmann, 'History of Religions Background', p. 27.

2. U. Wilckens, *Weisheit und Torheit* (BHT, 26; Tübingen: Mohr [Paul Siebeck], 1959).

3. R. Kittel, 'λέγω, λόγος, κτλ', *TDNT*, IV, pp. 124-28; Wilckens, 'σοφία, κτλ', pp. 514-22; cf. D.K. Clark, 'Signs and Wisdom in John', *CBQ* 45 (1983), pp. 201-209.

The *sophia*/Gnostic redeemer trajectory, as it developed in the Christian period, should, in my judgment, be traced as follows. 1. Jesus is viewed as possessing wisdom (synoptic tradition attests this). 2. Jesus comes to be viewed as Wisdom itself (synoptics hint at this, Paul asserts this). 3. Jesus, as God's Wisdom, is also God's *logos*, and therefore has the same functions as Word and Wisdom, for example, creation and redemption (pronounced in the Fourth Gospel, less developed in Paul). 4. The Pauline and Johannine Christologies, especially the latter, were much more attractive to emerging Gnostic speculations and probably provided the framework for the Gnostic redeemer myth. This myth likely did not take shape before the early part of the second century. The myth was not limited in its application to Jesus (such as in the *Apocryphon of John*), but could be applied to other ancient worthies (such as Seth or Adam). Indeed, the myth could influence Wisdom material (such as what originally made up the *Trimorphic Protennoia*). 5. In later, edited forms, these writings were secondarily Christianized (and in some cases Gnosticized).[1]

Conclusion

This study has led to the conclusion that the principal background against which the Johannine Prologue should be read is that of the Old Testament and various first-century interpretations and speculations relating to it. The context or provenance of the Prologue is the synagogue of the Diaspora. The specific antecedents of the Prologue consist of biblical texts relating to creation and the Sinai covenant interpreted against the Old Testament myth of Wisdom and ideas of God dwelling in Israel. The application of these traditions to Jesus was facilitated, if not suggested, by the style and content of some of Jesus' teaching: Jesus uttered Wisdom sayings and may very well have portrayed himself as God's Wisdom. This element was taken up early on, evidently exploited in the Diaspora setting (as evidenced by Paul), and reached its logical conclusion in its absolutized form in the Johannine

---

1.   For studies that have reached conclusions compatible with my proposal, see E.D. Freed, 'Theological Prelude to the Prologue of John's Gospel', *SJT* 32 (1979), pp. 257-69; W.R.G. Loader, 'The Central Structure of Johannine Christology', *NTS* 30 (1984), pp. 188-216; C.R. Koester, *The Dwelling of God: The Tabernacle in the Old Testament, Intertestamental Jewish Literature, and the New Testament* (CBQMS, 22; Washington: Catholic Biblical Association, 1989), pp. 100-15.

Prologue. At no point in this evolution is there a missing link which only Gnostic mythology can supply. Gnostic myths of a redeemed redeemer evidently originated in the second and third centuries, borrowing freely from Judaism, Christianity and passages from the Old and New Testaments. Parallels in some later traditions, such as those found in the targums and rabbinic writings, give indications of the continuity of several interpretive elements in the Fourth Gospel and only add conviction to the conclusion that the provenance of the Johannine community was the synagogue.

BIBLIOGRAPHY

Ackerman, J.S., 'The Rabbinic Interpretation of Psalm 82 and the Gospel of John: Jn 10.34', *HTR* 59 (1966), pp. 186-91.

Albright, W.F., 'Recent Discoveries in Palestine and the Gospel of John', in W.D. Davies and D. Daube (eds.), *The Background of the New Testament and its Eschatology* (Cambridge: Cambridge University Press, 1956), pp. 153-71.

Alexander, P.S., 'Rabbinic Judaism and the New Testament', *ZNW* 74 (1983), pp. 237-46.

Anderson, G., 'The Interpretation of Genesis 1.1 in the Targums', *CBQ* 52 (1990), pp. 21-29.

Ashton, J. (ed.), *The Interpretation of John* (London: SPCK; Philadelphia: Fortress Press, 1986).

—'The Transformation of Wisdom: A Study of the Prologue of John's Gospel', *NTS* 32 (1986), pp. 161-86.

Bacchiocchi, S., 'Matthew 11.28-30: Jesus' Rest and the Sabbath', *AUSS* 22 (1984), pp. 289-316.

Barrett, C.K., *The Gospel according to St. John* (London: SPCK; Philadelphia: Westminster Press, 2nd edn, 1978).

—*Das Johannesevangelium und das Judentum: Franz Delitzsch-Vorlesungen 1967* (Stuttgart: Kohlhammer, 1970); ET *The Gospel of John and Judaism* (London: SPCK; Philadelphia: Fortress Press, 1975).

—'The Old Testament in the Fourth Gospel', *JTS* 48 (1947), pp. 155-69.

—*The Prologue of St John's Gospel* (London: Athlone Press, 1971); repr. in C.K. Barrett, *New Testament Essays* (London: SPCK, 1972), p. 27-48.

—'*Shaliah* and Apostle', in E. Bammel *et al.* (eds.), *Donum Gentilicium: New Testament Studies in Honour of David Daube* (Oxford: Clarendon Press, 1978), pp. 88-102.

—'The Theological Vocabulary of the Fourth Gospel and of the Gospel of Truth', in W. Klassen and G.F. Snyder (eds.), *Current Issues in New Testament Interpretation: Essays in Honor of Otto A. Piper* (New York: Harper & Row; London: SCM Press, 1962), pp. 210-23.

Barton, G.A., '"A Bone of Him Shall Not Be Broken", John 19.36', *JBL* 49 (1930), pp. 13-19.

Bauer, W., *Das Johannesevangelium* (HNT, 6; Tübingen: Mohr [Paul Siebeck], 3rd edn, 1933).

Beasley-Murray, G.R., *John* (WBC, 36; Dallas: Word Books, 1987).

Becker, J. 'Beobachtungen zum Dualismus im Johannesevangelium', *ZNW* 65 (1974), pp. 71-87.

Behm, J., 'παράκλητος', *TDNT*, V, pp. 800-14.

Betz, O., *Jesus: Der Messias Israels: Aufsätze zur biblischen Theologie* (WUNT, 42; Tübingen: Mohr [Paul Siebeck], 1987).

—*Der Paraklet: Fürsprecher im häretischen Spätjudentum, im Johannesevangelium und in neu gefundenen gnostischen Schriften* (AGJU, 2; Leiden: Brill, 1963).

Beutler, J., 'Der alttestamentlich-jüdische Hintergrund der Hirtenrede in Johannes 10', in J. Beutler and R.T. Fortna (eds.), *The Shepherd Discourse of John 10 and its Context* (SNTSMS, 67; Cambridge: Cambridge University Press, 1991), pp. 18-32, 144-47.

—'Greeks Come to See Jesus (John 12,2f)', *Bib* 71 (1990), pp. 333-47.

Black, M., *An Aramaic Approach to the Gospels and Acts* (Oxford: Clarendon Press, 3rd edn, 1967).

—*The Scrolls and Christian Origins* (New York: Charles Scribner's Sons, 1961).

Böcher, O., *Der johanneische Dualismus im Zusammenhang des nachbiblischen Judentums* (Gütersloh: Gerd Mohn, 1965).

Boismard, M.-E., 'The First Epistle of John and the Writings of Qumran', in J.H. Charlesworth (ed.), *John and the Dead Sea Scrolls* (repr.; New York: Crossroad, 1990 [1972]), pp. 156-65.

—*Moïse ou Jésus: Essai de christologie johannique* (BETL, 84; Leuven: Leuven University Press, 1988).

—*Le Prologue de Saint Jean* (LD, 11; Paris: Cerf, 1953); ET *St. John's Prologue* (London: Blackfriars; Westminster: Newman, 1957).

Bonnet, J., *Le 'midrash' de l'Evangile de Saint Jean* (St-Etienne: Hénaff, 2nd edn, 1982).

Borgen, P., *Bread from Heaven: An Exegetical Study of the Concept of Manna in the Gospel of John and the Writings of Philo* (NovTSup, 10; Leiden: Brill, 1965).

—'God's Agent in the Fourth Gospel', in J. Neusner (ed.), *Religions in Antiquity* (NumSup, 14; Leiden: Brill, 1968), pp. 137-48; repr. in J. Ashton (ed.), *The Interpretation of John* (London: SPCK; Philadelphia: Fortress Press, 1986), pp. 67-78.

—'Logos var det sanne lys: Momenter til tolkning av Johannesprologen', *SEÅ* 35 (1970), pp. 79-95; ET 'Logos was the True Light', *NovT* 14 (1972), pp. 115-30.

—'Observations on the Midrashic Character of John 6', *ZNW* 54 (1963), pp. 232-40.

—'Observations on the Targumic Character of the Prologue of John', *NTS* 16 (1970), pp. 288-95.

—'Philo of Alexandria', in M.E. Stone (ed.), *Jewish Writings of the Second Temple Period* (CRINT, 2.2; Philadelphia: Fortress Press, 1984) 233-82.

—*Philo, John and Paul: New Perspectives on Judaism and Early Christianity* (BJS, 131; Atlanta: Scholars Press, 1987).

—'Some Jewish Exegetical Traditions as Background for Son of Man Sayings in John's Gospel (Jn 3, 13-14 and Context)', in M. de Jonge (ed.), *L'Evangile de Jean: Sources, rédaction, théologie* (BETL, 44; Gembloux: Duculot, 1977), pp. 243-59.

—'The Use of Tradition in John 12.44-50', *NTS* 26 (1979), pp. 18-35.

Borig, R., *Der wahre Weinstock: Untersuchungen zu Jo 15,1-10* (SANT, 16; Munich: Kösel, 1967).

Bornhäuser, K., *Das Johannesevangelium: Eine Missionsschrift für Israel* (BFCT, 2.15; Gütersloh: Bertelsmann, 1928).

Bornkamm, G., 'Der Paraklet im Johannes-Evangelium', in E. Wolf (ed.), *Festschrift*

Rudolf Bultmann zum 65. Geburtstag überreicht (Stuttgart: Kohlhammer, 1949), pp. 12-35; revised and repr. in G. Bornkamm, *Geschichte und Glaube*, III (GA; 3 vols.; Munich: Chr. Kaiser Verlag, 1968), pp. 68-89.

Bousset, W., *KYRIOS CHRISTOS: Geschichte des Christusglaubens von den Anfängen des Christentums bis Irenaeus* (Göttingen: Vandenhoeck & Ruprecht, 5th edn, 1965); ET *KYRIOS CHRISTOS: A History of the Belief in Christ from the Beginnings of Christianity to Irenaeus* (Nashville: Abingdon Press, 1970).

Bowker, J., *The Targums and Rabbinic Literature* (Cambridge: Cambridge University Press, 1969).

Braun, F.-M., 'Hermétisme et Johannisme', *RevThom* 55 (1955), pp. 22-42, 259-99.

Braun, H., *Qumran und das Neue Testament* (2 vols.; Tübingen: Mohr [Paul Siebeck], 1966).

Brown, R.E., 'The Dead Sea Scrolls and the New Testament', *ExpTim* 78 (1966), pp. 19-23; repr. in J.H. Charlesworth (ed.), *John and the Dead Sea Scrolls* (repr.; New York: Crossroad, 1990 [1972]), pp. 1-8.

—*The Gospel according to John* (AB, 29, 29a; 2 vols.; Garden City, NY: Doubleday, 1966–70).

—'The Gospel of Thomas and St John's Gospel', *NTS* 9 (1963), pp. 155-77.

—'The Qumran Scrolls and the Johannine Gospel and Epistles', *CBQ* 17 (1955), pp. 403-19, 559-74; repr. in K. Stendahl (ed.), *The Scrolls and the New Testament* (New York: Harper & Row, 1957; London: SCM Press, 1958), pp. 183-207; repr. in R.E. Brown, *New Testament Essays* (Garden City, NY: Doubleday, 1968), pp. 138-73.

—*The Semitic Background of 'Mystery' in the New Testament* (Philadelphia: Fortress Press, 1968).

Brownlee, W.H., 'The Habakkuk Midrash and the Targum of Jonathan', *JJS* 7 (1956), pp. 169-86.

—'Whence the Gospel According to John?', in J.H. Charlesworth (ed.), *John and the Dead Sea Scrolls* (repr.; New York: Crossroad, 1990 [1972]), pp. 166-94.

Brownson, J., 'The Odes of Solomon and the Johannine Tradition', *JSP* 2 (1988), pp. 49-69.

Bühner, J.-A., *Der Gesandte und sein Weg im 4. Evangelium: Die kultur- und religionsgeschichtlichen Grundlagen der johanneischen Sendungschristologie sowie ihre traditionsgeschichtliche Entwicklung* (WUNT, 2.2; Tübingen: Mohr [Paul Siebeck], 1977).

Bultmann, R., 'Die Bedeutung der neuerschlossenen mandäischen und manichäischen Quellen für das Verständnis des Johannesevangeliums', *ZTK* 24 (1925) 100-46; repr. in *Exegetica: Aufsätze zur Erforschung des Neuen Testaments* (ed. E. Dinkler; Tübingen: Mohr [Paul Siebeck], 1968), pp. 55-104.

—*Das Evangelium des Johannes* (KEK, 2; Göttingen: Vandenhoeck & Ruprecht, 1964); ET *The Gospel of John* (Oxford: Basil Blackwell; Philadelphia: Westminster Press, 1971).

—*Die Geschichte der synoptischen Tradition* (Göttingen: Vandenhoeck & Ruprecht, 2nd edn, 1931); ET *History of the Synoptic Tradition* (Oxford: Basil Blackwell, 1972).

—'γινώσκω, γνῶσις, κτλ', *TDNT*, I, pp. 689-719.

—'Johannesevangeliums', *RGG*, III, cols. 840-50.

—*Primitive Christianity in its Contemporary Setting* (London: Thames & Hudson; New York: Meridian, 1955).

—'Der religionsgeschichtliche Hintergrund des Prologs zum Johannesevangelium', in H. Schmidt (ed.), *EYXAPIΣTHPION: Studien zur Religion und Literatur des Alten und Neuen Testaments*, II (FRLANT, 36; 2 vols.; Göttingen: Vandenhoeck & Ruprecht, 1923), pp. 3-26; repr. in R. Bultmann, *Exegetica: Aufsätze zur Erforschung des Neuen Testaments* (ed. E. Dinkler; Tübingen: Mohr [Paul Siebeck], 1967), pp. 10-35; ET 'The History of Religions Background of the Prologue to the Gospel of John', in J. Ashton (ed.), *The Interpretation of John* (London: SPCK; Philadelphia: Fortress Press, 1986), pp. 18-35.

—*Theologie des Neuen Testaments* (Tübingen: Mohr [Paul Siebeck], 3rd edn, 1958); ET *Theology of the New Testament* (2 vols.; New York: Charles Scribner's Sons, 1951–55).

Burge, G.M., *The Anointed Community: The Holy Spirit in the Johannine Tradition* (Grand Rapids: Eerdmans, 1987).

Burkett, D., *The Son of Man in the Gospel of John* (JSNTSup, 56; Sheffield: JSOT Press, 1991).

Burkitt, F.C., *Church and Gnosis* (Cambridge: Cambridge University Press, 1932).

Burney, C.F., *The Aramaic Origin of the Fourth Gospel* (Oxford: Clarendon Press, 1922).

Caird, G.B., 'The Glory of God in the Fourth Gospel: An Exercise in Biblical Semantics', *NTS* 15 (1969), pp. 265-77.

Carey, G.L., 'Lamb of God and Atonement Theories', *TynBul* 32 (1981), pp. 97-122.

Carmignac, J., 'Les affinités qumrâniennes de la onzième Ode de Salomon', *RevQ* 3 (1961), pp. 71-102.

—'Un Qumrânien converti au Christianisme: l'auteurs des Odes de Salomon', in H. Bardtke (ed.), *Qumran-Probleme* (Berlin: Akademie Verlag, 1963), pp. 75-108.

Carson, D.A., *The Gospel according to John* (Grand Rapids: Eerdmans, 1991).

—'John and the Johannine Epistles', in D.A. Carson and H.G.M. Williamson (eds.), *It is Written: Scripture Citing Scripture: Essays in Honour of Barnabas Lindars, SSF* (Cambridge: Cambridge University Press, 1988), pp. 245-64.

Carter, W., 'The Prologue and John's Gospel: Function, Symbol and the Definitive Word', *JSNT* 39 (1990), pp. 35-58.

Casey, R.P., 'Gnosis, Gnosticism and the New Testament', in W.D. Davies and D. Daube (eds.), *The Background of the New Testament and its Eschatology: In Honour of Charles Harold Dodd* (Cambridge: Cambridge University Press, 1956), pp. 52-80.

Cathcart, K.J., and R.P. Gordon, *The Targum of the Minor Prophets* (ArBib, 14; Wilmington, DE: Michael Glazier, 1989).

Charlesworth, J.H., 'A Critical Comparison of the Dualism in 1QS 3.13–4.26 and the "Dualism" Contained in the Gospel of John', *NTS* 15 (1969), pp. 389-418; repr. in J.H. Charlesworth (ed.), *John and the Dead Sea Scrolls* (repr.; New York: Crossroad, 1990 [1972]), pp. 76-106.

—'The Jewish Roots of Christology: The Discovery of the Hypostatic Voice', *SJT* 39 (1986), pp. 19-41.

—'Odes of Solomon', in J.H. Charlesworth (ed.), *The Old Testament Pseudepigrapha*, II (2 vols.; Garden City, NY: Doubleday, 1983–85), pp. 725-71.

204 *Word and Glory*

—*The Odes of Solomon* (SBLTT: Pseudepigrapha Series, 7; Missoula, MT: Scholars Press, 1978).

—'The Odes of Solomon—Not Gnostic', *CBQ* 31 (1969), pp. 357-69.

—'Qumran, John and the Odes of Solomon', in J.H. Charlesworth (ed.), *John and the Dead Sea Scrolls* (repr.; New York: Crossroad, 1990 [1972]), pp. 107-36.

Charlesworth, J.H. (ed.), *John and the Dead Sea Scrolls* (repr.; New York: Crossroad, 1990 [1972]).

Charlesworth, J.H. and R.A. Culpepper, 'The Odes of Solomon and the Gospel of John', *CBQ* 35 (1973), pp. 298-322.

Chester, A., *Divine Revelation and Divine Titles in the Pentateuchal Targumim* (Tübingen: Mohr [Paul Siebeck], 1986).

Chilton, B.D., *A Galilean Rabbi and His Bible: Jesus' Use of the Interpreted Scripture of His Time* (GNS, 8; Wilmington, DE: Michael Glazier, 1984) = *A Galilean Rabbi and His Bible: Jesus' Own Interpretation of Isaiah* (London: SPCK, 1984).

—*The Glory of Israel: The Theology and Provenance of the Isaiah Targum* (JSOTSup, 23; Sheffield: JSOT Press, 1983).

—*The Isaiah Targum* (ArBib, 11; Wilmington, DE: Michael Glazier, 1987).

—'Recent and Prospective Discussion of *Memra*', in J. Neusner *et al.* (eds.), *From Ancient Israel to Modern Judaism: Intellect in Quest of Understanding* (BJS, 173; Atlanta: Scholars Press, 1989), pp. 119-37.

—'Typologies of *memra* and the Fourth Gospel', in P.V.M. Flesher (ed.), *Textual and Contextual Studies in the Pentateuchal Targums* (Targum Studies, 1; Atlanta: Scholars Press, forthcoming).

Clark, D.K., 'Signs and Wisdom in John', *CBQ* 45 (1983), pp. 201-209.

Colpe, C., 'Heidnische, jüdische und christliche Überlieferung in den Schriften aus Nag Hammadi, III', *JAC* 17 (1974), pp. 109-25.

—'New Testament and Gnostic Christology', in J. Neusner (ed.), *Religions in Antiquity* (NumSup, 14; Leiden: Brill, 1968), pp. 227-43.

—*Die religionsgeschichtliche Schule: Darstellung und Kritik ihres Bildes vom gnostischen Erlösermythus* (FRLANT, 60; Göttingen: Vandenhoeck & Ruprecht, 1961).

Colson, F.H., G.H. Whitaker, J.W. Earp and R. Marcus, *Philo* (LCL; 12 vols.; Cambridge, MA: Harvard University Press, 1929–53).

Conzelmann, H., 'Die Mutter der Weisheit', in E. Dinkler (ed.), *Zeit und Geschichte: Dankesgabe an Rudolf Bultmann zum 80. Geburtstag* (Tübingen: Mohr [Paul Siebeck], 1964), pp. 225-34; ET 'The Mother of Wisdom', in J.M. Robinson (ed.), *The Future of Our Religious Past* (New York and London: Harper & Row, 1971), pp. 230-43.

Crossan, J.D., *Four Other Gospels: Shadows on the Contours of Canon* (Minneapolis: Winston, 1985).

Cullmann, O., *Der johanneische Kreis: Sein Platz im Spätjudentum, in der Jüngerschaft und im Urchristentum* (Tübingen: Mohr [Paul Siebeck], 1975); ET *The Johannine Circle* (London: SCM Press; Philadelphia: Westminster Press, 1976).

—'L'Opposition contre le temple de Jérusalem, motif commun de la théologie johannique et du monde ambiant', *NTS* 5 (1959), pp. 157-73.

—'The Significance of the Qumran Texts for Research into the Beginnings of Christianity', *JBL* 74 (1955), pp. 213-26; repr. in K. Stendahl (ed.), *The Scrolls and the New Testament* (New York: Harper & Brothers; London: SCM Press, 1958), pp. 18-32.

—'The Theological Content of the Prologue to John in its Present Form', in R.T. Fortna and B.R. Gaventa (eds.), *The Conversation Continues: Studies in Paul and John in Honor of J. Louis Martyn* (Nashville: Abingdon Press, 1990), pp. 295-98.

Culpepper, R.A., 'The Pivot of John's Prologue', *NTS* 27 (1980), pp. 1-31.

Cumming, J.L., '"We Beheld His Glory": Some Aspects of the Old Testament/Semitic Background of Jn 1.14-18 and Exegetical Implications' (unpublished paper; Pasadena, CA: Fuller Theological Seminary, 1991).

Dahl, N.A., 'Der Erstgeborene Satans und der Vater des Teufels (Polyk. 7.1 und Joh 8.44)', in U. Eickelberg *et al.* (eds.), *Apophoreta: Festschrift für Ernst Haenchen zu seinem siebzigsten Gehurtstag* (BZNW, 30; Berlin: Töpelmann, 1964), pp. 70-84.

Dalman, G., *Die Worte Jesu* (Leipzig: Hinrichs, 2nd edn, 1930); ET *The Words of Jesus* (Edinburgh: T. & T. Clark, 1902).

Daube, D., *The New Testament and Rabbinic Judaism* (repr.; New York: Arno, 1973).

Davies, W.D., and D.C. Allison, *The Gospel according to Matthew VIII–XVIII* (ICC; Edinburgh: T. & T. Clark, 1991).

—'The Use of the Word χριστός in the Johannine Epistles', in A.S. Geyser *et al.* (eds.), *Studies in John: Presented to Professor Dr J.N. Sevenster on the Occasion of his Seventieth Birthday* (NovTSup, 24; Leiden: Brill, 1970), pp. 66-74.

Deeks, D., 'The Prologue of St. John's Gospel', *BTB* 6 (1976), pp. 62-78.

Demke, C., 'Der sogennante Logos-Hymnus im johanneischen Prolog', *ZNW* 58 (1967), pp. 45-68.

Dettwiler, A., 'Le prologue johannique (Jean 1,1-18)', in J.-D. Kaestli *et al.* (eds.), *La communauté johannique et son histoire: La trajectoire de l'évangile de Jean aux deux premiers siècles* (MB; Geneva: Labor & Fides, 1990), pp. 185-203.

Deutsch, C. *Hidden Wisdom and the Easy Yoke: Wisdom, Torah and Discipleship in Matthew 11.25-30* (JSNTSup, 18; Sheffield: JSOT Press, 1987).

Díaz, J.R., 'Targum Palestinense y Nuevo Testamento', *EstBíb* 21 (1962), pp. 337-42; ET 'Palestinian Targum and the New Testament', *NovT* 6 (1963), pp. 75-80.

Díez Macho, A., 'El Logos y el Espíritu Santo', *Atlántida* 1 (1963), pp. 381-96.

Dodd, C.H., *The Interpretation of the Fourth Gospel* (Cambridge: Cambridge University Press, 1953).

—'The Prologue of the Fourth Gospel and Christian Worship', in F.L. Cross (ed.), *Studies in the Fourth Gospel* (London: Mowbrays, 1957), pp. 9-22.

Duke, P.D., *Irony in the Fourth Gospel* (Atlanta: John Knox, 1985).

Duncan, R.L., 'The Logos: From Sophocles to the Gospel of John', *Christian Scholar's Review* 9 (1979), pp. 121-30.

Dunn, J.D.G., *Christology in the Making: A New Testament Inquiry into the Origins of the Doctrine of the Incarnation* (London: SCM Press, 1980).

—'Let John Be John—A Gospel for its Time', in P. Stuhlmacher (ed.), *Das Evangelium und die Evangelien: Vorträge vom Tübinger Symposium 1982* (Tübingen: Mohr [Paul Siebeck], 1983), pp. 309-34; repr. in P. Stuhlmacher (ed.), *The Gospel and the Gospels* (Grand Rapids: Eerdmans, 1991), pp. 293-322.

Eltester, W., 'Der Logos und sein Prophet: Fragen zur heutigen Erklärung des johanneischen Prologs', in U. Eickelberg *et al.* (eds.), *Apophoreta: Festschrift für Ernst Haenchen zu seinen siebzigsten Geburtstag* (BZNW, 30; Berlin: Töpelmann, 1964), pp. 109-34.

Emerton, J.A., 'Notes on some Passages in the Odes of Solomon', *JTS* 28 (1977), pp. 507-19.

Epp, E.J., 'Wisdom, Torah, Word: The Johannine Prologue and the Purpose of the Fourth Gospel', in G. F. Hawthorne (ed.), *Current Issues in Biblical and Patristic Interpretation* (Grand Rapids: Eerdmans, 1975), pp. 128-46.

Epstein, I. (ed.), *The Babylonian Talmud* (18 vols.; London: Soncino, 1978).

Epstein, J.N., and E.Z. Melamed, *Mekhilta D'Rabbi Sim'on b. Jochai* (Jerusalem: Mekize Nirdamim, 1955).

Evans, C.A., 'Current Issues in Coptic Gnosticism for New Testament Study', *Studia Biblica et Theologica* 9.2 (1979), pp. 95-129.

—'Obduracy and the Lord's Servant: Some Observations on the Use of the Old Testament in the Fourth Gospel', in C.A. Evans and W.F. Stinespring (eds.), *Early Jewish and Christian Exegesis: Studies in Memory of William Hugh Brownlee* (Homage, 10; Atlanta: Scholars Press, 1987), pp. 221-36.

—'On the Prologue of John and the *Trimorphic Protennoia*', *NTS* 27 (1981), pp. 395-401.

—'On the Quotation Formulas in the Fourth Gospel', *BZ* 26 (1982), pp. 79-83.

—'On the Vineyard Parables of Isaiah 5 and Mark 12', *BZ* 28 (1984), pp. 82-86.

—*To See and Not Perceive: Isaiah 6.9-10 in Early Jewish and Christian Interpretation* (JSOTSup, 64; Sheffield: JSOT Press, 1989).

Fascher, E., 'Christologie und Gnosis im vierten Evangelium', *TLZ* 93 (1968), cols. 721-30.

Faure, A., 'Die alttestamentlichen Zitate im 4. Evangelium und die Quellenscheidungshypothese', *ZNW* 21 (1922), pp. 99-122.

Feuillet, A., *Le Prologue du Quatrième Evangile: Etude de Théologie Johannique* (Paris: Desclée de Brouwer, 1968).

Finkel, A., *The Pharisees and the Teacher of Nazareth: A Study of their Background, their Halachic and Midrashic Teachings, the Similarities and Differences* (AGJU, 4; Leiden: Brill, 1964).

Fischel, H.A., 'Jewish Gnosticism in the Fourth Gospel', *JBL* 65 (1946), pp. 157-74.

Fischer, K.M., 'Der johanneische Christus und der gnostische Erlöser: Überlegungen auf Grund von Joh 10', in K.-W. Tröger (ed.), *Gnosis und Neues Testament: Studien aus Religionswissenschaft und Theologie* (Gütersloh: Gerd Mohn; Berlin: Evangelische Verlagsanstalt, 1973), pp. 245-67.

Fitzmyer, J.A., *The Genesis Apocryphon of Qumran Cave I* (BibOr, 18a; Rome: Pontifical Biblical Institute Press, 2nd edn, 1971).

—*The Gospel according to Luke X–XXIV* (AB, 28a; Garden City, NY: Doubleday, 1985).

Fohrer, G., 'σοφία, κτλ', *TDNT*, VII, pp. 489-92.

Ford, J.M. '"Mingled Blood" from the Side of Christ (John xix. 34)', *NTS* 15 (1969), pp. 337-38.

Forestell, J.T., *Targumic Traditions and the New Testament* (SBL Aramaic Studies, 4; Chico, CA: Scholars Press, 1979).

Fortna, R.T., *The Fourth Gospel and its Predecessor* (Philadelphia: Fortress Press, 1988).

—*Gospel of Signs: A Reconstruction of the Narrative Source Underlying the Fourth Gospel* (SNTSMS, 11; Cambridge: Cambridge University Press, 1970).

Freed, E.D., *Old Testament Quotations in the Gospel of John* (NovTSup, 11; Leiden: Brill, 1965).

—'Some Old Testament Influences on the Prologue of John', in H.N. Bream *et al.* (eds.), *A Light Unto My Path: Old Testament Studies in Honor of Jacob M. Myers* (GTS, 4; Philadelphia: Temple University Press, 1974), pp. 145-61.

—'Theological Prelude to the Prologue of John's Gospel', *SJT* 32 (1979), pp. 257-69.

Freedman, H., and M. Simon (eds.), *Midrash Rabbah* (10 vols.; London: Soncino, 1983).

Frye, R.N., 'Reitzenstein and Qumrân Revisited by an Iranian', *HTR* 55 (1962), pp. 261-68.

Gaylord, H.E., '3 (Greek Apocalypse of) Baruch', in J.H. Charlesworth (ed.), *The Old Testament Pseudepigrapha*, I (2 vols.; Garden City, NY: Doubleday, 1983–85), pp. 653-79.

Gese, H., 'Der Johannesprolog', in *Zur biblischen Theologie: Alttestamentliche Vorträge* (BEvT, 78; Munich: Chr. Kaiser Verlag, 1977), pp. 152-201.

Giblin, C.H., 'Two Complementary Literary Structures in Jn 1.1-18', *JBL* 104 (1985), pp. 87-103.

Glasson, T.F., *Moses in the Fourth Gospel* (SBT, 40; London: SCM Press, 1963).

Goodenough, E.R., *An Introduction to Philo Judaeus* (Oxford: Basil Blackwell, 1962).

—*By Light, Light: The Mystic Gospel of Hellenistic Judaism* (New Haven and London: Yale University Press, 1935).

—'John a Primitive Gospel', *JBL* 64 (1945), pp. 145-82.

Grant, R.M., *Gnosticism: A Sourcebook of Heretical Writings from the Early Christian Period* (New York: Harper & Brothers, 1961).

Grässer, E., 'Die antijüdische Polemik im Johannesevangelium', *NTS* 11 (1964), pp. 74-90.

Grimm, W., *Jesus und das Danielbuch* (ANTJ, 6.2; Frankfurt am Main: Peter Lang, 1984).

Grossfeld, B., *The Targum Onqelos* (ArBib, 6-9; 4 vols.; Wilmington, DE: Michael Glazier, 1988).

Grundmann, W., *Das Evangelium nach Johannes* (ed. E. Fascher; THKNT, 4; Berlin: Evangelische Verlagsanstalt, 1968).

—*Der Zeuge der Weisheit: Grundzüge der Christologie des Johannesevangeliums* (ed. W. Wiefel; Berlin: Evangelische Verlagsanstalt, 1985).

Gundry, R.H., *Matthew: A Commentary on his Literary and Theological Art* (Grand Rapids: Eerdmans, 1982).

Gunkel, H., 'Die Oden Salomos', *Deutsche Rundschau* 154 (1913), pp. 25-47.

—'Die Oden Salomos', *ZNW* 11 (1910), pp. 291-328.

Haenchen, E., 'Gab es eine vorchristliche Gnosis?', *ZTK* 49 (1952), pp. 316-49; repr. in *Gott und Mensch: Gesammelte Aufsätze* (Tübingen: Mohr [Paul Siebeck], 1965), pp. 265-98.

—*Das Johannesevangelium* (ed. U. Busse; Tübingen: Mohr [Paul Siebeck], 1980); ET *John 1: A Commentary on the Gospel of John* (Hermeneia; Philadelphia: Fortress Press, 1984).

—'Probleme des johanneischen "Prologs"', *ZTK* 60 (1963) 305-34; repr. in *Gott und Mensch: Gesammelte Aufsätze* (Tübingen: Mohr [Paul Siebeck], 1965), pp. 114-43.

Hagner, D.A., 'The Vision of God in Philo and John', *JETS* 14 (1971), pp. 81-93.

Hamp, V., *Der Begriff 'Wort' in den aramäischen Bibelübersetzungen: Ein exegetischer Beitrag zur Hypostasen-Frage und zur Geschichte der Logos Spekulation* (Munich: Filser, 1938).

Hanson, A.T., *Grace and Truth: A Study in the Doctrine of the Incarnation* (London: SPCK, 1975).

—'Jn 1,14-18 and Exodus 34', *NTS* 23 (1976), pp. 90-101; repr. in *The New Testament Interpretation of Scripture* (London: SPCK, 1980), pp. 97-109.

—'John's Citation of Psalm LXXXII: John X.33-36', *NTS* 11 (1965), pp. 158-62.

—'John's Citation of Psalm LXXXII Reconsidered', *NTS* 13 (1967), pp. 363-67.

—*The Prophetic Gospel: A Study of John and the Old Testament* (Edinburgh: T. & T. Clark, 1991).

Harnack, A. von, 'Über das Verhältnis des Prologs des vierten Evangeliums zum ganzen Werk', *ZTK* 2 (1892), pp. 189-231.

Harris, J.R., *The Origin of the Prologue to St. John's Gospel* (Cambridge: Cambridge University Press, 1917).

Harrison, E.F., 'A Study of Jn 1.14', in R.A. Guelich (ed.), *Unity and Diversity in New Testament Theology* (Grand Rapids: Eerdmans, 1978), pp. 23-36.

Harvey, A.E., 'Christ as Agent', in L.D. Hurst and N.T. Wright (eds.), *The Glory of Christ in the New Testament: Studies in Christology* (Oxford: Clarendon Press, 1987), pp. 239-50.

Hayward, C.T.R., 'The Holy Name of the God of Moses and the Prologue of St John's Gospel', *NTS* 25 (1978), pp. 16-32.

Hayward, R., 'Memra and Shekhina: A Short Note', *JJS* 31 (1980), pp. 210-13.

Hedrick, C.W. (ed.), *Nag Hammadi Codices XI, XII and XIII* (NHS, 28; Leiden: Brill, 1990).

Hengel, M. 'Christological Titles in Early Christianity', in J.H. Charlesworth (ed.), *The Messiah: Developments in Earliest Judaism and Christianity* (Minneapolis: Fortress Press, 1992), pp. 425-48.

—*Crucifixion in the Ancient World and the Folly of the Message of the Cross* (Philadelphia: Fortress Press, 1977).

—'Jesus als messianischer Lehrer der Weisheit und die Anfänge der Christologie', in J. Leclant *et al.* (eds.), *Sagesse et Religion: Colloque de Strasbourg, Octobre 1976* (Paris: Bibliothèque des Centres d'Etudes Supérieures Spécialisés, 1979), pp. 147-88.

—*The Johannine Question* (London: SCM Press; Philadelphia: Trinity Press International, 1989).

—'Die Schriftauslegung des 4. Evangeliums auf dem Hintergrund der urchristlichen Exegese', *JBT* 4 (1989) 249-89; abridged ET 'The Old Testament in the Fourth Gospel', *HBT* 12 (1990), pp. 19-41.

—*Der Sohn Gottes: Die Entstehung der Christologie und die jüdisch-hellenistische Religionsgeschichte* (Tübingen: Mohr [Paul Siebeck], 1975); ET *Son of God* (Philadelphia: Fortress Press, 1976).

—'The Wine Miracle at Cana', in L.D. Hurst and N.T. Wright (eds.), *The Glory of Christ in the New Testament: Studies in Christology in Memory of George Bradford Caird* (Oxford: Clarendon Press, 1987), pp. 83-112.

—*Die johanneische Frage: Ein Lösungsversuch* (WUNT, 67; Tübingen: Mohr [Paul Siebeck], 1993).

Hofius, O., 'Struktur und Gedankengang des Logos-Hymnus in John 1 1-18', *ZNW* 78 (1987), pp. 1-25.

Hofrichter, P., *Im Anfang war der 'Johannesprolog': Das urchristliche Logosbekenntnis —die Basis neutestamentlicher und gnostischer Theologie* (Regensburg: Pustet, 1986).

Hooker, M.D., 'The Johannine Prologue and the Messianic Secret', *NTS* 21 (1975), pp. 40-58.

—'John the Baptist and the Johannine Prologue', *NTS* 16 (1970), pp. 354-58.

Horbury, W., 'The Benediction of the Minim and Early Jewish–Christian Controversy', *JTS* 33 (1982), pp. 19-61.

Horsley, R.A., and J.S. Hanson, *Bandits, Prophets, and Messiahs: Popular Movements at the Time of Jesus* (San Francisco: Harper & Row, 1985).

Hoskyns, E.C., *The Fourth Gospel* (ed. F.N. Davey; 2 vols.; London: Faber & Faber, 2nd edn, 1947).

Humann, R.J., 'The Function and Form of the Explicit Old Testament Quotations in the Gospel of John', *LTR* 1 (1988–89), pp. 31-54.

Hunter, A.M., 'Crux Criticorum—Matt. 11.25-30', *NTS* 8 (1962), pp. 241-49.

Hurtado, L., *One God, One Lord: Early Christian Devotion and Ancient Jewish Monotheism* (Philadelphia: Fortress Press, 1988).

Janssens, Y., *La Protennoia Trimorphe* (Bibliothèque copte de Nag Hammadi: Section 'Textes' 4; Québec: Laval University Press, 1978).

—'Une source gnostique du Prologue?', in M. de Jonge (ed.), *L'Evangile de Jean: Sources, rédaction, théologie* (BETL, 44; Leuven: Leuven University Press, 1977), pp. 355-58.

Jaubert, A., 'The Calendar of Qumran and the Passion Narrative in John', in J.H. Charlesworth (ed.), *John and the Dead Sea Scrolls* (repr.; New York: Crossroad, 1990 [1972]), pp. 62-75.

—'L'image de la vigne (Jean 15)', in F. Christ (ed.), *Oikonomia: Heilsgeschichte als Thema der Theologie: O. Cullmann zum 65. Geburtstag gewidmet* (Hamburg: Reich, 1967), pp. 93-99.

—'La symbolique du puits de Jacob', in *L'homme devant Dieu* (Théologie, 56; Paris: Aubier, 1963), pp. 63-73.

Jeremias, J., *Der Prolog des Johannesevangeliums (Johannes 1,1-18)* (CH, 88; Stuttgart: Calwer Verlag, 1967).

—'The Revealing Word', in *The Central Message of the New Testament* (London: SCM Press; Philadelphia: Fortress Press, 1965), pp. 71-90.

Jonge, M. de (ed.), *L'Evangile de Jean: Sources, rédaction, théologie* (BETL, 44; Leuven: Leuven University Press, 1977).

Kaestli, J.-D., 'L'exégèse valentinienne du quatrième évangile', in J.-D. Kaestli *et al.* (eds.), *La communauté johannique et son histoire: La trajectoire de l'évangile de Jean aux deux premiers siècles* (MB; Geneva: Labor & Fides, 1990), pp. 323-50.

Käsemann, E., 'Aufbau und Anliegen des johanneischen Prologs', in W. Matthias and E. Wolf (eds.), *Libertas Christiana* (BEvT, 26; Munich: Chr. Kaiser Verlag, 1957), pp. 75-99; repr. in *Exegetische Versuche und Besinnungen* (Göttingen: Vandenhoeck & Ruprecht, 2nd edn, 1965), pp. 155-80; ET 'The Structure and Purpose of the Prologue to John's Gospel', in *New Testament Questions of Today* (London: SCM; Philadelphia: Fortress Press, 1969), pp. 138-67.

—*Jesu letzter Wille nach Johannes 17* (Tübingen: Mohr [Paul Siebeck], 1966); ET *The*

Testament of Jesus: A Study of the Gospel of John in the Light of Chapter 17 (London: SCM Press; Philadelphia: Fortress Press, 1968).

Kilpatrick, G.D., 'The Religious Background of the Fourth Gospel', in F.L. Cross (ed.), *Studies in the Fourth Gospel* (London: Mowbrays, 1957), pp. 36-44.

—'What John Tells us about John', in A.S. Geyser *et al.* (eds.), *Studies in John: Presented to Professor Dr J.N. Sevenster on the Occasion of his Seventieth Birthday* (NovTSup, 24; Leiden: Brill, 1970), pp. 75-87.

Kimelman, R., '*Birkat Ha-Minim* and the Lack of Evidence for an anti-Christian Jewish Prayer in Late Antiquity', in E.P. Sanders *et al.* (eds.), *Jewish and Christian Self-Definition*, II (3 vols.; Philadelphia: Fortress Press, 1980–82), pp. 226-44, 391-403.

King, J.S., 'The Prologue to the Fourth Gospel: Some Unsolved Problems', *ExpTim* 86 (1974), pp. 372-75.

Kittel, G., and von Rad, G., 'δοκέω, δόξα, κτλ', *TDNT*, II, pp. 232-55.

—'λέγω, λόγος, κτλ (Word and Speech in the New Testament)', *TDNT*, IV, pp. 100-136.

Klein, M.L., *The Fragment-Targums of the Pentateuch* (AnBib, 76; 2 vols.; Rome: Pontifical Biblical Institute Press, 1980).

—'The Preposition קדם ("Before"): A Pseudo-Anti-Anthropomorphism in the Targums', *JTS* 20 (1979), pp. 502-507.

Kleinknecht, H., 'λέγω, λόγος, κτλ (The Logos in the Greek and Hellenistic World)', *TDNT*, IV, pp. 77-91.

Klijn, A.F.J., *Seth in Jewish, Christian and Gnostic Literature* (NovTSup, 46; Leiden: Brill, 1977).

Kloppenborg, J.S., *The Formation of Q: Trajectories in Ancient Wisdom Collections* (Studies in Antiquity & Christianity; Philadelphia: Fortress Press, 1987).

Klostermann, E., *Das Matthäusevangelium* (HNT, 4; Tübingen: Mohr [Paul Siebeck], 4th edn, 1971).

Koester, C.R., *The Dwelling of God: The Tabernacle in the Old Testament, Intertestamental Jewish Literature, and the New Testament* (CBQMS, 22; Washington: Catholic Biblical Association, 1989).

Koester, H. 'Les discours d'adieu de l'évangile de Jean: leur trajectoire au premier et au deuxième siècle', in J.-D. Kaestli *et al.* (eds.), *La communauté johannique et son histoire: La trajectoire de l'évangile de Jean aux deux premiers siècles* (MB; Geneva: Labor & Fides, 1990), pp. 269-80.

—*Einführung in das Neue Testament* (Berlin: deGruyter, 1980); ET *Introduction to the New Testament* (2 vols.; New York: deGruyter, 1982).

Kruije, T.C. de,'The Glory of the Only Son (John i 14)', in A.S. Geyser *et al.* (eds.), *Studies in John: Presented to Professor Dr J.N. Sevenster on the Occasion of his Seventieth Birthday* (NovTSup, 24; Leiden: Brill, 1970), pp. 111-23.

Kuhn, K.G., 'Die in Palästina gefundenen hebräischen Texte und das Neue Testament', *ZTK* 47 (1950), pp. 192-211.

—'Johannesevangelium und Qumrantexte', in A.N. Wilder *et al.* (eds.), *Neotestamentica et Patristica: Eine Freundesgabe Herrn Professor Dr Oscar Cullmann zu seinem 60. Geburtstag Überreicht* (NovTSup, 6; Leiden: Brill, 1962), pp. 111-22.

Kuyper, L.J., 'Grace and Truth: An Old Testament Description of God and Its Use in the Johannine Gospel', *Int* 18 (1964), pp. 3-19.

Kysar, R., 'The Background of the Prologue of the Fourth Gospel: A Critique of Historical Methods', *CJT* 16 (1970), pp. 250-55.

—*The Fourth Evangelist and His Gospel: An Examination of Contemporary Scholarship* (Minneapolis: Augsburg, 1975).

Ladd, G.E., *A Theology of the New Testament* (Grand Rapids: Eerdmans, 1967).

Lamarche, P., 'Le Prologue de Jean', *RSR* 52 (1964), pp. 497-537; ET 'The Prologue of John', in J. Ashton (ed.), *The Interpretation of John* (London: SPCK; Philadelphia: Fortress Press, 1986), pp. 36-52.

Langkammer, P.H., 'Zur Herkunft des Logostitels im Johannesprolog', *BZ* 9 (1965), pp. 91-94.

LaSor, W.S., *The Dead Sea Scrolls and the New Testament* (Grand Rapids: Eerdmans, 1972).

Lausberg, H., *Minuscula philologia (V): Jesaja 55,10–11 im Evangelium nach Johannes* (Nachrichten der Akademie der Wissenschaften in Göttingen, Philologisch-historische Klasse, 7; Göttingen: Vandenhoeck & Ruprecht, 1979).

Lauterbach, J.Z., *Mekilta de-Rabbi Ishmael* (3 vols.; Philadelphia: Jewish Publication Society, 1933).

Layton, B., *The Gnostic Scriptures* (Garden City, NY: Doubleday, 1987).

Le Déaut, R., *The Message of the New Testament and the Aramaic Bible* (SubBib, 5; Rome: Pontifical Biblical Institute Press, 1982).

—'Targumic Literature and New Testament Interpretation', *BTB* 4 (1974), pp. 243-89.

Leaney, A.R.C., 'The Johannine Paraclete and the Qumran Scrolls', in J.H. Charlesworth (ed.), *John and the Dead Sea Scrolls* (repr.; New York: Crossroad, 1990 [1972]), pp. 38-61.

Levey, S.H., *The Messiah: An Aramaic Interpretation: The Messianic Exegesis of the Targum* (MHUC, 2; Cincinnati: Hebrew Union College/Jewish Institute of Religion, 1974)

Lidzbarski, M., *Ginza: Der Schatz order das grosse Buch der Mandäer* (QR, 13; Göttingen: Vandenhoeck & Ruprecht; Leipzig: Hinrichs, 1925).

—*Das Johannesbuch der Mandäer* (2 vols.; repr.; Giessen: Töpelmann, 1966 [1905–15]); ET in G. Meade, *The Gnostic John the Baptizer* (London: Watkins, 1924).

—*Mandäische Liturgien* (repr.; Berlin: Weidmann, 1962 [1920]).

Lietzmann, H., 'Ein Beitrag zur Mandäerfrage', *Sitzungsberichte der Preussischen Akademie der Wissenschaft: Phil.-Hist. Klasse* 17 (1930), pp. 595-608.

Lindars, B., *The Gospel of John* (NCB; London: Marshall, Morgan & Scott; Grand Rapids: Eerdmans, 1972).

—'Traditions behind the Fourth Gospel', in M. de Jonge (ed.), *L'Evangile de Jean: Sources, rédaction, théologie* (BETL, 44; Leuven: Leuven University Press, 1977), pp. 107-24.

Loader, W.R.G., 'The Central Structure of Johannine Christology', *NTS* 30 (1984), pp. 188-216.

Mack, B.L. 'The Christ and Jewish Wisdom', in J.H. Charlesworth (ed.), *The Messiah: Developments in Earliest Judaism and Christianity* (The First Princeton Symposium on Judaism and Christian Origins; Minneapolis: Fortress Press, 1992), pp. 192-221.

MacRae, G.W., 'The Fourth Gospel and *Religionsgeschichte*', *CBQ* 32 (1970), pp. 13-24.

—'Gnosticism and New Testament Studies', *Bible Today* 38 (1968), pp. 2623-30.

—'The Jewish Background of the Gnostic Sophia Myth', *NovT* 12 (1970), pp. 86-101.

Malina, B.J., *The Palestinian Manna Tradition: The Manna Tradition in the Palestinian Targums and its Relationship to the New Testament Writings* (AGSU, 7; Leiden: Brill, 1968).

Mansoor, M., 'The Nature of Gnosticism in Qumran', in U. Bianchi (ed.), *Le Origini dello Gnosticismo* (NumSup, 12; Leiden: Brill, 1967), pp. 389-400.

Martyn, J.L., 'Glimpses into the History of the Johannine Community', in M. de Jonge (ed.), *L'Evangile de Jean: Sources, rédaction, théologie* (BETL, 44; Leuven: Leuven University Press, 1977), pp. 149-75.

—*History and Theology in the Fourth Gospel* (Nashville: Abingdon Press, 2nd edn, 1979).

—*The Gospel of John in Christian History* (New York: Paulist Press, 1978).

McCaffrey, J., *The House with Many Rooms: The Temple Theme of Jn. 14,2-3* (AnBib, 114; Rome: Pontifical Biblical Institute, 1988).

McNamara, M., '*Logos* of the Fourth Gospel and *Memra* of the Palestinian Targum (Ex. 12.42)', *ExpTim* 79 (1968), pp. 115-17.

—*The New Testament and the Palestinian Targum to the Pentateuch* (AnBib, 27; Rome: Pontifical Biblical Institute Press, 1966).

—*Palestinian Judaism and the New Testament* (GNS, 4; Wilmington, DE: Michael Glazier, 1983).

—*Targum and Testament* (Shannon: Irish University Press; Grand Rapids: Eerdmans, 1972).

Meade, G., *The Gnostic John the Baptizer* (London: Watkins, 1924).

Meagher, J.C., 'John 1.14 and the New Temple', *JBL* 88 (1969), pp. 57-68.

Meeks, W.A., '"Am I a Jew?" Johannine Christianity and Judaism', in J. Neusner (ed.), *Christianity, Judaism and Other Greco-Roman Cults* (SJLA, 12; Leiden: Brill, 1975), pp. 163-86.

—'The Man from Heaven in Johannine Sectarianism', *JBL* 91 (1972), pp. 44-72.

—*The Prophet-King: Moses Traditions and the Johannine Christology* (NovTSup, 14; Leiden: Brill, 1967).

—'The Divine Agent and his Counterfeit in Philo and the Fourth Gospel', in E. Schüssler Fiorenza (ed.), *Aspects of Religious Propaganda in Judaism and Early Christianity* (London and Notre Dame: University of Notre Dame Press, 1976), pp. 43-67.

Meier, J.P., *A Marginal Jew: Rethinking the Historical Jesus* (ABRL; Garden City, NY: Doubleday, 1991).

Menken, M.J.J., 'Die Form des Zitates aus Jes 6,10 in Joh 12,40', *BZ* 32 (1988), pp. 189-209.

Michaelis, W., *Einleitung in das Neue Testament* (Bern: Haller, 3rd edn, 1961).

—'σκηνή, κτλ', *TDNT*, VII, pp. 368-94.

Michel, O., 'Der aufsteigende und herabsteigende Gesandte', in W.C. Weinrich (ed.), *The New Testament Age: Essays in Honor of Bo Reicke*, II (2 vols.; Macon: Mercer University Press, 1984), pp. 335-61.

Middleton, R., 'Logos and Shekina in the Fourth Gospel', *JQR* 29 (1933), pp. 101-33.

Miller, E.L., *Salvation-History in the Prologue of John: The Significance of John 1.3/4* (NovTSup, 60; Leiden: Brill, 1989).

Montgomery, J.A., 'Hebrew Hesed and Greek Charis', *HTR* 32 (1939), pp. 97-102.

Moore, G.F., 'Intermediaries in Jewish Theology', *HTR* 15 (1922), pp. 41-85.

—*Judaism in the First Centuries of the Christian Era* (3 vols.; Cambridge, MA: Harvard University Press, 1927–30).

Muñoz León, D., *Dios Palabra: Memrá en los Targumim del Pentateuco* (Institución San Jerónimo, 4; Granada: Editorial Santa Rita, 1974).

—*Palabra y Gloria: Excursus en la Biblia y en la Literatura Intertestamentaria* (Verbum Gloriae, 4; Madrid: Consejo Superior de Investigaciones Científicas Instituto 'Francisco Suárez', 1983).

Nagel, W., '"Die Finsternis hat's nicht begriffen" (Joh i 5)', *ZNW* 50 (1959), pp. 132-37.

Negoïtsa, A., and C. Daniel, 'L'Agneau de Dieu est le Verbe de Dieu (Ad Jo. i 29 et 36)', *NovT* 13 (1971), pp. 24-37.

Neusner, J., *A History of the Mishnaic Law of Appointed Times. Part One: Sabbath* (SJLA, 34; Leiden: Brill, 1981).

—*A History of the Mishnaic Law of Purities. Part Twenty-Two: The Mishnaic System of Uncleanness* (SJLA, 6; Leiden: Brill, 1977).

—*A History of the Mishnaic Law of Women. Part One: Yebamot* (SJLA, 33; Leiden: Brill, 1980).

—*Rabbinic Traditions about the Pharisees before 70* (3 vols.; Leiden: Brill, 1971).

—'The Use of the Later Rabbinic Evidence for the Study of Paul', in W.S. Green (ed.), *Approaches to Ancient Judaism II* (BJS, 9; Chico, CA: Scholars Press, 1980), pp. 43-63.

Neusner, J. (ed.), *The Talmud of the Land of Israel* (35 vols.; Chicago: University of Chicago Press, 1982–).

Neyrey, J.H., 'I said "You are Gods": Psalm 82.6 and John 10', *JBL* 108 (1989), pp. 647-63.

—*An Ideology of Revolt: John's Christology in Social-Science Perspective* (Philadelphia: Fortress Press, 1988).

—'The Jacob Allusions in John 1.51', *CBQ* 44 (1982), pp. 586-605.

—'Jacob Traditions and the Interpretation of John 4.10-26', *CBQ* 41 (1979), pp. 419-37.

Nicholson, G.C., *Death as Departure: The Johannine Descent–Ascent Schema* (SBLDS, 63; Chico, CA: Scholars Press, 1983).

Nicol, W., *The Semeia in the Fourth Gospel: Tradition and Redaction* (NovTSup, 32; Leiden: Brill, 1972).

Nock, A.D., *Essays on Religion and the Ancient World* (2 vols.; Cambridge, MA: Harvard University Press, 1972).

Odeberg, H., *The Fourth Gospel: Interpreted in its Relation to Contemporaneous Religious Currents in Palestine and in the Hellenistic-Oriental World* (repr.; Amsterdam: Grüner; Chicago: Argonaut, 1968 [1929]).

Olmstead, A.T., 'Could an Aramaic Gospel be Written?', *JNES* 1 (1942), pp. 41-75.

O'Neill, J.C., 'The Prologue to St John's Gospel', *JTS* 20 (1969), pp. 41-52.

—'The Word Did Not "Become" Flesh', *ZNW* 82 (1991), pp. 125-27.

O'Rourke, J., 'Explicit Old Testament Citations in the Gospels', *Studia Montis Regii* 7 (1964), pp. 37-60.

—'John's Fulfilment Texts', *ScEccl* 19 (1967), pp. 433-43.

Pagels, E.H., *The Johannine Gospel in Gnostic Exegesis: Heracleon's Commentary on John* (SBLMS, 17; Nashville: Abingdon Press, 1973).

Painter, J., 'Christology and the Fourth Gospel: A Study of the Prologue', *AusBR* 31 (1983), pp. 45-62.

—'Christology and the History of the Johannine Community in the Prologue of the Fourth Gospel', *NTS* 30 (1984), pp. 460-74.

Pamment, M., 'The Meaning of *doxa* in the Fourth Gospel', *ZNW* 74 (1983), pp. 12-16.

Perkins, P., 'Gnostic Christologies and the New Testament', *CBQ* 43 (1981), pp. 590-606.

—'New Testament Christologies in Gnostic Transformation', in B.A. Pearson (ed.), *The Future of Early Christianity* (Minneapolis: Fortress Press, 1991), pp. 433-41.

Pétrement, S., *Le Dieu séparé: Les origines du gnosticisme* (Paris: Cerf, 1984); ET *A Separate God: The Christian Origins of Gnosticism* (London: Darton, Longman & Todd, 1991).

Pinto, B. de, 'Word and Wisdom in St. John', *Scr* 19 (1967), pp. 19-27.

Piper, R.A., *Wisdom in the Q Tradition: The Aphoristic Teaching of Jesus* (SNTSMS, 61; Cambridge: Cambridge University Press, 1989).

Pollard, T.E., 'Cosmology and the Prologue of the Fourth Gospel', *VC* 12 (1958), pp. 147-53.

—*Johannine Christology and the Early Church* (SNTSMS, 13; Cambridge: Cambridge University Press, 1970).

Potterie, I. de la, 'Structure du Prologue de Saint Jean', *NTS* 30 (1984), pp. 354-81.

Price, J.L., 'Light from Qumran upon some Aspects of Johannine Theology', in J.H. Charlesworth (ed.), *John and the Dead Sea Scrolls* (repr.; New York: Crossroad, 1990 [1972]), pp. 9-37.

Quispel, G., 'Qumran, John and Jewish Christianity', in J.H. Charlesworth (ed.), *John and the Dead Sea Scrolls* (repr.; New York: Crossroad, 1990 [1972]), pp. 137-55.

Reicke, B., 'Da'at and Gnosis in Intertestamental Literature', in E.E. Ellis and M. Wilcox (eds.), *Neotestamentica et Semitica: Studies in Honour of Matthew Black* (Edinburgh: T. & T. Clark, 1969), pp. 245-55.

—'Traces of Gnosticism in the Dead Sea Scrolls?', *NTS* 1 (1954), pp. 137-41.

Reim, G., 'Joh. 8.44—Gotteskinder/Teufelskinder: Wie antijudaistisch ist "Die wohl antijudaistischste Äusserung des NT"?', *NTS* 30 (1984), pp. 619-24.

—'Johannesevangelium und Synagogengottesdienst—ein Beobachtung', *BZ* 27 (1983), p. 101.

—*Studien zum alttestamentlichen Hintergrund des Johannesevangeliums* (SNTSMS, 22; Cambridge: Cambridge University Press, 1974).

—'Targum und Johannesevangelium', *BZ* 27 (1983), pp. 1-13.

Reitzenstein, R., *Das iranische Erlösungsmysterium* (Bonn: Marcus & Weber, 1921).

Reitzenstein, R. and H.H. Schaeder, *Studien zum antiken Synkretismus aus Iran und Griechenland* (repr.; Darmstadt: Wissenschaftliche Buchgesellschaft, 1965 [1926]).

Richter, G., 'Die alttestamentlichen Zitate in der Rede vom Himmelsbrot John 6,26-51a', in J. Ernst (ed.), *Schriftauslegung: Beiträge zur Hermeneutik des Neuen Testaments und im Neuen Testament* (Munich: Schöningh, 1972), pp. 193-279.

—'Die Fleischwerdung des Logos im Johannes-Evangelium', *NovT* 13 (1971), pp. 81-126; 14 (1972), pp. 257-76; repr. in *Studien zum Johannesevangelium* (ed. J. Hainz; BU, 13; Regensburg: Pustet, 1977), pp. 149-98.

Ridderbos, H., 'The Structure and Scope of the Prologue to the Gospel of John', *NovT* 8 (1966), pp. 180-201.

Ringgren, H., 'Qumran and Gnosticism', in U. Bianchi (ed.), *Le Origini dello Gnosticismo* (NumSup, 12; Leiden: Brill, 1967), pp. 379-84.

Rissi, M., 'John 1,1-18', *Int* 31 (1977), pp. 395-401.

—'Die Logoslieder im Prolog des vierten Evangeliums', *TZ* 31 (1975), pp. 321-36; 32 (1976), pp. 1-13.

Robinson, G. (see also G. Schenke), 'The Trimorphic Protennoia and the Prologue of the Fourth Gospel', in J.E. Goehring *et al.* (eds.), *Gnosticism and the Early Christian World* (Sonoma, CA: Polebridge Press, 1990), pp. 37-50.

Robinson, J.A.T., 'The Destination and Purpose of St John's Gospel', *NTS* 6 (1960), pp. 117-31; repr. in *Twelve New Testament Studies* (SBT, 34; London: SCM Press, 1962), pp. 107-25.

—'The New Look on the Fourth Gospel', in K. Aland *et al.* (eds.), *Studia Evangelica: Papers Presented to the International Congress on 'The Four Gospels' in 1957* (TU, 73; Berlin: Akademie Verlag, 1959) 338-50; repr. in J.A.T. Robinson, *Twelve New Testament Studies* (SBT, 34; London: SCM Press, 1962), pp. 94-106.

—'The Parable of the Shepherd (John 10.1-5)', *ZNW* 46 (1955), pp. 233-40; repr. in *Twelve New Testament Studies* (SBT, 34; London: SCM Press, 1962), pp. 67-75.

—'The Relation of the Prologue to the Gospel of St John', *NTS* 9 (1963), pp. 120-29; repr. in *Twelve More New Testament Studies* (London: SCM Press, 1984), pp. 65-76.

Robinson, J.M., 'Gnosticism and the New Testament', in B. Aland (ed.), *Gnosis: Festschrift für Hans Jonas* (Göttingen: Vandenhoeck & Ruprecht, 1978), pp. 125-43.

—*The Nag Hammadi Library in English* (Leiden: Brill; San Francisco: Harper & Row, 3rd edn, 1988).

—'The Prologue of John and the Trimorphic Protennoia', in P.J. Achtemeier (ed.), *Society of Biblical Literature, 1978, Abstracts* (Missoula, MT: Scholars Press, 1978), p. 29.

—'Sethians and Johannine Thought: The *Trimorphic Protennoia* and the Prologue of the Gospel of John', in B. Layton (ed.), *The Rediscovery of Gnosticism: Proceedings of the International Conference on Gnosticism at Yale, New Haven, Connecticut, March 28-31, 1978; Volume Two: Sethian Gnosticism* (NumSup, 41; Leiden: Brill, 1981), pp. 643-62.

Robinson, J.M., and H. Koester, *Trajectories through Early Christianity* (Philadelphia: Fortress Press, 1971).

Rochais, G., 'La Formation du Prologue (Jn 1, 1-18)', *ScEs* 37 (1985), pp. 5-44, 161-87.

Romaniuk, C., 'Le thème de la sagesse dans les documents de Qumran', *RevQ* 15 (1978), pp. 429-35.

Rosenthal, F., *A Grammar of Biblical Aramaic* (Wiesbaden: Otto Harrassowitz, 1974).

Rowland, C., 'Jn 1.51, Jewish Apocalyptic and Targumic Tradition', *NTS* 30 (1984), pp. 498-507.

Rubinkiewicz, R., 'Apocalypse of Abraham', in J.H. Charlesworth (ed.), *The Old Testament Pseudepigrapha*, I (2 vols.; Garden City, NY: Doubleday, 1983–85), pp. 681-705.

Ruckstuhl, E., 'Kritische Arbeit am Johannesprolog', in W.C. Weinrich (ed.), *The New*

Testament Age: Essays in Honor of Bo Reicke, II (2 vols.; Macon: Mercer University Press, 1984), pp. 443-54.

Rudolph, K., *Die Gnosis: Wesen und Geschichte einer spätantiken Religion* (Leipzig: Koehler & Amelang, 2nd edn, 1980); ET *Gnosis: The Nature and History of Gnosticism* (Edinburgh: T. & T. Clark; San Francisco: Harper & Row, 1983).

—*Die Mandäer* (FRLANT, 56; 2 vols.; Göttingen: Vandenhoeck & Ruprecht, 1960–61).

—'Problems of a History of the Development of the Mandaean Religion', *History of Religions* 8 (1969), pp. 210-35.

—'War der Verfasser der Oden Salomos ein "Qumran-Christ"? Ein Beitrag zur Diskussion um die Anfänge der Gnosis', *RevQ* 4 (1964), pp. 523-55.

Sabourin, L., 'The MEMRA of God in the Targums', *BTB* 6 (1976), pp. 79-85.

Sanders, J.N., and B.A. Mastin, *A Commentary on the Gospel according to St. John* (BNTC; London: A. & C. Black; HNTC; New York: Harper & Brothers, 1968).

Sanders, J.T., 'Nag Hammadi, Odes of Solomon, and NT Christological Hymns', in J.E. Goehring *et al.* (eds.), *Gnosticism and the Early Christian World: In Honor of James M. Robinson* (Sonoma, CA: Polebridge Press, 1990), pp. 51-66.

—*The New Testament Christological Hymns: Their Historical Religious Background* (SNTSMS, 15; Cambridge: Cambridge University Press, 1971).

Sandmel, S., *Philo of Alexandria* (New York: Oxford University Press, 1979).

Schenke, G. (see also G. Robinson), '"Die dreigestaltige Protennoia": Eine gnostische Offenbarungsrede in koptischer Sprache aus dem Fund von Nag Hammadi', *TLZ* 99 (1974), cols. 731-46.

Schenke, H.-M., 'Die neutestamentliche Christologie und der gnostische Erlöser', in K.-W. Tröger (ed.), *Gnosis und Neues Testament: Studien aus Religionswissenschaft und Theologie* (Berlin: Evangelische Verlagsanstalt, 1973), pp. 205-29.

—'Die zweite Schrift des Codex Jung und die Oden Salomos', in *Die Herkunft des sogenannten Evangelium Veritatis* (Göttingen: Vandenhoeck & Ruprecht, 1959), pp. 26-29.

Schimanowski, G., *Weisheit und Messias: Die jüdischen Voraussetzungen der urchristlichen Präexistenzchristologie* (WUNT, 2.17; Tübingen: Mohr [Paul Siebeck], 1985).

Schlatter, A., *Der Evangelist Johannes* (Stuttgart: Calwer Verlag, 1920).

—*Die Sprache und Heimat des vierten Evangelisten* (Gütersloh: Bertelsmann, 1902); repr. in K.H. Rengstorf (ed.), *Johannes und sein Evangelium* (WF, 82; Darmstadt: Wissenschaftliche Buchgesellschaft, 1973), pp. 28-201.

Schlier, H., '"Im Anfang war das Wort" im Prolog des Johannesevangeliums', *Wort und Wahrheit* 9 (1954) 169-80; repr. as 'Im Anfang war das Wort: Zum Prolog des Johannesevangeliums', in *Die Zeit der Kirche: Exegetische Aufsätze und Vorträge* (Freiburg: Herder, 5th edn, 1972), pp. 274-86.

Schmithals, W., 'Der Prolog des Johannesevangeliums', *ZNW* 70 (1979), pp. 16-43.

Schnackenburg, R., *Das Johannesevangelium* (HTKNT, 4.1-3; 3 vols.; Freiburg: Herder, 1965–75); ET *The Gospel according to St John* (3 vols.; repr.; New York: Crossroad, 1987 [1980]).

—'Logos-Hymnus und johanneischer Prolog', *BZ* 1 (1957), pp. 69-109.

—'Und das Wort ist Fleisch geworden', *IKZ* 8 (1979), pp. 1-9.

—'Zur christologischen Schriftauslegung des vierten Evangelisten', in H. Baltensweiler and B. Reicke (eds.), *Neues Testament und Geschichte* (Tübingen: Mohr [Paul Siebeck], 1972), pp. 167-77.

Schneider, H., '"The Word Was Made Flesh": An Analysis of the Theology of Revelation in the Fourth Gospel', *CBQ* 31 (1969), pp. 344-56.

Schneider, J., *Das Evangelium nach Johannes* (THKNT; Berlin: Evangelische Verlagsanstalt, 1976).

Schnelle, U., *Antidocetic Christology in the Gospel of John* (Philadelphia: Fortress Press, 1988)

Schoonenberg, P., 'A Sapiential Reading of John's Prologue: Some Reflections on Views of Reginald Fuller and James Dunn', *TD* 33 (1986), pp. 403-21.

Schottroff, L., *Der Glaubende und die feindliche Welt: Beobachtungen zum gnostischen Dualismus und seiner Bedeutung für Paulus und das Johannes-evangelium* (WMANT, 37; Neukirchen–Vluyn: Neukirchener Verlag, 1970).

Schrage, W., *Das Verhältnis des Thomas-Evangeliums zur synoptischen Tradition und zu den koptischen Evangelienübersetzungen* (BZNW, 29; Berlin: Töpelmann, 1964).

Schubert, K., *Die Gemeinde vom Toten Meer: Ihre Entstehung und ihre Lehren* (Munich: Reinhardt, 1958) 131-33; ET *The Dead Sea Community: Its Origin and Teachings* (London: A. & C. Black, 1959), pp. 151-54.

—'Der Sektenkanon von En-Feschcha und die Anfänge der jüdischen Gnosis', *TLZ* 78 (1953), cols. 495-506.

Schuchard, B.G., *Scripture within Scripture: The Interrelationship of Form and Function in the Explicit Old Testament Citations in the Gospel of John* (SBLDS, 133; Atlanta: Scholars Press, 1992).

Schulz, S., 'Die Komposition des Johannesprologs und die Zusammensetzung des vierten Evangeliums', in K. Aland *et al.* (eds.), *Studia Evangelica: Papers Presented to the International Congress on 'The Four Gospels' in 1957* (TU, 73; Berlin: Akademie Verlag, 1959), pp. 351-62.

Schweizer, E., *Ego Eimi: Die religionsgeschichtliche Herkunft und theologische Bedeutung der johanneischen Bildreden, zugleich ein Beitrag zur Quellenfrage des vierten Evangeliums* (FRLANT, 38; Göttingen: Vandenhoeck & Ruprecht, 1930 [2nd edn, 1968]).

—'The Concept of the Church in the Gospel and Epistles of St. John', in A.J.B. Higgins (ed.), *New Testament Essays: Studies in Memory of T.W. Manson* (Manchester: Manchester University Press, 1959), pp. 230-45.

—'Jesus der Zeuge Gottes: Zum Problem des Doketismus im Johannesevangelium', in A.S. Geyser *et al.* (eds.), *Studies in John: Presented to Professor Dr J.N. Sevenster on the Occasion of his Seventieth Birthday* (NovTSup, 24; Leiden: Brill, 1970), pp. 161-68.

—*Neotestamentica* (Zürich: Zwingli-Verlag, 1963).

Scott, M., *Sophia and the Johannine Jesus* (JSNTSup, 71; Sheffield: JSOT Press, 1992).

Segal, A.F., *Two Powers in Heaven: Early Rabbinic Reports about Christianity and Gnosticism* (SJLA, 25; Leiden: Brill, 1977).

Sevrin, J.-M., 'Le quatrième évangile et le gnosticisme: questions de méthode', in J.-D. Kaestli *et al.* (eds.), *La communauté johannique et son histoire: La trajectoire de l'évangile de Jean aux deux premiers siècles* (MB; Geneva: Labor & Fides, 1990), pp. 251-68.

Smith, D.M., 'Johannine Christianity: Some Reflections on its Character and

Delineation', *NTS* 21 (1975), pp. 222-48; repr. in *Johannine Christianity: Essays on its Setting, Sources, and Theology* (Columbia: University of South Carolina Press, 1984), pp. 1-36.

—'The Setting and Shape of a Johannine Narrative Source', *JBL* 95 (1976), pp. 231-41; repr. in *Johannine Christianity: Essays on its Setting, Sources, and Theology* (Columbia: University of South Carolina Press, 1984), pp. 80-93.

Smith, R.H., 'Exodus Typology in the Fourth Gospel', *JBL* 81 (1962), pp. 329-42.

Snodgrass, K.R., *The Parable of the Wicked Tenants: An Inquiry into Parable Interpretation* (WUNT, 27; Tübingen: Mohr [Paul Siebeck], 1983).

Spicq, C., 'Le Siracide et la structure littéraire du Prologue de saint Jean', in *Mémorial Lagrange: Cinquantenaire de l'école biblique et archéologique française de Jérusalem (15 novembre 1890 – 15 novembre 1940)* (Paris: Gabalda, 1940), pp. 183-95.

Stein, E., *Philo und Midrasch* (BZAW, 57; Giessen: Töpelmann, 1931).

Stendahl, K. (ed.), *The Scrolls and the New Testament* (New York: Harper & Brothers; London: SCM Press, 1958).

Stenning, J.F., *The Targum of Isaiah* (Oxford: Clarendon Press, 1949).

Strachan, R.H., *The Fourth Gospel: Its Significance and Environment* (London: SCM Press, 3rd edn, 1941).

Talbert, C.H., 'The Myth of a Descending–Ascending Redeemer in Mediterranean Antiquity', *NTS* 22 (1976), pp. 418-40.

Teeple, H.M., 'Qumran and the Origin of the Fourth Gospel', *NovT* 4 (1960), pp. 6-25.

Testuz, M. (ed.), *Papyrus Bodmer VII-IX* (Cologne and Geneva: Bibliothèque Bodmer, 1959).

Theobald, M., *Im Anfang war das Wort: Textlinguistische Studie zum Johannesprolog* (SBS, 106; Stuttgart: Katholisches Bibelwerk, 1983).

Thoma, C., 'Biblisches Erbe im Gottesdienst der Synagoge', in H.H. Henrix (ed.), *Jüdische Liturgie: Geschichte—Struktur—Wesen* (QD, 86; Freiburg: Herder, 1979), pp. 47-65.

Thomas, J.C., 'The Fourth Gospel and Rabbinic Judaism', *ZNW* 82 (1991), pp. 159-82.

Thompson, M.M., *The Humanity of Jesus in the Fourth Gospel* (Philadelphia: Fortress Press, 1988).

—'Signs and Faith in the Fourth Gospel', *BBR* 1 (1991), pp. 89-108.

Thyen, H., 'Aus der Literatur zum Johannesevangelium', *TRu* 39 (1975), pp. 53-69, 222-52.

—'Johannes 10 im Kontext des vierten Evangeliums', in J. Beutler and R.T. Fortna (eds.), *The Shepherd Discourse of John 10 and its Context* (SNTSMS, 67; Cambridge: Cambridge University Press, 1991), pp. 116-34, 163-68.

Tobin, T.H., 'The Prologue of John and Hellenistic Jewish Speculation', *CBQ* 52 (1990), pp. 252-69.

Townsend, J.T., *Midrash Tanhuma* (Hoboken, NJ: Ktav, 1989).

Tröger, K.-W., 'Ja oder Nein zur Welt: War der Evangelist Johannes Christ oder Gnostiker?', *Theologische Versuche* 7 (1976), pp. 61-77.

Tuckett, C.M., *Nag Hammadi and The Gospel Tradition* (Studies of the New Testament and Its World; Edinburgh: T. & T. Clark, 1986).

—'Thomas and the Synoptics', *NovT* 30 (1988), pp. 132-57.

Turner, H.E.W., 'The Gospel of Thomas: Its History, Transmission and Sources', in

H. Montefiore and H.E.W. Turner, *Thomas and the Evangelists* (SBT, 35; London: SCM Press, 1962), pp. 11-39.

—*The Pattern of Christian Truth* (London: Mowbrays, 1954).

Turner, J.D., 'The History of Religions Background of John 10', in J. Beutler and R.T. Fortna (eds.), *The Shepherd Discourse of John 10 and its Context* (SNTSMS, 67; Cambridge: Cambridge University Press, 1991), pp. 33-52, 147-50.

Turner, N., *A Grammar of New Testament Greek. IV. Style* (Edinburgh: T. & T. Clark, 1976).

Unnik, W.C. van, 'The Purpose of St John's Gospel', in K. Aland *et al.* (eds.), *Studia Evangelica: Papers Presented to the International Congress on 'The Four Gospels' in 1957* (TU, 73; Berlin: Akademie Verlag, 1959), pp. 382-411.

Vawter, B., 'What Came to Be in Him Was Life (Jn 1, 3b-4a)', *CBQ* 25 (1963), pp. 401-406.

Vermes, G., 'He is the Bread: Targum Neofiti Ex. 16.15', in E.E. Ellis and M. Wilcox (eds.), *Neotestamentica et Semitica: Studies in Honour of Matthew Black* (Edinburgh: T. & T. Clark, 1969), pp. 256-63.

—*Scripture and Tradition in Judaism* (SPB, 4; Leiden: Brill, 2nd edn, 1973).

Wengst, K., *Bedrängte Gemeinde und verherrlichter Christus: Der historische Ort des Johannesevangeliums als Schlüssel zu seiner Interpretation* (BTSt, 5; Neukirchen–Vluyn: Neukirchener Verlag, 2nd edn, 1983).

—*Christologische Formeln und Lieder im Urchristentums* (SNT, 7; Gütersloh: Gerd Mohn, 1972).

Westcott, B.F., *An Introduction to the Study of the Gospels* (London: Macmillan, 4th edn, 1874).

—*The Gospel according to St John* (repr.; Grand Rapids: Eerdmans, 1973 [1881]).

Whitacre, R.A., *Johannine Polemic: The Role of Tradition and Theology* (SBLDS, 67; Chico, CA: Scholars Press, 1982).

Wilckens, U., *Weisheit und Torheit* (BHT, 26; Tübingen: Mohr [Paul Siebeck], 1959).

—'σοφία, κτλ', *TDNT*, VII, pp. 465-76, 496-528.

Wilson, R.M., 'The *Trimorphic Protennoia*', in M. Krause (ed.), *Gnosis and Gnosticism* (NHS, 8; Leiden: Brill, 1977), pp. 50-54.

Witherington, B., *The Christology of Jesus* (Minneapolis: Fortress Press, 1990).

Wolfson, H.A., *Philo* (2 vols.; Cambridge, MA: Harvard University Press, 1948).

Wrede, W., *Charakter und Tendenz des Johannesevangeliums* (Tübingen: Mohr [Paul Siebeck], 2nd edn, 1933).

Yamauchi, E.M., *Gnostic Ethics and Mandaean Origins* (HTS, 24; Cambridge, MA: Harvard University Press, 1970).

—'Jewish Gnosticism? The Prologue of John, Mandaean Parallels, and the Trimorphic Protennoia', in R. van den Broek and M.J. Vermaseren (eds.), *Studies in Gnosticism and Hellenistic Religions* (EPRO, 91; Leiden: Brill, 1981), pp. 467-97.

—*Pre-Christian Gnosticism: A Survey of the Proposed Evidences* (Grand Rapids: Baker, 2nd edn, 1983).

Young, F.W., 'A Study of the Relation of Isaiah to the Fourth Gospel', *ZNW* 46 (1955), pp. 215-33.

Ziener, G., 'Weisheitsbuch und Johannesevangelium', *Bib* 38 (1957), pp. 396-418.

Zimmermann, H., 'Christushymnus und johanneischer Prolog', in J. Gnilka (ed.), *Neues Testament und Kirche: Für Rudolf Schmackenburg* (Freiburg: Herder, 1974), pp. 249-65.

INDEXES

INDEX OF REFERENCES

OLD TESTAMENT

NEW TESTAMENT

b. Šab.		48b	164	2.4	153
15a	168			5.3	23
32a	108	b. Suk.		8.6	130
87a	138	27b	153		
116a	25	52a	163	y. Ma'as. Š.	
116b	25			5.15	32
151b	154	b. Yeb.			
		120a	167	y. Meg.	
b. Sanh.				4.9	23
43a	168, 181	b. Yom.			
61b	26	4a	151	y. Sanh.	
70a	44	9b	164	1.1	168
93b	177	38b	131	7.1	168
100a	154				
101a	120	b. Zeb.		y. Ta'an.	
103a	25	7b	108	2.1	25
				4.5	33, 177
b. Soṭ.		y. Ber.			
12a	131	2.3	22		

TOSEFTA

t. Hul.		t. Pe'ah		13.3	164
2.24	25	4.21	108	14.5-6	32
t. Me'il.		t. Sanh.		t. Suk.	
1.16	23	7.11	152	3.15	23
t. Men.		t. Soṭ.		t. Zeb.	
13.18-22	32	13.2	158	11.16-17	32

MIDRASHIM

Gen. R.		81.6	22	35.1	131
1.1	115	94.6	167	36.3	118
2.3	131				
2.4	131	Exod. R.		Lev. R.	
2.5	123	1.15	154	6.5	158
3.6	130, 131	1.20	131	18.1	167
8.2	120	2.2	34	20.6	151
11.10	163	3.4	142	27.6	154
15.7	44	3.14	142	36.2	40
44.22	163	5.21	138		
56.3	164	18.3	108	Num. R.	
63.6	154	21.3	166	12.11	97
68.12	159	25.2	163	21.3	167
70.5	155, 163	29.5	25		
70.8	163	30.9	163		

GNOSTIC WRITINGS

JOURNAL FOR THE STUDY OF THE NEW TESTAMENT

Supplement Series